A Therapist's Guide to Integrative Therapy

The Yanni Integration Approach:
A Practical Framework for
Real-World Clinical Decision-Making

Joseph R. Yanni, Psy.D.

Published by Psychological Services of New York, P.C.

ISBN 979-8-9960954-0-7, Paperback
ISBN 979-8-9960954-1-4, Hardcover
ISBN 979-8-9960954-2-1, Ebook

Author's Note

For inquiries or professional consultations regarding the Yanni Integration Approach (YIA), please contact:

Joseph R. Yanni, Psy.D.
Psychological Services of New York, P.C.
14 Harwood Court, Suite 226, Scarsdale, NY 10583
29 Marble Avenue, 2nd Floor, Pleasantville, NY 10570
Email: drjoeyanni52@gmail.com
Website: www.psychologicalservicesofnewyork.com

Acknowledgments

A Therapist's Guide to Integrative Therapy would not have been possible without the support, guidance, and encouragement of the many people who have shaped my personal and professional journey.

First and foremost, I want to express my deepest gratitude to my mom and dad. Their unwavering love, guidance, and belief in me provided the foundation for who I am today. They instilled in me the values of hard work, compassion, and integrity, all of which have guided my approach to both life and therapy. My mother set up my first meeting with the psychologist at the school she worked at, and I knew then this was the field for me. My father has been a constant support who encouraged me to keep working hard to reach my potential. I am also grateful for my siblings, whose presence and shared life experiences have contributed to the person I have become.

To my wife, Deborah, your endless support, patience, and encouragement have been my anchor. You have stood beside me through the long hours, the challenges, and the triumphs, always believing in my vision. You met me when I was still looking for a job as a psychologist and look how far we have come. Your love and partnership make everything possible.

To my five incredible children, Mckenzie, Maggie, Molly, Joey, and Anthony, you are my greatest inspiration. Your curiosity, resilience, and boundless energy remind me every day of why this work is so important. I hope that through this journey, you see the value of helping others and the importance of pursuing your passion.

To Granny, thank you for always believing in me and being the best friend a person could ever have had. Your love and humor have taken me very far.

I also want to extend my gratitude to the families and clients who have trusted me over the years. Your courage and willingness to engage in the therapeutic process have not only shaped my career but also reinforced my belief in the power of integrative therapy. Thank you for allowing me to be part of your journeys.

To my colleagues and the interns I have had the privilege of supervising, your dedication and passion for the field have deeply influenced my own practice. Each of you has taught me something valuable, and I am grateful for the conversations, challenges, and shared growth that have shaped my perspective on therapy.

A special thanks to my professors and classmates, whose insights and encouragement honed my clinical skills and deepened my understanding of therapy. The academic discussions and collaborations we engaged in have played a critical role in the development of my approach to mental health.

Finally, to all mental health professionals who dedicate their lives to supporting others, I honor your commitment to this work. I hope that this book serves as a useful resource and supports you in your practice as you continue to make a meaningful impact in the lives of those you serve. Thank you all for being part of this endeavor. Your support, wisdom, and encouragement have made this book a reality.

Preface

Throughout my career as a psychologist, I have had the privilege of working in educational settings with children and adolescents facing complex emotional and behavioral challenges. Many of the students I have served were classified as emotionally disabled, presenting with a wide range of needs that required flexibility, creativity, and an individualized therapeutic approach. In working with these children, I quickly realized that no single therapeutic model could fully address their diverse struggles: What worked for one student often failed to resonate with another. This experience solidified my belief that an integrative approach, one that draws from multiple evidence-based frameworks, was essential for effective treatment.

In addition to my direct work with students and clients, I have supervised many interns and early-career professionals over the years. While teaching them how to help clients was a fundamental part of supervision, I also made it a priority to instill the importance of self-care, professional reflection, and maintaining a sustainable workload. Too often, I have seen dedicated therapists become overwhelmed and exhausted, sacrificing their own well-being in their efforts to support others. *A Therapist's Guide to Integrative Therapy* is written not only to guide mental health professionals in providing high-quality, integrative care but also to ensure that they take care of themselves in the process.

This book is intended for a wide range of mental health professionals, including psychologists, counselors, social workers, and therapists working in educational or clinical settings. It is also valuable for students preparing to enter the field, as it provides a practical foundation for understanding how to apply multiple therapeutic models in real-world practice. Whether you are working with children, adolescents, or adults, the principles outlined in this book will help you develop a more flexible and client-centered approach to therapy.

HOW TO USE

A Therapist's Guide to Integrative Therapy

This book is designed as both a comprehensive guide and a practical resource for mental health professionals at various stages of their careers. The chapters are structured to build upon one another, introducing key concepts of integrative therapy before exploring their application in practice. The Yanni Integration Approach (YIA) presented in this book blends cognitive behavioral therapy (CBT), psychodynamic therapy, humanistic therapy, person-centered therapy, and lifestyle-based interventions, offering a framework that allows therapists to tailor their approach to the unique needs of each client.

Readers are encouraged to use this book in the way that best supports their learning and clinical practice:

- For new therapists and students, this book provides a structured approach to therapy, including foundational knowledge, case examples, and strategies for effective intervention.
- For experienced clinicians, this book offers advanced insights into integrating multiple therapy models, refining case formulation, and managing complex client presentations.

- For supervisors and educators, this book can serve as a teaching tool, offering practical guidance on training interns and early-career professionals in integrative methods while emphasizing therapist self-care.

While the book can be read sequentially, each chapter also functions as a standalone resource, allowing readers to reference specific topics as needed. Case studies, practical exercises, and therapist reflection questions are included throughout to help bridge theory and practice.

Ultimately, my hope is that this book provides a comprehensive, adaptable, and sustainable approach to therapy, one that benefits both clients and the professionals who support them. Integration is not just about combining techniques; it is about cultivating a mindset of flexibility, responsiveness, and self-awareness that allows therapists to provide the highest level of care while preserving their own well-being.

I appreciate the time and dedication of every mental health professional who seeks to improve their practice, and I hope this book serves as a valuable resource in that journey.

Disclaimer

This book is intended as a resource for mental health professionals, students, and individuals interested in therapy. The information provided reflects evidence-based approaches, clinical experience, and professional insights, but it should not be used as a substitute for formal training, clinical supervision, or professional consultation. Therapists are encouraged to exercise their own clinical judgment and refer to professional guidelines, ethical standards, and continuing education when implementing any strategies discussed.

Furthermore, this book does not provide medical, psychological, or psychiatric diagnoses, nor does it replace consultation with a qualified healthcare professional. Individuals experiencing mental health concerns should seek guidance from a licensed therapist, psychiatrist, or physician.

All case studies included in this book are composite narratives, drawn from professional experience and research, and do not depict any specific real-life individuals. Identifying details have been altered or fictionalized to protect confidentiality while illustrating key therapeutic concepts.

The author and publisher assume no responsibility or liability for the use or misuse of the information provided in this book. The application of any therapeutic techniques or strategies remains the sole responsibility of the reader or practitioner.

Table of Contents

CHAPTER 1:

An Introduction to the Yanni Integration Approach

Introduction

A client walks into your office struggling with anxiety. Over the next few sessions, you realize their distress is more than just cognitive distortions. It is deeply rooted in childhood attachment wounds, reinforced by current relationship struggles, and worsened by poor sleep and chronic stress. A single therapeutic model may help, but would it be enough?

Therapists often face complex, multidimensional client concerns that require more than a single-modality approach. Yet, many clinicians are trained in one dominant theoretical model, which may limit their ability to meet clients where they are. What if therapy could be structured, research-driven, and flexible, while allowing clinicians to adapt to each client's evolving needs?

The Yanni Integration Approach (YIA) was developed in response to this challenge. YIA is a structured yet adaptable model that combines cognitive behavioral therapy (CBT) (A. T. Beck, 1976), psychodynamic therapy (Freud, 1917), humanistic therapy (Maslow, 1968), person-centered therapy (Rogers, 1951), and lifestyle-based interventions (Ratey, 2008) into a seamless, integrative practice. It provides practical, evidence-based strategies that therapists can apply immediately in clinical work, ensuring that therapy is both symptom-focused and insight-driven, structured and exploratory, collaborative and directive.

This chapter introduces the key principles of YIA, explains why an integrative approach is essential, and sets the foundation for a new vision for therapy, one that is adaptable, research-backed, and deeply client-centered.

How This Book Helps Both New and Seasoned Therapists

A Therapist's Guide to Integrative Therapy serves as a comprehensive guide for both new and experienced therapists, equipping them with the knowledge, tools, and confidence to implement an integrative therapeutic approach that is both structured and flexible.

For New Therapists

This book provides:

- A clear roadmap for structuring sessions, from the first meeting to ongoing therapy and termination.
- Step-by-step guidance on how to apply multiple therapeutic models together, rather than relying on just one.
- Practical examples, case studies, and probing questions to help develop confidence and build a strong therapeutic alliance.
- Research-backed techniques to help navigate common client challenges, such as anxiety, depression, trauma, and relational issues.
- Self-reflection tools and strategies to refine their approach over time and prevent burnout.

For Seasoned Therapists

This book offers:

- A deeper understanding of integration, showing how blending these five therapeutic models leads to stronger client outcomes.
- Advanced insights into case formulation and holistic assessment, helping uncover deeper patterns in client behavior.
- Strategies for managing complex cases, including resistance, transference, and countertransference.
- A focus on therapist-client collaboration, strengthening client engagement and ensuring long-term change.
- Research and lifestyle-based interventions to enhance therapy beyond just talk-based methods.

By merging foundational knowledge with real-world application, this book bridges the gap between theory and practice, helping therapists at all levels enhance their effectiveness, improve client outcomes, and grow as professionals.

A New Vision for Therapy

For decades, therapy has been shaped by diverse theoretical models, each offering valuable insights into human psychology. However, many traditional approaches focus primarily on either deep psychodynamic exploration, structured behavioral change, or holistic wellness, often missing the opportunity to seamlessly integrate these elements.

The Yanni Integration Approach (YIA) provides a structured yet flexible framework to blend:

- Cognitive behavioral therapy (CBT) (A. T. Beck, 1976)

- Person-centered therapy (Rogers, 1951)
- Psychodynamic therapy (Freud, 1917)
- Humanistic therapy (Maslow, 1968)
- Lifestyle-based interventions (Ratey, 2008)

This combination ensures that clients receive both short-term symptom relief and long-term transformation. Unlike traditional integrative models that remain largely theoretical, YIA is designed to be immediately applicable for therapists and clients alike, offering clear, research-based strategies to enhance therapy outcomes and promote overall well-being.

What Makes YIA Unique?

Although several models claim to be integrative, YIA stands apart by offering a structured, practical, and immediately usable framework. It is not just a mix of techniques but a scaffolded approach that ensures therapeutic interventions are seamlessly woven together to meet each client's unique needs.

Key Differentiators of YIA

- **Structured, Intentional Integration**: YIA is more than just a mix of techniques; it is a cohesive system that blends therapeutic approaches in a way that enhances their individual strengths (Norcross & Goldfried, 2019).
- **Beyond Traditional Integrative Therapy**: Unlike conventional models that focus solely on integrating various psychological perspectives, YIA incorporates lifestyle-based interventions as a foundational element, ensuring that therapy addresses both mental and physical well-being (Linehan, 1993; Ratey, 2008).

- **Immediate Real-World Application**: YIA provides therapists with practical tools, structured session guidelines, and evidence-based interventions that can be implemented immediately in clinical practice (Weisz & Kazdin, 2017).
- **Bridging the Gap Between Insight and Action**: By combining psychodynamic depth, behavioral structure, and lifestyle interventions, YIA ensures therapy is both reflective and results-driven, allowing clients to achieve meaningful, lasting change (Shedler, 2010).

A Call for Research and Collaboration

Although YIA presents an innovative approach to psychotherapy, further empirical research is needed to validate its effectiveness, refine its interventions, and explore long-term outcomes. Future research should assess:

- The comparative effectiveness of YIA against other integrative models (Beutler & Harwood, 2000).
- How YIA can be adapted across various cultural and socioeconomic contexts (Naeem, 2012).
- Best practices for training clinicians in YIA's structured framework (Norcross & Lambert, 2019b).
- The long-term impact of YIA on client mental health and overall quality of life (Prochaska & DiClemente, 1983).

As you embark on this journey through the Yanni Integration Approach, my hope is that this book provides you with the knowledge, tools, and confidence to integrate multiple therapeutic approaches in a way that is both seamless and effective.

Together, we can advance psychotherapy, ensuring that every client receives treatment that is not only evidence-based but also deeply personalized, practical, and transformative.

CHAPTER 2:

Why an Integrated Approach Matters

Introduction

Imagine a day in a therapist's office. In the morning, you support a middle school student struggling with panic attacks. By noon, you're helping a high school senior with intrusive thoughts related to obsessive-compulsive disorder. Before the day ends, you intervene in a crisis with a student experiencing suicidal ideation. Each case demands a different approach, yet traditional therapy models often expect therapists to fit clients into one rigid modality.

How can we adapt in real time to meet our clients where they are?

As discussed in Chapter 1, the Yanni Integration Approach (YIA) was developed in response to the limitations of single-modality therapy. Although cognitive behavioral therapy (CBT) (A. T. Beck, 1976), psychodynamic therapy (Freud, 1917), humanistic therapy (Maslow, 1968), person-centered therapy (Rogers, 1951), and lifestyle-based interventions (Ratey, 2008) each offer proven benefits, no single approach is sufficient for every client's needs. Successful therapy requires integration, allowing therapists to shift seamlessly between models to respond to each client's unique emotional, cognitive, and behavioral challenges.

This chapter explores the real-world challenges that led to the development of YIA, bridging theory and practice while highlighting the limitations of traditional therapy models. By the end of this chapter, therapists will understand why an integrative approach is essential and how YIA enhances flexibility, effectiveness, and therapeutic outcomes.

The Journey to the Yanni Integration Approach

Throughout my career as a psychologist, particularly in fast-paced educational settings, I have worked with individuals and families facing a wide range of emotional, social, and psychological challenges. Unlike private practice, school settings require therapists to adapt rapidly, one minute supporting a highly anxious student, the next managing a crisis, and later helping a teen with a thought disorder navigate daily functioning.

These varied experiences reinforced a key realization:

No single therapeutic model is sufficient for every situation.

Relying solely on CBT techniques would often leave relational wounds unaddressed. A purely psychodynamic approach might help students gain insight into their struggles but fail to provide them with immediate coping tools. I realized that successful therapy depends not on rigid loyalty to one model, but on the ability to integrate multiple approaches seamlessly.

Bridging Theory and Practice

In addition to direct therapy, working in schools meant collaborating with teachers, families, administrators, and support staff. These collaborations required me to:

- Quickly assess and identify key concerns while tailoring interventions to each child's unique needs.
- Adapt interventions to be practical, ensuring they were effective within a classroom environment.

- Translate complex psychological concepts into clear, actionable strategies for parents and educators.
- Recognize the limitations of therapy sessions alone, focusing on how daily routines, relationships, and lifestyle factors impact mental health.

These experiences reinforced that therapy does not end in the office, it extends into the client's relationships, daily habits, and lived environment. This realization led to a major shift in my thinking:

If therapy is to be truly effective, it must be adaptable, not only within a session but also beyond the therapy room.

Thus, I began to formalize these insights into a cohesive framework, developing what would become the Yanni Integration Approach (YIA).

The Birth of the Yanni Integration Approach (YIA)

YIA was built on the premise that combining multiple well-established therapeutic models leads to a more robust, client-centered intervention. Instead of forcing clients into a single approach, YIA allows therapists to pull from multiple evidence-based models based on client needs, session goals, and evolving challenges.

YIA integrates the following:

- **Cognitive Behavioral Therapy (CBT)** → Provides structured interventions and thought restructuring (A. T. Beck, 1976).
- **Psychodynamic Therapy** → Uncovers unconscious patterns and past influences (Shedler, 2010).
- **Humanistic Therapy** → Fosters self-actualization and personal growth (Rogers, 1961).
- **Person-Centered Therapy** → Creates a trusting, empathetic, and collaborative therapeutic space (Elliott et al., 2004).

- **Lifestyle-Based Interventions** → Supports long-term well-being through nutrition, sleep, exercise, and social engagement (Walsh, 2011).

By seamlessly integrating these approaches, YIA provides a structured yet flexible framework that ensures therapy remains comprehensive, practical, and responsive to each client's needs.

The Limitations of Traditional Therapy Models

While each therapy model has proven strengths, using them in isolation often leaves significant gaps in treatment.

Therapy Model	Strengths	Limitations
Cognitive Behavioral Therapy (CBT)	Highly structured and effective for modifying thoughts and behaviors.	May overlook deeper emotional wounds and unconscious influences (A. T. Beck, 1976).
Psychodynamic Therapy	Explores early life experiences and relational patterns.	Lacks immediate symptom relief strategies (Shedler, 2010).
Humanistic Therapy	Encourages personal growth and self-acceptance.	Can feel too unstructured for clients needing goal-oriented interventions (Rogers, 1961).
Person-Centered Therapy	Provides a nonjudgmental, supportive space.	Some clients require more directive approaches (Elliott et al., 2004).

Lifestyle-Based Interventions	Improves sleep, nutrition, and emotional regulation.	Cannot replace deeper emotional work for trauma and relational issues (Walsh, 2011).

Conclusion: The Future of Therapy Is Integrated

The Yanni Integration Approach (YIA) is more than a theoretical concept, it is a practical model designed for real-world therapy. Rigid, one-size-fits-all methods no longer meet the growing complexity of mental health needs (Norcross & Goldfried, 2019).

By drawing from CBT, Psychodynamic Therapy, Humanistic Therapy, Person-Centered Therapy, and Lifestyle Interventions, YIA ensures:

- Personalized, research-backed treatment.
- A structured yet flexible approach to therapy.
- Sustainable change through both immediate interventions and long-term growth.

As mental health continues to evolve, so must our therapeutic approaches. Integration is the future of therapy, empowering both clients and therapists to work more effectively toward meaningful, lasting transformation.

CHAPTER 3:

The Foundation of Effective Therapy: Preparing for Integrative Practice

Introduction

Effective therapy is shaped long before the first words of a session are spoken. Success in therapy requires a strong foundation of preparation, self-awareness, and adaptability, qualities that allow therapists to anticipate client needs, establish trust, and engage in meaningful post-session reflection.

In Chapter 2, we explored why a single-modality approach often falls short and how the Yanni Integration Approach (YIA) provides a flexible, client-centered framework for therapy. Now, we turn our attention to the therapist, examining how a prepared and self-reflective mindset ensures the success of integrative practice.

By integrating cognitive behavioral therapy (CBT) (A. T. Beck, 1976), psychodynamic therapy (Freud, 1915), humanistic therapy (Rogers, 1961, 1957), person-centered therapy (Elliott et al., 2004; Mearns et al., 2013), and lifestyle-based interventions (Walsh, 2011), therapists can create an adaptable and effective treatment structure. This chapter explores how therapists can prepare before, during, and after sessions, ensuring thoughtful, effective, and client-centered care.

Therapist Mindset: Confidence, Professionalism, and Continuous Learning

Effective therapy begins with a solid therapist mindset. A strong therapist embodies self-assurance, professionalism, and the willingness to evolve. This does not mean always having the "right" answer; rather, it involves trusting the therapeutic process and recognizing that therapy is a collaborative effort where clients play an active role in their own healing.

With this foundational mindset, it is essential to balance confidence with humility, a quality that opens the door to ongoing learning and self-improvement.

Balancing Confidence and Humility

Each therapeutic model offers valuable insights into the therapist's role:

- **CBT Approach:** Recognizing and challenging automatic negative thoughts (e.g., *"I need to say the perfect thing"*) helps manage self-doubt and imposter syndrome (A. T. Beck, 1976).
- **Psychodynamic Perspective:** Acknowledging countertransference, our own emotional reactions to clients, is vital, and processing these feelings in supervision is key (Gelso & Hayes, 2007).
- **Humanistic Approach:** Authenticity and vulnerability build genuine connections, showing that presence matters more than perfection (Rogers, 1957, 1961).
- **Person-Centered Therapy:** Relying on deep listening rather than expertise allows clients to lead their own progress (Elliott et al., 2004; Mearns et al., 2013).
- **Lifestyle Changes:** Regular self-care, ongoing professional development, and mindfulness practices help prevent burnout and sustain engagement (Walsh, 2011).

In addition to balancing confidence with humility, great therapists remain committed to continuous learning and adaptability. Recognizing what we do not know is not a weakness, but rather an invitation to deepen our knowledge and refine our approach.

Continuous Learning and Adaptability

Great therapists never stop learning. Engaging in ongoing training, supervision, and research helps us remain responsive to emerging challenges and innovative methodologies. For example, attending workshops on the latest integrative techniques or participating in peer consultations can provide fresh insights that enhance practice (Norcross & Goldfried, 2019).

With a mindset anchored in continuous growth, it is equally important to prepare for each session with intentionality.

Integrating Models Before the Session: Anticipating Needs and Potential Strategies

Entering each session with a clear plan and flexible preparation is crucial. Therapists must anticipate a client's unique concerns, reflect on past session themes, and consider potential interventions. However, it is important to remain adaptable, as clients often bring unexpected emotions and challenges.

Assessing the Client's Needs Using an Integrative Lens

- **CBT:** Identify patterns of negative thought distortions and maladaptive behaviors (A. T. Beck, 1976).
- **Psychodynamic:** Consider relational dynamics, unconscious conflicts, and transference issues (Shedler, 2010).

- **Humanistic:** Prepare to offer unconditional positive regard, creating a space where the client feels fully accepted (Rogers, 1961).
- **Person-Centered:** Let the client guide the session rather than imposing a predetermined agenda (Elliott et al., 2004).
- **Lifestyle Changes:** Review whether factors such as sleep, exercise, nutrition, or social engagement might be impacting the client's mental health (Walsh, 2011).

Before a session with a client experiencing anxiety, a therapist might review past notes on cognitive distortions while also considering whether recent changes in the client's sleep patterns could be contributing to heightened stress.

Once the client's needs are assessed, the next step is to build trust while maintaining necessary professional boundaries.

Building Trust While Maintaining Boundaries

Therapy is most effective when clients feel safe, heard, and respected. This requires a delicate balance of warmth and professional boundaries. Clients need to know that their therapist cares about them while understanding that ethical and structural boundaries are in place.

Establishing Trust Through an Integrative Approach

- **Cognitive-Behavioral Therapy (CBT):** Consistent, structured interventions help clients see measurable progress, reinforcing a sense of security and predictability in the therapeutic relationship (A. T. Beck, 1976; Dobson, 2010).
- **Psychodynamic Therapy:** Helping clients explore unconscious fears and defenses without judgment builds deep trust, as they feel understood on a fundamental level (Freud, 1915; Shedler, 2010).

- **Humanistic Therapy:** Empathy, authenticity, and unconditional positive regard are essential in creating an emotionally secure environment where clients feel accepted and valued (Rogers, 1951, 1957).
- **Person-Centered Therapy:** A collaborative approach empowers clients and reinforces that therapy is a joint effort, helping them feel heard and actively involved in their healing process (Mearns et al., 2013).
- **Lifestyle Changes:** Encouraging self-care outside of sessions demonstrates that the therapist is invested in the client's overall well-being, fostering a sense of trust that extends beyond the therapy room (Seligman, 2011; Prochaska & DiClemente, 1983).

In addition to these structured strategies, thoughtful self-disclosure can further enhance the therapeutic relationship when used appropriately. Self-disclosure, when relevant and intentional, can normalize client experiences and strengthen the therapeutic alliance by demonstrating authenticity and mutual respect (Hill & Knox, 2001).

The Role of Self-Disclosure in Enhancing the Therapeutic Relationship

While traditional psychoanalytic models have often discouraged self-disclosure, contemporary research supports its potential benefits when used appropriately. When genuine, relevant, and client-centered, self-disclosure can:

- **Normalize Client Experiences:** For example, saying "Many people struggle with self-doubt, including myself at times" helps clients feel less isolated.
- **Enhance the Therapeutic Alliance:** Authentic self-disclosure demonstrates vulnerability and relatability, strengthening the connection between therapist and client (Goldfried et al., 2003).

- **Model Healthy Vulnerability:** Sharing personal experiences in a measured way can provide a model for emotional regulation, particularly for clients who struggle with trust (Barnett, 2011).

Therapists must exercise self-awareness when using self-disclosure, ensuring that it supports, rather than distracts from, the client's healing process.

Cultural Considerations in Self-Disclosure

- Some clients welcome therapist self-disclosure, while others prefer a more neutral, structured dynamic.
- Therapists should assess each client's comfort level before sharing personal insights.

When used effectively, self-disclosure enhances connection while maintaining professional integrity.

Finally, continuous improvement in practice requires reflective self-evaluation after each session.

Reflecting on Strengths and Areas of Growth Post-Session

Self-reflection is a cornerstone of effective therapy. After each session, therapists should take time to assess:

- What strategies worked well?
- Where did challenges arise?
- What adjustments can be made for future sessions?

A psychodynamic therapist might reflect on their countertransference response to a client, while a CBT-focused therapist might evaluate the effectiveness of a cognitive restructuring technique used in session. Engaging in regular self-reflection helps identify strengths, reduce blind spots, and leads to better overall session outcomes (Norcross & Goldfried, 2019).

A therapist might keep a reflective journal noting that a particular intervention worked well with a client but also identifying moments where rigidity in approach hindered progress, thus informing adjustments in future sessions.

Conclusion

The foundation of effective therapy lies in the therapist's preparation, mindset, and ability to reflect. Success in integrative therapy begins long before a session starts and continues well beyond its conclusion. The Yanni Integration Approach (YIA) thrives on a therapist's ability to balance confidence with humility, remain open to continuous learning, and approach each session with flexibility and intentionality.

Preparation is key: Anticipating client needs through an integrative lens allows therapists to enter sessions with clarity while remaining adaptable to the evolving therapeutic process. Establishing trust, maintaining professional boundaries, and using self-disclosure thoughtfully further enhance the therapeutic relationship, creating a space where clients feel safe and empowered. Additionally, self-reflection after sessions strengthens a therapist's ability to refine their approach, ensuring ongoing personal and professional growth.

By integrating Cognitive Behavioral Therapy, Psychodynamic Therapy, Humanistic and Person-Centered approaches, and Lifestyle-Based Interventions, therapists can create a dynamic, responsive, and effective framework for client care. The work of therapy is not simply about mastering techniques; it is about cultivating a mindset that embraces learning, connection, and adaptability.

CHAPTER 4:

First Impressions and Initial Rapport

Introduction

The first session is a critical opportunity to build trust, establish collaboration, and set the foundation for long-term therapeutic success. Research consistently shows that the strength of the therapeutic alliance, especially during the early stages of therapy, is one of the strongest predictors of positive outcomes (Horvath & Bedi, 2002). In this initial encounter, therapy goes beyond gathering information; it is about creating a safe, supportive space where clients feel truly heard and understood.

In chapter 3, we explored the importance of therapist preparation and adaptability. Now, we apply these principles to one of the most critical moments in therapy: the first session. This is where preparation becomes action, and the foundation for the therapeutic alliance is established.

The Yanni Integration Approach (YIA) emphasizes using multiple therapeutic models from the very beginning. Humanistic empathy fosters trust and emotional safety, CBT provides structure and early problem-solving, and Psychodynamic insight allows for deeper exploration of relational and emotional patterns. Together, these models lay the groundwork for both short-term symptom relief and long-term growth. This chapter outlines strategies for making a strong first impression by focusing on rapport-building, active listening, nonverbal communication, and setting clear expectations.

With this framework in mind, the following section discusses the importance of presenting oneself as a neutral yet empathetic guide, a vital first step in building client rapport.

Presenting as a Blank Slate

Clients often enter therapy with preexisting assumptions or fears based on past experiences. Some may project negative expectations, worrying they will be judged or dismissed; others might idealize the therapist, expecting immediate solutions. These projections, rooted in past relational experiences, often manifest as transference, where clients unconsciously assign roles or expectations to the therapist (Luborsky & Crits-Christoph, 1998).

In Psychodynamic therapy, these projections offer opportunities for insight (Freud, 1911; Kernberg, 1975), while Humanistic approaches remind us to balance neutrality with empathy (Rogers, 1957). The goal is to create a safe space where clients can explore their experiences without fear of judgment.

Clients may unknowingly project expectations onto the therapist based on past relationships with caregivers, authority figures, or even prior therapists (Levenson, 1995; Shedler, 2010). Recognizing these projections early can provide valuable insight into relational patterns (Safran et al., 2011). A therapist might say, *"I notice you seem hesitant to trust me. Has that been a pattern in past relationships as well?"* This approach balances curiosity with empathy, making room for deeper exploration.

Strategies to Balance Neutrality and Empathy:

- **Acknowledge Anxiety:** For example, *"Starting therapy can feel like a big step. How has this process been for you so far?"* (Mearns et al., 2013).

- **Invite Openness:** Use open-ended questions such as, "*What would you like to focus on today?*" to let the client guide the session (W. R. Miller & Rollnick, 2013; Rogers, 1951).

Once the client feels safe to share, the next step is to establish a collaborative relationship that empowers them in the therapeutic process.

Establishing Equality and Collaboration

Therapy is most effective when clients feel empowered to actively participate in their healing. The traditional "expert" model, in which the therapist dictates the course of therapy, can undermine client agency. Research supports a collaborative approach where both therapist and client contribute to goal-setting and decision-making (Bordin, 1979).

The YIA emphasizes balancing Humanistic empowerment with CBT's structured guidance, while also incorporating Psychodynamic exploration, Lifestyle Changes, and Person-Centered Therapy to enhance collaboration. When clients know their input is valued, they are more engaged and invested in their progress.

Strategies to Foster Collaboration:

- **Humanistic Goal-Setting:** Ask, "*What would you like to work on together over the next few sessions?*" (Rogers, 1951).
- **CBT Problem Focus:** Inquire, "*What's one situation that's been particularly stressful for you lately?*" (A. T. Beck, 1976).
- **Psychodynamic Exploration:** If resistance or hesitancy is present, explore underlying relational patterns. "*Have there been times in past relationships where you felt unheard or dismissed?*" (Shedler, 2010).

- **Lifestyle Considerations:** Encourage active participation in self-care. *"What's one small habit you can start outside of therapy that might support your progress?"* (Seligman, 2011).
- **Person-Centered Collaboration:** Reinforce the client's autonomy and shared decision-making. *"It's important that this process feels right for you. How do you feel about the direction we're taking?"* (Rogers, 1957).

Balancing Models for Initial Rapport

Building rapport in the first session involves integrating techniques from several therapeutic models to address both immediate and long-term needs. Each model contributes unique strengths:

- **Humanistic Approach:** Prioritizes empathy, acceptance, and validation to help clients feel emotionally safe. Genuine warmth encourages clients to open up (Rogers, 1957).
- **CBT Techniques:** Provide structure by identifying key problems, which can be particularly useful when clients seek immediate strategies for managing stress, anxiety, or depression (Dobson, 2010).
- **Psychodynamic Insight:** Attends to deeper emotional or relational themes. For example, if a client frequently mentions feeling rejected, gently explore whether this is a recurring pattern (Levenson, 1995).
- **Lifestyle Integration:** Acknowledges the client's daily routines and self-care habits, reinforcing the role of well-being beyond the therapy session (Seligman, 2011).
- **Person-Centered Approach:** Maintains an unconditional positive regard that allows the client to feel truly heard and valued, fostering intrinsic motivation for growth (Mearns et al., 2013).

In addition to blending verbal strategies, effective nonverbal communication plays a crucial role in establishing rapport.

Active Listening and Reflection

Active listening demonstrates that you are fully present with the client, reinforcing trust and engagement. Studies show that clients who feel deeply understood by their therapist are more likely to form a strong therapeutic alliance and remain engaged in therapy (Elliott et al., 2011).

Core Active Listening Techniques:

- **Paraphrasing:** *"So you're feeling unsure about where to go from here, right?"*
- **Reflecting Emotions:** *"It sounds like there's a lot of sadness beneath that frustration."*
- **Summarizing:** *"What I'm hearing is that you've been feeling overwhelmed by both work and family pressures. Is that accurate?"*

Alongside attentive listening, nonverbal communication further reinforces the message of empathy and understanding.

Body Language and Nonverbal Communication

Nonverbal cues, such as eye contact, posture, and facial expressions, play a significant role in conveying empathy and building trust. Research indicates that clients often interpret these nonverbal behaviors as key indicators of a therapist's presence and engagement (J. A. Hall et al., 1995).

Nonverbal Strategies for Building Rapport:

- **Maintain Steady Eye Contact:** Signal attentiveness while adjusting based on the client's comfort.
- **Adopt an Open Posture:** Convey receptivity and engagement.
- **Mirror Subtle Facial Expressions:** Reflect the client's emotional state to reinforce empathy.

Be mindful that cultural differences can influence norms around eye contact and personal space (Sue & Sue, 2016). Adapting nonverbal communication to match the client's cultural background enhances connection and safety. For instance, while direct eye contact is seen as a sign of engagement in Western cultures, it may be perceived as confrontational in other cultures. Therapists should observe a client's comfort level and adjust accordingly, ensuring nonverbal behaviors align with the client's communication style.

Finally, setting clear expectations and boundaries helps consolidate the initial rapport and provides structure for the session.

Setting Expectations and Boundaries

Clients often come to therapy with varied expectations about the process. Setting clear expectations regarding session structure, confidentiality, and communication helps reduce anxiety and establish trust (Zur, 2007).

Key Areas to Address:

- **Session Length:** *"Our sessions will last about 45 minutes."*
- **Confidentiality:** *"Everything we discuss here is confidential, except in cases where safety might be at risk. I'll explain those exceptions in detail."*

- **Between-Session Contact:** *"For urgent matters, you can reach out; for non-urgent updates, we'll discuss them during our sessions."*

Providing this predictable structure is particularly important for clients who have experienced instability or trauma.

Conclusion

The first session is a crucial opportunity to build trust, establish collaboration, and set the groundwork for long-term change. The Yanni Integration Approach (YIA) emphasizes blending humanistic empathy, CBT's structure, psychodynamic insight, person-centered empowerment, and lifestyle changes to create a comprehensive, client-centered experience. By presenting yourself as a neutral yet empathetic guide, engaging in active listening, using both verbal and nonverbal communication effectively, incorporating practical strategies for well-being, and setting clear expectations, you foster immediate engagement and lay a solid foundation for long-term growth.

CHAPTER 5:

Understanding the Client's World

Introduction

Building upon the principles discussed in chapter 4, the therapeutic process moves from establishing trust and connection to developing a deeper, more nuanced understanding of the client's world. The early sessions are not just about gathering information, they are about uncovering the complex interplay between thoughts, emotions, behaviors, and relationships that shape a client's experience (A. T. Beck, 1976; Rogers, 1951).

Effective assessment requires more than structured questioning; it demands active listening, reflection, and collaboration to reveal patterns, clarify goals, and identify both strengths and challenges (Ackerman & Hilsenroth, 2003; Elliott et al., 2011). The Yanni Integration Approach (YIA) facilitates this process by synthesizing cognitive behavioral therapy (CBT), psychodynamic therapy, humanistic therapy, person-centered therapy, and lifestyle changes into a cohesive framework. This allows therapists to move beyond surface-level concerns and explore the deeper psychological, relational, and behavioral dynamics influencing a client's well-being.

Understanding the client's world is not merely an introductory step, it is the foundation upon which effective interventions are built (Fonagy et al., 2002;

Walsh, 2011). A comprehensive, integrative assessment enables therapists to tailor their approach, ensuring that treatment is both meaningful and impactful.

With this in mind, the following sections outline strategies for fostering a safe therapeutic space, gathering holistic client information, and synthesizing that data into a well-informed case formulation.

Creating a Safe Space for Assessment

Clients are often hesitant to share personal information during early sessions, especially if previous experiences with professionals were negative. Research indicates that clients are more likely to disclose sensitive details when they feel emotionally supported and validated (Ackerman & Hilsenroth, 2003). A safe space, one characterized by unconditional positive regard, empathy, and authenticity, is essential (Rogers, 1957).

Strategies to Create a Safe Space:

- **Normalize the Process:** *"The first few sessions are about getting to know each other. We'll take our time to explore what's important to you."*
- **Acknowledge Vulnerability:** *"It can be hard to open up to someone new. I appreciate you being here and sharing what you can."*
- **Clarify Boundaries and Confidentiality:** Explain that the session is judgment-free and that everything shared remains confidential (except in certain, predefined situations).
- **Address Cultural Considerations:** Some clients come from backgrounds where therapy may not be a common or trusted resource. Therapists should assess a client's comfort level with therapy, acknowledge any concerns about stigma, and tailor the conversation accordingly (Sue & Sue, 2016).

Once clients feel safe, they are more willing to engage in a deeper conversation. The next step is to gather comprehensive information in a way that feels natural and client-centered.

Gathering Comprehensive Information

Effective assessment must cover multiple aspects of a client's life, including emotional well-being, thought patterns, behaviors, relationships, and external circumstances, while remaining conversational rather than clinical. Research supports the use of open-ended, exploratory questions that encourage clients to share their story (Elliott et al., 2011).

Using the YIA Model to Guide Information Gathering

- **Humanistic Approach:** Explore the client's values, aspirations, and sense of self (Rogers, 1961).
  <u>Example:</u> *"What's most important to you in your life right now?"*

- **CBT Tools:** Identify problematic thought patterns and behaviors (A. T. Beck, 1976).
  <u>Example:</u> *"When you're feeling stressed, what thoughts tend to go through your mind?"*

- **Psychodynamic Insight:** Explore recurring emotional themes and relational patterns (Shedler, 2010).
  <u>Example:</u> *"Are there situations where you notice the same kinds of feelings or conflicts coming up repeatedly?"*

- **Person-Centered Therapy:** Encourage client autonomy in how they frame and describe their experiences (Cain, 2010).
  <u>Example:</u> *Allow the client to lead the conversation about their background.*

- **Lifestyle Changes:** Assess daily habits that may influence mental health, such as sleep, exercise, nutrition, and social engagement (Walsh, 2011).
  <u>Example:</u> *"How do you feel your current sleep or exercise habits impact your mood?"*

After gathering detailed information, it is important to also focus on the client's strengths and resilience, which sets the stage for a balanced assessment.

Identifying Strengths and Resilience

Although assessments often focus on areas of difficulty, it is equally important to explore the client's strengths. Research shows that clients who recognize and build on their strengths tend to achieve better outcomes (Saleebey, 2012). The Humanistic model reminds us that each client possesses inherent potential for growth.

Strategies to Identify Strengths:

- **Ask Reflective Questions:** *"Can you think of a time when you faced a challenge and successfully overcame it?"*
- **Highlight Existing Strengths:** *"It sounds like you've been incredibly resourceful in balancing everything on your plate."*
- **Encourage Self-Recognition:** *"What do you think others would say are your greatest strengths?"*

With strengths identified, the next step is to explore how relational patterns and emotional themes contribute to the client's current experiences.

Exploring Relational Patterns and Emotional Themes

Many issues clients face stem from relational dynamics. Psychodynamic theory emphasizes that early attachment experiences shape how individuals relate to others and manage emotions (Fonagy et al., 2002).

Key Areas to Explore:

- **Attachment History:** *"How would you describe your relationships with your family growing up?"*
- **Current Relationships:** *"What are your relationships like now, with your partner, friends, or coworkers?"*
- **Emotional Regulation:** *"How do you typically respond when you're feeling overwhelmed or hurt?"*

In addition to exploring relational dynamics, it is essential to assess lifestyle factors, as these also play a crucial role in mental health.

Assessing Lifestyle Factors

A client's mental health is deeply connected to daily lifestyle factors such as sleep, nutrition, exercise, and social support. The YIA Model stresses that even small lifestyle changes can significantly enhance well-being (Walsh, 2011).

Probing Questions for Lifestyle Factors:

- **Sleep:** *"How many hours of sleep do you usually get? Do you wake up feeling rested?"*
- **Nutrition:** *"Do you feel that your eating habits support your energy and mental clarity?"*
- **Exercise:** *"How active are you throughout the week? Are there any activities you enjoy that help you unwind?"*

After gathering and exploring all these facets, the next step is to synthesize the information into a coherent, holistic understanding of the client's world.

Synthesizing the Assessment into a Holistic Understanding

Gathering information is only the first step. The true power of assessment comes from synthesizing this data into a coherent understanding of the client's internal and external world. This process involves identifying recurring themes, patterns, and connections that may not be immediately obvious but are essential for developing an effective treatment plan. Collaboration with the client during this synthesis process ensures that the case formulation accurately reflects their lived experience, strengths, and priorities.

Let's explore how to identify key themes and patterns from the collected information.

Identifying Themes and Patterns

A crucial step in synthesis is recognizing recurring themes in the client's thoughts, emotions, relationships, and behaviors. For example, a client who frequently experiences a sense of abandonment might develop a core belief such as, "I'm not worthy of love or support." Such beliefs often arise from early attachment experiences and can perpetuate maladaptive coping strategies (Fonagy et al., 2002).

Using the Five YIA Components to Identify Patterns:

- **CBT:** Identifies negative thought loops and cognitive distortions (A. T. Beck, 1976).
- **Psychodynamic:** Explores attachment patterns and unconscious relational themes (Shedler, 2010).
- **Humanistic:** Examines the client's sense of self, meaning, and authenticity (Rogers, 1961).

- **Person-Centered:** Utilizes non-directive approaches that help clients uncover their own patterns (Elliott et al., 2011).
- **Lifestyle Changes:** Assesses how factors like diet, sleep, exercise, and social support influence emotional patterns (Walsh, 2011).

Probing Questions to Uncover Patterns:

- *"Do you notice any recurring thoughts or emotions across different areas of your life?"*
- *"Are there specific situations where you feel stuck or encounter similar challenges repeatedly?"*
- *"What themes seem to appear in your relationships, and how do you typically respond to them?"*

Recognizing these patterns allows us to draw connections between different aspects of the client's experience.

Highlighting Connections Between Factors

Clients often present with multiple, seemingly unrelated concerns. A key part of a holistic assessment is linking these issues to help the client understand how various aspects of their life interact. For example, work-related anxiety coupled with insomnia may indicate an underlying pattern of perfectionism affecting multiple areas of life.

Steps to Highlight Connections:

1. **Identify Intersecting Issues:** *"How do you think your stress at work might be affecting your sleep?"*

2. **Link Emotional and Relational Dynamics:** *"It sounds like feeling overwhelmed at work mirrors the pressure you've experienced in personal relationships. Does that resonate with you?"*
3. **Summarize for Clarity:** *"It seems like there's a recurring theme of self-criticism affecting both your professional and personal life. Let's explore how that might be shaping your overall well-being."*

With these connections in place, the next step is to collaboratively develop clear treatment goals.

Developing Collaborative Goals

A key principle of the Yanni Integration Approach is the importance of collaboration in setting treatment goals. When clients actively participate in goal-setting, they tend to be more engaged and motivated, which leads to better outcomes (Swift & Greenberg, 2015).

Strategies for Collaborative Goal-Setting:

- **Cognitive Behavioral Therapy (CBT):** Establish SMART (Specific, Measurable, Achievable, Relevant, Time-bound) goals to effectively manage symptoms. This structured approach facilitates clear and attainable objectives, promoting measurable progress in therapy (Locke & Latham, 2002; J. S. Beck, 2011).
- **Psychodynamic Therapy:** Focus on long-term insight and relational healing during the goal-setting process. This approach emphasizes increasing client self-awareness and understanding the influence of past experiences on present behavior (Shedler, 2010; Gabbard, 2014).
- **Humanistic Therapy:** Encourage self-actualization and personal growth as foundational goals. This perspective centers on helping clients uncover their authentic selves and realize their full potential, leading to a more fulfilling and meaningful life (Maslow, 1943; Rogers, 1951).

- **Person-Centered Therapy:** Empower clients to determine their therapeutic focus, fostering a self-directed approach to mental health. This method aims to encourage clients to reflect on and overcome their challenges, promoting autonomy in the therapeutic process (Rogers, 1957; Cain, 2010).
- **Lifestyle Changes:** Suggest small, sustainable habit modifications that enhance mental well-being. Implementing positive behavioral changes, such as adopting healthier lifestyle habits, can significantly improve mental health outcomes (Prochaska & DiClemente, 1983; Walsh, 2011).

Probing Questions for Goal-Setting:

- *"What would you say is the most important issue for us to focus on right now?"*
- *"We can work on immediate strategies to help you feel more in control, but we can also explore deeper patterns. How does that sound?"*
- *"How are you feeling about the progress we've made so far? Are there other areas you'd like to focus on?"*

With collaborative goals in place, it is time to create a comprehensive case formulation.

Creating a Working Case Formulation

A case formulation is a dynamic roadmap that integrates insights from all five YIA components into a structured treatment plan.

Components of a YIA Case Formulation:

1. **Presenting Concerns:** A summary of the client's primary symptoms and challenges.

2. **Key Patterns:** Identification of core beliefs, relational dynamics, and emotional triggers.
3. **Maintaining Factors:** Recognition of cognitive distortions, avoidance behaviors, and external stressors that perpetuate symptoms.
4. **Strengths and Resources:** An outline of personal qualities and support systems the client can draw upon.
5. **Goals and Interventions:** A flexible, yet structured plan incorporating CBT, psychodynamic, humanistic, person-centered, and lifestyle change approaches.

Research indicates that well-structured, integrative case formulations lead to better treatment outcomes because they allow interventions to be tailored to the client's evolving needs (Eells, 2015).

Collaboration remains key even after the initial formulation.

Collaborating with the Client to Refine the Synthesis

While therapists bring clinical insights to case formulation, it is crucial to involve clients in refining the treatment plan. This collaboration ensures the plan reflects the client's lived experience, priorities, and goals.

Questions to Invite Collaboration:

- *"Does this summary of what we've discussed so far feel accurate to you?"*
- *"Are there any important parts of your story that you feel I've missed?"*
- *"Does this approach to therapy make sense to you, or would you like to adjust our focus?"*

Collaborative refinement not only reinforces trust but also empowers clients by making them active participants in their healing process.

The Power of a Holistic Understanding

Synthesizing assessment information into a holistic, integrative case formulation is vital for effective therapy. The Yanni Integration Approach (YIA) ensures that therapists:

- Identify core themes in thoughts, behaviors, and emotions.
- Draw meaningful connections between life experiences and mental health.
- Develop collaborative, personalized treatment goals.
- Continuously adapt and refine the case formulation over time.

By merging insights from CBT, psychodynamic, humanistic, person-centered, and lifestyle change models, therapists create dynamic, individualized interventions that empower clients to achieve long-term growth and healing.

Conclusion

A holistic assessment lays the foundation for effective therapy. The Yanni Integration Approach ensures that therapists explore the client's background, emotions, thought patterns, relationships, and lifestyle factors while also identifying their strengths and goals. By integrating multiple therapeutic models, therapists can provide personalized, flexible, and impactful treatment plans that foster lasting change.

CHAPTER 6:

Using the Yanni Integrated Approach

Introduction

This chapter is the core of the Yanni Integration Approach (YIA), demonstrating how cognitive behavioral therapy (CBT), humanistic therapy, person-centered therapy, psychodynamic therapy, and lifestyle changes work together to support clients. Each model offers unique strengths, and by integrating them, therapists can address both immediate symptoms and deeper underlying issues in a holistic manner.

In Chapter 5, we explored how to develop a deep understanding of the client's world through a thorough and integrative assessment process. With this foundation in place, the next step is to determine how best to intervene. A strong assessment informs treatment by guiding the selection of therapeutic techniques that align with the client's needs, goals, and personality. In this chapter, we move from assessment to application, ensuring that interventions are not only evidence-based but also tailored to the client's evolving progress.

Furthermore, lifestyle changes, such as improvements in sleep, nutrition, exercise, and social connections, are increasingly recognized as essential components of mental health treatment. Research shows that clients who adopt small but sustainable lifestyle modifications often experience significant improvements in overall well-being (Walsh, 2011). When combined with traditional therapeutic models, these changes can lead to lasting transformation.

A skilled therapist using YIA does not simply apply different techniques in isolation; rather, they fluidly navigate between models based on the client's evolving needs. This approach ensures a balance between structured interventions, emotional exploration, and practical, real-world changes.

With this integrative framework in mind, the following sections illustrate how each model contributes to therapy through research, case studies, and practical examples.

Cognitive Behavioral Therapy (CBT): Creating Structure and Practical Solutions

CBT is an evidence-based approach that helps clients identify and challenge negative thought patterns and behaviors contributing to emotional distress. Clients often present with automatic, self-defeating thoughts, such as *"I'm a failure"* or *"Everyone is judging me."* By examining and restructuring these thoughts, CBT enables clients to adopt more realistic and adaptive beliefs. Research shows that CBT is effective in treating anxiety, depression, and PTSD (Hofmann et al., 2012).

However, CBT may fall short when a client's core issues stem from unconscious conflicts or longstanding emotional wounds. Integrating Psychodynamic techniques allows exploration of how unresolved past experiences influence current thought patterns, while Humanistic and Person-Centered approaches build empathy and trust. In addition, Lifestyle Changes, by addressing physical and environmental factors, further strengthen the impact of CBT. For example, regular physical activity can reduce anxiety and depressive symptoms by regulating stress hormones and improving sleep quality (Carek et al., 2011).

Case Study: Maria's Social Anxiety

Maria, a 29-year-old graphic designer, struggles with social anxiety. She fears judgment from others, which causes her to avoid networking events at work. As a result, she feels exhausted and experiences difficulty sleeping after anxiety-provoking situations.

Integrated Approach:

1. **CBT:** Maria's therapist helps her identify and challenge automatic thoughts such as *"They'll think I'm incompetent."* Together, they develop cognitive strategies for reframing these thoughts.
2. **Humanistic:** The therapist validates Maria's fear of judgment by stating, *"It makes sense that you'd feel anxious when you're worried about being judged. That's a very human reaction."*
3. **Psychodynamic:** Maria reveals that her father frequently criticized her, leading her to believe she was never good enough. The therapist explores how these early experiences shape her current self-image.
4. **Person-Centered Therapy:** Maria is encouraged to take an active role in setting goals that align with her values. The therapist asks, *"What would feeling more confident in social situations look like for you?"* This empowers Maria to define her own path for growth, ensuring therapy remains collaborative and attuned to her personal aspirations.
5. **Lifestyle Changes:** The therapist suggests small steps, such as incorporating evening walks to reduce stress and improve sleep, and recommends mindfulness exercises to manage anxiety before social events.

While CBT provides structure and practical tools, humanistic therapy further deepens the therapeutic relationship by fostering empathy and self-actualization.

Humanistic Therapy: Fostering Empathy and Self-Actualization

Humanistic therapy emphasizes empathy, authenticity, and unconditional positive regard. The goal is to create a supportive environment where clients feel safe to explore their emotions and values. Carl Rogers (1957) argued that clients can achieve self-actualization when they are fully understood and accepted. Research supports that empathy and a strong therapeutic alliance are key predictors of positive outcomes (Elliott et al., 2004).

For clients experiencing acute distress, emotional exploration alone may not suffice. Integrating CBT provides tools for managing symptoms, while psychodynamic methods help uncover the unconscious origins of emotional pain. Moreover, lifestyle changes can boost physical and mental energy, further supporting self-actualization.

Case Study: David's Low Self-Esteem

David, a 38-year-old teacher, struggles with low self-worth and often compares himself unfavorably to his peers. He feels trapped in a cycle of self-criticism and exhaustion.

Integrated Approach:

1. **Humanistic:** The therapist provides empathy and acceptance, saying, *"It sounds like you've been carrying a lot of self-doubt for a long time. That can feel overwhelming."*
2. **CBT:** David identifies recurring negative thoughts, such as *"I'll never be successful,"* and the therapist helps him challenge these beliefs by focusing on his achievements.

3. **Psychodynamic:** The therapist explores how David's perfectionism and self-criticism stem from early experiences with a critical parent.
4. **Person-Centered Therapy:** The therapist fosters a non-directive, client-led space where David feels fully heard and accepted. Instead of imposing solutions, the therapist provides unconditional positive regard, allowing David to explore his thoughts and emotions at his own pace. Through reflective listening, the therapist acknowledges David's struggles, saying, *"I hear that you feel like you're always falling short compared to others. That sounds really painful. What do you feel would help you feel more at peace with yourself?"* By emphasizing self-exploration and personal growth, David begins to trust his own voice and recognize his inner strengths.
5. **Lifestyle Changes:** David is encouraged to adopt small self-care practices, like setting work boundaries and scheduling time for activities he enjoys, such as hiking.

In addition to fostering empathy, person-centered therapy empowers clients by giving them control over their therapeutic process.

Person-Centered Therapy: Empowering Clients to Lead the Process

Person-centered therapy prioritizes client autonomy by allowing clients to lead in exploring their thoughts and feelings. The therapist's role is to provide active listening and reflection, creating a safe space for clients to develop greater self-awareness. Research indicates that when clients control the therapeutic process, their motivation and engagement increase (Deci & Ryan, 2000; Elliott et al., 2011).

Some clients, however, may initially struggle to find direction without structure. Integrating CBT and Psychodynamic approaches can offer concrete tools for goal-setting and self-reflection, while Lifestyle Changes encourage healthier routines and self-discovery.

Case Study: Jenna's Career Uncertainty

Jenna, a 26-year-old marketing professional, feels unfulfilled in her career but is uncertain about which path to pursue. She worries about disappointing her family if she makes a change.

Integrated Approach:

1. **Person-Centered:** The therapist encourages Jenna to explore her feelings without judgment, noting, *"It sounds like you're feeling a lot of pressure to meet others' expectations."*
2. **CBT:** The therapist helps Jenna clarify her goals by asking, *"What activities or roles have made you feel most energized and fulfilled in the past?"*
3. **Psychodynamic:** Jenna connects her difficulty in decision-making to a childhood pattern of seeking parental approval.
4. **Humanistic Therapy:** The therapist acknowledges Jenna's desire for meaning and fulfillment, emphasizing her innate capacity for growth. They explore what truly excites and inspires her, reinforcing the idea that self-discovery is an evolving process. The therapist reassures Jenna, saying, *"It's completely natural to question your path. Your feelings of uncertainty don't mean you're lost, they mean you're searching for something more meaningful."* This validation encourages Jenna to embrace her journey rather than viewing it as a failure.
5. **Lifestyle Changes:** The therapist suggests journaling and mindful walks to help Jenna reflect on her values and priorities.

In contrast, psychodynamic therapy delves deeper into underlying emotional and relational patterns.

Psychodynamic Therapy: Exploring Deep Emotional and Relational Patterns

Psychodynamic Therapy focuses on uncovering unconscious conflicts and relational patterns. Clients often bring unresolved emotional wounds into their current relationships, which can manifest as anxiety, depression, or self-sabotaging behaviors. Research suggests that bringing these unconscious patterns to light can lead to improved emotional regulation and healthier relationships (Fonagy et al., 2002).

Nevertheless, deep introspection may overwhelm some clients. Integrating CBT provides grounding techniques, while humanistic approaches offer the empathy needed to explore painful memories safely. Lifestyle changes support overall emotional regulation by promoting physical well-being.

Case Study: Eric's Fear of Intimacy

Eric, a 34-year-old software engineer, has a pattern of withdrawing from relationships when emotions run high. Torn between a desire for connection and a fear of vulnerability, Eric experiences significant distress.

Integrated Approach:

1. **Psychodynamic:** The therapist explores Eric's fear of intimacy by asking, *"Do you think this fear of getting close to others might be linked to earlier experiences of rejection?"*
2. **Humanistic:** The therapist offers empathy, stating, *"It's understandable that you'd want to protect yourself from being hurt again."*
3. **CBT:** Eric learns grounding techniques to manage anxiety in emotionally charged situations.
4. **Person-Centered Therapy:** The therapist ensures Eric feels fully heard and respected, fostering unconditional positive regard to help him develop

self-trust. Instead of pushing solutions, the therapist gently asks, *"What feels safe for you when it comes to emotional closeness?"* This question allows Eric to explore intimacy at his own pace, helping him build confidence in his ability to navigate relationships.

5. **Lifestyle Changes:** The therapist recommends regular physical activities, such as yoga, to reduce stress and promote relaxation.

Finally, a flexible session can incorporate lifestyle changes seamlessly with other therapeutic techniques to meet shifting client needs.

Bringing the Models Together with Lifestyle Changes

Therapy often requires adapting to a client's evolving needs within a single session. The Yanni Integration Approach (YIA) emphasizes flexibility and responsiveness, enabling therapists to move fluidly among empathy, problem-solving, deep exploration, lifestyle coaching, and client empowerment to create a holistic and personalized experience.

Research highlights that the most effective therapy adapts to the individual, emphasizing an integrative and client-responsive approach rather than a rigid adherence to a single model (Norcross & Wampold, 2018).

Example Session Flow:

1. **Humanistic Empathy:** Begin by validating the client's experience. *"It sounds like this week has been particularly overwhelming for you."*
2. **CBT:** Introduce practical strategies if the client feels stuck. *"What's one small step you could take to feel more in control?"*
3. **Psychodynamic Exploration:** If the client is ready, delve into deeper themes. *"Does this struggle feel familiar from other times in your life?"*

4. **Person-Centered Therapy:** Allow space for the client to take the lead, ensuring the session remains aligned with their needs. The therapist asks, *"What feels most important for you to focus on today?"* This approach reinforces self-determination and trust in the client's own ability to direct their healing process, rather than imposing an external agenda.
5. **Lifestyle Changes:** Collaborate on a self-care plan. *"Are there any activities you could add to your routine that might help you recharge?"*

By integrating these five approaches, therapists can adapt in real time to meet clients where they are emotionally, cognitively, and behaviorally, ensuring each session is both deeply validating and solution-focused.

Conclusion

The Yanni Integration Approach blends CBT, humanistic, person-centered, and psychodynamic models with lifestyle changes. CBT tackles distorted conscious thoughts, Psychodynamic therapy uncovers unconscious patterns, and humanistic and person-centered approaches foster empathy and autonomy. Meanwhile, lifestyle changes support physical and emotional resilience. Together, these integrated strategies enable clients to achieve both immediate symptom relief and sustained long-term growth. This comprehensive framework is firmly grounded in research and empowers clients to lead healthier, more fulfilling lives.

CHAPTER 7:

Key Steps During the Session

Introduction

Building upon the structured assessment and conceptualization process outlined in chapter 6, the focus now shifts to the real-time application of the Yanni Integration Approach (YIA) within sessions. While understanding a client's needs and background lays the groundwork for therapy, it is within the session itself that true integration occurs, where therapists blend multiple therapeutic models, respond to client needs fluidly, and guide meaningful progress.

Each session is unique, shaped by the client's emotional state, ongoing challenges, and evolving goals. However, certain key steps create a foundation for effective therapy, ensuring that interventions are not only adaptable but also intentional. The YIA framework emphasizes both structure and flexibility, allowing therapists to remain responsive while keeping sessions focused, productive, and collaborative.

Research suggests that symptoms across various psychological disorders, including anxiety, depression, trauma, and self-esteem challenges, often share common cognitive, emotional, and behavioral patterns (Harvey et al., 2004). These shared mechanisms support the need for a holistic and integrative approach that allows for flexibility in therapeutic interventions (Norcross & Goldfried, 2019). Additionally, research has confirmed that no single therapy model works best for all clients, reinforcing the value of integrative approaches (Wampold, 2015). Studies have shown that integrating multiple therapeutic approaches enhances client outcomes across various populations (Norcross & Goldfried, 2019).

This chapter explores how to seamlessly integrate therapeutic approaches at each stage of a session, from establishing rapport and setting goals to interventions, reflection, and closure.

With this overall framework in mind, the first step is to establish a warm and collaborative tone at the beginning of each session.

Introducing Yourself and Setting the Tone

The start of each session is critical for establishing trust and setting a collaborative atmosphere. Research shows that early interactions can significantly influence a client's engagement and openness (Norcross & Wampold, 2011a). The YIA encourages therapists to be warm, attentive, and professional while emphasizing that therapy is a partnership.

For example, in initial sessions, you might say:

"I've worked with many individuals facing similar challenges, and I'm here to help support you through this process."

Strategies for Starting a Session:

- **Reflective Statements:** Acknowledge the client's current emotional state.
- **Simple Check-Ins:** Ask, *"How have things been since we last met?"* to help the client transition into the session.

Once the tone is set, clarifying the session's goals is the next vital step.

Clarifying Goals for the Session

After establishing rapport, it's important to clarify what the client hopes to achieve during the session. Research indicates that collaboratively setting goals increases client motivation and engagement (Swift & Greenberg, 2012). Therapists who explicitly discuss session goals with clients report improved session focus and better treatment adherence (Geurtzen et al., 2020). This process is especially valuable in CBT, which emphasizes structured goal-setting, but it also applies to Humanistic and Psychodynamic frameworks.

Example Questions to Clarify Goals:

- *"What's most important for us to focus on today?"*
- *"Are there any specific issues or situations that have arisen since our last session?"*

This step ensures that both therapist and client are aligned on priorities, setting a clear direction for the session.

With goals established, it's essential to integrate different therapeutic approaches seamlessly during the session.

Integration Across Models

Different models contribute unique strengths:

- **CBT:** Uses concrete goals to guide problem-solving and specific interventions.
- **Humanistic:** Maintains a flexible, client-centered approach that allows the session to evolve naturally.
- **Psychodynamic:** Remains attuned to recurring themes that may influence the client's current priorities, even if these themes are not immediately conscious.

- **Person-Centered Therapy:** Prioritizes the client's autonomy by allowing them to direct the session based on what feels most important to them in the moment, ensuring that their experience remains at the forefront of the therapeutic process (Rogers, 1951).
- **Lifestyle Changes:** Encourages small, sustainable habit adjustments that reinforce mental well-being outside of the session, such as incorporating self-care routines, stress management techniques, or physical activity to support long-term progress (Walsh, 2011).

Research has shown that blending multiple therapeutic models enhances client outcomes across various disorders (Leichsenring & Steinert, 2017).

A structured approach helps therapists determine which model to emphasize based on the client's presentation.

Decision-Making for Model Selection

A key refinement to this process is ensuring therapists have a structured way to determine which model to prioritize in a given session. A simple decision-making framework can help:

1. If the client presents with immediate distress or crisis → Prioritize CBT for grounding and symptom relief.
2. If the client is processing deeper relational or unconscious themes → Integrate psychodynamic techniques.
3. If the client needs emotional validation and connection → Emphasize humanistic and person-centered approaches.
4. If the client is discussing lifestyle-related stressors → Introduce lifestyle interventions. (Wachtel, 2011).

By combining these approaches, you create a balanced session that offers both structure and room for exploration.

With a clear structure in place, the next step is implementing interventions that address both immediate symptoms and underlying issues.

Implementing Interventions

The core of each session involves using interventions tailored to the client's goals and emotional readiness. The YIA emphasizes balancing practical strategies with deeper reflection. For instance, if a client is overwhelmed by anxiety, you might begin with CBT techniques to reduce immediate distress, then transition to exploring underlying emotional triggers using psychodynamic principles, while also incorporating humanistic, person-centered, and lifestyle change strategies to create a holistic and sustainable approach.

Intervention Strategies by Model:

- **CBT:** Focus on cognitive restructuring, behavioral activation, or exposure exercises.
  Example: *"Let's examine some of the thoughts that came up during your anxiety this week. Were there any patterns?"*

- **Humanistic:** Offer empathy and active listening, creating space for emotional processing.
  Example: *"It sounds like you've been feeling really alone with all of this. Let's talk more about that."*

- **Psychodynamic:** Explore unconscious patterns and relational dynamics.
  Example: *"Do you think these feelings might connect to past experiences where you felt similarly stuck or rejected?"*

- **Person-Centered Therapy:** Prioritize client autonomy, allowing them to guide the direction of the session while fostering self-trust.
  Example: *"What feels most important for you to explore today? Where would you like to start?"*

- **Lifestyle Changes:** Encourage sustainable daily habits that support mental and emotional regulation beyond the session.
  Example: *"Are there any small routines or self-care practices that help you feel more grounded?"*

Case Study: Sarah's Anxiety Management

Sarah, a 32-year-old lawyer, experiences anxiety that affects both her work and personal life. In one session, she describes a recent panic attack during a client meeting.

Integrated Approach:

1. **CBT:** The therapist helps Sarah identify the automatic thought triggering her panic: *"I'm going to fail in front of everyone."* Together, they examine and challenge this thought, helping her reframe it into a more balanced perspective.
2. **Humanistic:** The therapist validates Sarah's fear, stating, *"That must have been terrifying. You're carrying so much pressure right now."* This acknowledgment normalizes her experience and reduces feelings of isolation.
3. **Psychodynamic:** Sarah reveals that she experienced similar anxiety when her parents criticized her as a child; the therapist explores how this dynamic continues to influence her reactions to authority, helping her recognize and reprocess these deeper emotional triggers.

4. **Person-Centered:** The therapist asks, *"What feels most important for you right now in understanding your anxiety?"* By encouraging self-exploration and autonomy, Sarah begins to develop a sense of ownership over her healing process.
5. **Lifestyle Changes:** The therapist suggests deep-breathing exercises and reducing caffeine intake to manage physical anxiety symptoms. They also explore the impact of her work-life balance and discuss practical stress-reduction techniques tailored to her routine.

By integrating all five YIA components, the therapist ensures Sarah receives a comprehensive, personalized intervention that addresses immediate symptom relief, emotional validation, deeper self-awareness, personal agency, and sustainable lifestyle adjustments.

With interventions implemented, it is important to encourage client reflection during the session.

Encouraging Reflection and Insight

Midway through the session, pausing to encourage reflection can deepen client self-awareness and emotional regulation. Research shows that clients who regularly engage in reflective thinking during therapy develop a stronger sense of self (Elliott et al., 2011).

Questions to Prompt Reflection:

- *"What's standing out to you most from today's session?"*
- *"How do you think this connects to other challenges you've faced?"*
- *"What are you learning about yourself as we talk through this?"*

After reflection, planning concrete action steps is the next critical phase.

Planning Action Steps and Applying Lifestyle Changes

Toward the end of the session, collaborate with the client to develop actionable steps to take between sessions. Research supports goal-oriented planning in maintaining therapeutic momentum (Michie et al., 2009). Lifestyle changes, in particular, are key for reinforcing both emotional and physical well-being, ensuring that therapeutic insights translate into meaningful, real-world adjustments. (Cuijpers et al., 2014).

Examples of Action Steps:

- **CBT:** Set a goal to challenge negative thoughts in specific situations.
  <u>*Example:*</u> *"Next time you notice yourself thinking, 'I can't do this,' try replacing it with, 'I'm still learning, and I can handle this step by step.'"*

- **Humanistic Therapy:** Encourage the client to engage in self-care activities that bring them joy.
  <u>*Example:*</u> *"What is something you enjoy doing that you haven't made time for lately?"*

- **Psychodynamic Therapy:** Help clients recognize patterns influencing their present behaviors and how small shifts can break these cycles.
  <u>*Example:*</u> *"You mentioned feeling guilty when you take a break. Do you think that connects to messages you received growing up about productivity?"*

- **Person-Centered Therapy:** Empower the client to take the lead in identifying what feels most meaningful to them in their progress.
  <u>*Example:*</u> *"What small step feels right for you this week? You know yourself best."*

- **Lifestyle Changes:** Suggest small, sustainable habit adjustments that support overall well-being.
  <u>*Example:*</u> *"How would it feel to set a consistent bedtime this week to improve your sleep?"*

Case Study: Alex's Burnout Recovery

Alex, a 40-year-old business executive, experiences chronic fatigue and emotional numbness due to work demands. Through therapy, he recognizes that neglecting his basic needs is contributing to his burnout and that change is necessary to regain balance.

Integrated Approach:

1. **Humanistic:** The therapist validates Alex's exhaustion, acknowledging, *"You've been pushing yourself so hard for so long—it makes sense that you feel drained."* They help him reconnect with his core values, such as prioritizing personal fulfillment over external expectations.
2. **CBT:** Alex identifies thought patterns that reinforce overwork, such as *"If I don't push myself, I'll fall behind."* Together, they work on reframing these beliefs, shifting toward a more sustainable mindset: *"Taking breaks allows me to be more effective in the long run."*
3. **Psychodynamic Therapy:** Alex reflects on childhood messages about success and self-worth, recognizing that his tendency to overwork is linked to early experiences where rest was seen as laziness. Understanding this pattern helps him release some of the internal pressure he places on himself.
4. **Person-Centered Therapy:** The therapist asks, *"What does balance look like to you?"* This ensures that Alex's own values and desires shape the changes he implements, rather than simply following prescriptive advice.
5. **Lifestyle Changes:** The therapist collaborates with Alex to create a manageable routine that includes regular sleep, exercise, and time for social connection.

With action steps in place, it is essential to close the session in a manner that reinforces progress and prepares the client for future growth. By integrating these five approaches, therapists help clients implement meaningful change in a way that is both structured and self-directed, ensuring long-term benefits beyond the therapy room.

Closing the Session

Ending the session on a reflective and hopeful note helps clients feel grounded as they transition back into daily life. Summarizing key takeaways reinforces progress and builds continuity between sessions (Norcross & Lambert, 2019b).

Strategies for Closing:

- **Summarize Key Points:** *"We talked today about how your anxiety is connected to both current pressures and past experiences. You've already taken important steps by recognizing those patterns."*
- **Plan Next Steps:** *"Next time, we can check in on how those coping strategies are working and explore any new challenges."*
- **Reaffirm Client's Agency:** *"You're making really meaningful progress. I'm here to support you as you continue working toward your goals."*

Research suggests that clear session closure improves client satisfaction and promotes continued engagement with therapy (Norcross & Lambert, 2019b).

Conclusion

Now that we have explored how to structure a session using YIA, the next step is understanding how these principles apply to specific client concerns. While every session is unique, certain psychological struggles, such as anxiety, depression, and trauma, frequently arise in therapy. Chapter 8 will illustrate how YIA's integrative framework tailors interventions to address these common issues effectively, ensuring that therapists can respond flexibly to diverse client needs.

CHAPTER 8:

Addressing Common Client Issues

Introduction

Clients seek therapy for a variety of struggles, yet many underlying cognitive, emotional, and behavioral patterns remain consistent across issues such as anxiety, depression, trauma, relationship difficulties, and self-esteem challenges. Although no two clients are exactly alike, similar psychological mechanisms often underlie their symptoms. The Yanni Integration Approach (YIA) offers a comprehensive, evidence-based framework for addressing these concerns by blending cognitive behavioral therapy (CBT), psychodynamic therapy, humanistic therapy, person-centered therapy, and lifestyle changes. Research has shown that integrative psychotherapy approaches can be highly effective in improving clinical outcomes across various disorders (Norcross & Goldfried, 2019). This integrated approach allows therapists to tackle both immediate symptoms and deeper-rooted issues, promoting sustainable healing and personal growth.

Building on the structured approach to sessions discussed in Chapter 7, this chapter focuses on how YIA adapts to specific client presentations. Every session involves a dynamic balance of symptom relief and deeper exploration, and understanding common client issues allows therapists to choose the right therapeutic tools at the right moment.

The following sections detail how the integration of these models creates a holistic response to common mental health concerns, supported by research and illustrated through case studies.

Anxiety: Managing Symptoms and Uncovering Root Causes

Anxiety disorders affect millions of individuals and often manifest as chronic worry, panic attacks, avoidance behaviors, and physiological symptoms like rapid heartbeat and restlessness (Kessler et al., 2005). While CBT is well recognized for helping clients modify maladaptive thought patterns (Hofmann et al., 2012), anxiety is not solely cognitive, it frequently involves deep-seated emotional experiences, unconscious fears, and lifestyle habits.

It is also important to note that anxiety frequently coexists with other conditions, such as depression and trauma-related disorders. Studies indicate that nearly 60% of individuals diagnosed with major depressive disorder also meet criteria for an anxiety disorder (Kalin, 2020). This highlights the necessity of using an integrative approach that adapts to overlapping symptoms.

Integrated Approach to Anxiety

- **CBT:** Identifies and challenges irrational thought patterns (e.g., catastrophizing, overgeneralization).
- **Psychodynamic:** Explores unconscious fears and childhood experiences that contribute to chronic anxiety.
- **Humanistic:** Provides a nonjudgmental space for expressing emotions and reducing shame.
- **Person-Centered:** Encourages client autonomy in developing self-awareness and coping strategies.

- **Lifestyle Changes:** Emphasizes techniques such as breathing exercises, improved sleep, regular exercise, and dietary adjustments to regulate anxiety responses.

Case Study: Michael's Performance Anxiety

Michael, a 35-year-old marketing director, experiences severe panic attacks before public speaking engagements. He avoids networking events due to a fear of judgment and failure, limiting his professional growth despite his competence in his field. His anxiety leads to physical symptoms, such as shortness of breath and an elevated heart rate, making each presentation a distressing experience.

Integrated Intervention:

1. **CBT:** The therapist helps Michael identify and challenge automatic negative thoughts, such as *"Everyone will think I'm incompetent"*. Using evidence from past successful presentations, Michael gradually learns to replace catastrophic thinking with a more balanced perspective. Through exposure exercises, he starts practicing small speaking engagements in controlled settings, increasing his confidence over time.
2. **Psychodynamic:** Exploration reveals that Michael's highly critical father played a significant role in shaping his deep-seated fears of failure and rejection. He recalls early experiences where his achievements were dismissed or met with excessive scrutiny, leading him to internalize the belief that his worth was tied to perfection. Therapy helps Michael unpack these past experiences, allowing him to recognize how they continue to influence his anxiety in professional settings.
3. **Humanistic:** The therapist provides a supportive, non-judgmental space where Michael can express his emotions freely. Rather than viewing his anxiety as a personal flaw, he learns to see it as a natural response to past

experiences. Through self-compassion exercises, Michael begins to embrace his strengths while acknowledging that mistakes are part of growth, rather than reflections of inadequacy.

4. **Person-Centered:** Recognizing the importance of autonomy, Michael is encouraged to take an active role in selecting coping strategies that align with his values. He experiments with different techniques, such as visualization, self-affirmation, and reframing, until he finds what works best for him. This collaborative, client-driven approach reinforces his sense of control over his progress.
5. **Lifestyle Changes:** To complement his therapeutic work, Michael integrates breathing exercises and mindfulness techniques to regulate his anxiety before speaking engagements. He also adopts a structured pre-presentation routine, including light physical exercise, hydration, and controlled breathing, to ground himself before stepping onto the stage. As his confidence grows, he starts attending networking events with more ease, expanding his professional opportunities.

Follow-Up: Michael's Progress and Continued Development

After several months of therapy, Michael experiences a noticeable reduction in the intensity of his panic attacks before public speaking. He begins approaching networking events and presentations with less avoidance and more confidence, relying on the coping strategies he has developed in therapy. While moments of anxiety still arise, he no longer perceives them as insurmountable obstacles but rather as manageable experiences that he has the tools to navigate.

Despite these improvements, Michael occasionally doubts his ability to handle high-pressure situations. Therapy continues to reinforce cognitive restructuring techniques, helping him recognize when self-doubt is creeping in and replace automatic negative thoughts with more balanced perspectives. He also engages in gradual exposure exercises, where he challenges himself to take on increasing levels of public engagement, reinforcing his confidence through experience.

As Michael gains a stronger sense of self-efficacy, he begins to explore how his leadership and communication skills extend beyond public speaking. Rather than viewing presentations as moments of personal scrutiny, he starts to reframe them as opportunities for connection and knowledge-sharing. This shift in mindset allows him to approach his professional role with greater enthusiasm and a renewed sense of purpose.

Although Michael may always experience some level of performance anxiety, he now feels in control rather than controlled by it. Through YIA, he has strengthened his confidence, refined his communication skills, and learned to navigate high-stakes situations with greater ease and resilience.

In addition to addressing anxiety, an integrated approach is also vital for treating depression by breaking negative thought cycles and facilitating emotional expression.

Depression: Breaking Negative Thought Cycles and Encouraging Emotional Expression

Depression is characterized by persistent sadness, low motivation, and self-critical thought patterns (American Psychiatric Association, 2013). Although CBT is effective in challenging negative automatic thoughts, depression often involves deeper emotional wounds that require further exploration through Psychodynamic therapy and emotional validation via Humanistic techniques.

Additionally, many individuals struggling with depression experience symptoms of emotional numbness or dissociation, making it difficult for them to engage in therapy. Integrating Humanistic Therapy, which focuses on self-actualization, emotional depth, and self-compassion, can help clients reconnect with their emotions in a safe, supportive space. Person-Centered Therapy, emphasizing client autonomy and non-directive support, ensures that individuals feel empowered to set their own pace in healing without pressure or judgment. Utilizing these approaches early in treatment can help build rapport and motivation before engaging in deeper emotional work (Gilbert & Simos, 2022).

Integrated Approach to Depression

- **CBT:** Challenges maladaptive thought patterns such as *"I'm not good enough."*
- **Psychodynamic:** Identifies early attachment wounds, unresolved grief, and other emotional conflicts.
- **Humanistic:** Encourages self-compassion and acceptance.
- **Person-Centered:** Allows clients to set their own pace for healing.
- **Lifestyle Changes:** Incorporates exercise, social connection, and mindfulness practices to improve overall well-being.

Case Study: Lisa's Chronic Sadness

Lisa, a 42-year-old teacher, has struggled with depression since her divorce. She isolates herself, experiences persistent feelings of sadness, and believes she is unworthy of happiness. Despite wanting to rebuild her life, she finds it difficult to engage in social activities or establish new relationships due to deep-seated fears of rejection and emotional numbness.

Integrated Intervention:

1. **CBT:** The therapist helps Lisa identify and challenge self-defeating thoughts such as *"I will always be alone"* and *"I am not good enough."* Through cognitive restructuring, Lisa begins replacing these automatic negative thoughts with more balanced, evidence-based beliefs. By reviewing past relationships and identifying moments of meaningful connection, she gradually starts to reframe her self-perception.

2. **Psychodynamic:** Exploration reveals that Lisa's fear of abandonment stems from her emotionally distant parents, leading her to internalize a sense of unworthiness. The therapist helps Lisa recognize how these early relational experiences contribute to her current struggles with self-doubt and trust. Processing unresolved grief from her divorce also becomes a critical component of her healing process.
3. **Humanistic:** A key aspect of Lisa's progress involves fostering self-compassion and acceptance. Her therapist provides an empathetic, judgment-free space where she can express her sadness and frustration without fear of invalidation. Through unconditional positive regard, Lisa gradually learns to embrace her emotions without self-judgment, allowing her to rebuild a sense of intrinsic worth.
4. **Person-Centered:** Recognizing the importance of autonomy in the healing process, Lisa is encouraged to take the lead in setting her own goals. The therapist provides support without imposing directives, allowing Lisa to regain a sense of control over her life. She identifies small, manageable steps toward reconnecting with friends and engaging in activities that bring her joy.
5. **Lifestyle Changes:** To complement her therapeutic work, Lisa integrates daily outdoor activities and a consistent sleep routine into her lifestyle. She also begins incorporating mindfulness exercises, which help her regulate emotions and increase present-moment awareness. As she reconnects with supportive friends and builds healthier habits, she notices an improvement in both her mood and overall well-being.

Follow-Up: Lisa's Progress and Continued Growth

After several months of therapy, Lisa notices a gradual shift in her emotional state. She becomes more open to social interactions, no longer feeling as overwhelmed by the thought of reconnecting with others. Her self-perception improves, and she begins to see herself as capable of forming meaningful relationships rather than believing she is unworthy of love and connection. Although moments of sadness still occur, she now views them as temporary emotional experiences rather than evidence of personal failure.

Despite this progress, Lisa occasionally struggles with feelings of doubt and reluctance to trust others. Therapy continues to focus on reinforcing self-confidence and emotional regulation, helping her recognize when old patterns of avoidance emerge. Through consistent practice, she becomes more comfortable setting boundaries and expressing her needs without fear of rejection.

As Lisa gains a stronger sense of self, she begins to reflect on what brings her fulfillment. Rather than focusing solely on overcoming depression, she turns her attention toward rediscovering her passions and personal aspirations. She starts engaging in activities that once brought her joy, such as creative writing and outdoor exploration, using them as outlets for emotional expression.

While Lisa understands that depression may resurface at times, she feels better equipped to manage it. Through YIA, she has developed a greater sense of emotional agency, self-awareness, and the ability to embrace life with renewed optimism and purpose.

While anxiety and depression are common, trauma presents its own unique challenges that require a sensitive, multi-layered approach.

Trauma: Addressing Triggers and Processing Deep-Rooted Emotional Wounds

Trauma often results in emotional dysregulation, flashbacks, and avoidance behaviors (van der Kolk, 2014). While CBT can help reframe trauma-related thoughts, deeper healing typically requires the emotional processing offered by Psychodynamic therapy, along with the support of Humanistic and Lifestyle Change interventions.

Furthermore, trauma can underlie many other presenting concerns. Research suggests that individuals with a history of trauma are at significantly higher risk for developing anxiety and depressive disorders (McLaughlin et al., 2019). Even if trauma is not the primary reason for seeking therapy, it is essential to assess for past distressing experiences that may be influencing current symptoms.

Integrated Approach to PTSD

- **CBT:** Challenges trauma-related maladaptive thought patterns, such as *"I am permanently damaged"* or *"I will never be safe."* Through cognitive restructuring, clients learn to identify and replace distorted beliefs, develop distress tolerance skills, and gradually confront trauma-related triggers in a structured, manageable way.
- **Psychodynamic:** Explores early attachment wounds, suppressed emotions, and unconscious defense mechanisms that may have developed in response to past trauma. Processing unresolved grief, shame, and fear helps clients gain insight into how their past experiences shape their current emotional responses and behaviors.
- **Humanistic:** Encourages self-compassion and emotional validation, helping clients accept their trauma history without self-blame. A key focus is on restoring a sense of personal identity and agency, fostering an environment where clients feel empowered to heal at their own pace.
- **Person-Centered:** Allows clients to dictate the pace of their trauma work, ensuring therapy remains empowering rather than overwhelming. The therapist provides unconditional positive regard and non-directive support, creating a safe, judgment-free space where clients can process emotions without pressure.
- **Lifestyle Changes:** Incorporates body-based and mindfulness interventions to help regulate the nervous system. Clients engage in regular physical activity, deep-breathing exercises, meditation, and social connection, which have been shown to reduce PTSD symptoms, promote emotional stabilization, and improve overall well-being.

Case Study: James's PTSD from Childhood Abuse

James, a 30-year-old veteran, sought therapy after experiencing recurring panic attacks, nightmares, and emotional numbness related to his childhood abuse. Though his initial motivation for therapy was to manage anxiety in social settings, deeper exploration revealed unresolved trauma that had significantly impacted his self-worth, relationships, and ability to trust others.

Integrated Intervention:

1. **CBT:** The therapist introduced grounding techniques, such as the 5-4-3-2-1 sensory awareness method, to help James stay present during panic episodes. Trauma-focused exposure exercises were gradually introduced to help him reframe distressing memories and reduce avoidance behaviors. Through cognitive restructuring, James began identifying and challenging maladaptive beliefs, such as *"I am unlovable"* or *"I will always be in danger"* (Foa et al., 2007). Research has consistently demonstrated that CBT is one of the most effective interventions for PTSD, helping individuals reprocess trauma-related thoughts and reduce distressing symptoms (Ehlers et al., 2005).
2. **Psychodynamic:** As therapy progressed, James unearthed deeply repressed emotions of anger and sadness toward his abuser. He explored the defense mechanisms, such as emotional detachment and hyper-independence, that he had developed as a child to survive. Processing these emotions in a safe therapeutic space helped James release long-held shame and self-blame (Schottenbauer et al., 2008). Psychodynamic therapy has been shown to aid in resolving unconscious conflicts and facilitating long-term emotional processing in trauma survivors (Fonagy et al., 2002).
3. **Humanistic:** A key component of James's healing was receiving consistent, unconditional support from his therapist. By experiencing acceptance and validation, James gradually internalized a new, healthier self-narrative, one

that recognized his resilience and intrinsic worth, rather than defining himself solely by his past trauma. The humanistic approach, as described by Rogers (1951), emphasizes that a non-judgmental and empathetic therapeutic environment fosters emotional healing and self-acceptance.

4. **Person-Centered:** Recognizing the importance of autonomy in trauma recovery, the therapist allowed James to dictate the pace of his trauma work. Some sessions were focused solely on self-regulation and present-moment coping, while others delved deeper into processing painful memories. This flexible approach ensured that therapy remained empowering rather than overwhelming (Elliott et al., 2004). Person-centered therapy has been widely recognized for its effectiveness in fostering self-efficacy and emotional resilience, particularly in individuals recovering from trauma.
5. **Lifestyle Changes:** To complement his therapeutic work, James integrated physical and mindfulness-based practices. Yoga helped him reconnect with his body in a non-threatening way, while daily deep-breathing exercises became a cornerstone of his emotional stabilization. Additionally, he began prioritizing sleep hygiene and social connection, both of which significantly improved his overall well-being. Research has demonstrated that yoga, mindfulness, and breathwork can help trauma survivors regulate emotions, reduce physiological arousal, and improve overall mental health (van der Kolk, 2014).

Follow-Up: James's Progress and Ongoing Work

After several months of therapy, James reported a noticeable decrease in the frequency and intensity of his panic attacks. His nightmares, while still present, became less distressing as he worked through trauma-related memories. However, challenges remained, James struggled with vulnerability in relationships, often defaulting to emotional withdrawal when confronted with conflict.

To address this, therapy shifted toward helping James practice healthy relational boundaries and effective communication. By using role-playing exercises, he gained confidence in expressing his needs and fears to trusted individuals in his life.

Additionally, as James felt more in control of his emotions, he expressed a desire to find deeper meaning in his experiences. Therapy expanded to include discussions about post-traumatic growth, how he could channel his resilience into mentoring others or engaging in advocacy work.

While James' trauma would never be entirely erased, he no longer felt defined by it. Through YIA, he transformed his relationship with his past, gaining the tools to navigate life with greater self-compassion and emotional stability.

Bringing together these diverse approaches helps create a comprehensive treatment plan that addresses both immediate symptoms and long-term healing.

Conclusion

The case studies presented in this chapter illustrate how an integrative model can transform lives, helping clients rebuild confidence, reframe their experiences, and develop resilience. By addressing both the cognitive and emotional layers of distress, YIA ensures that therapy is not just about symptom reduction but about empowering individuals to reclaim their sense of self, cultivate healthier relationships, and embrace a more fulfilling life.

As the field of psychotherapy continues to evolve, an integrative, adaptable approach like YIA remains essential. The ability to blend evidence-based techniques with a client-driven, compassionate framework makes YIA a powerful tool for fostering deep and lasting healing.

CHAPTER 9:

Therapist-Client Collaboration and Growth

Introduction

A strong therapeutic alliance is one of the most significant predictors of successful treatment outcomes (Norcross & Lambert, 2019a). While initial trust-building is essential, sustaining therapist-client collaboration over time determines the depth and effectiveness of therapy. Clients must feel supported not only in moments of progress but also through setbacks, as therapy is not a linear journey.

In chapter 8, we explored how an integrative approach effectively addresses client concerns such as anxiety, depression, and trauma. However, therapy is more than just resolving immediate distress, it is about ensuring lasting progress. This chapter focuses on sustaining engagement, navigating challenges, and fostering long-term growth in collaboration with clients.

The Yanni Integration Approach (YIA) emphasizes that growth in therapy requires a balance between structured interventions (cognitive behavioral therapy), deep self-exploration (psychodynamic therapy), emotional validation (humanistic therapy), client autonomy (person-centered therapy), and practical lifestyle modifications (lifestyle changes). This comprehensive, integrated model ensures that therapy remains adaptive and dynamic, fostering long-term self-efficacy and resilience.

This chapter explores strategies for maintaining the therapeutic alliance, helping clients reflect on progress, and empowering them to sustain long-term emotional well-being.

Sustaining the Therapeutic Alliance Over Time

The therapist-client relationship evolves throughout the course of therapy. Initial rapport-building gives way to deeper, more complex work that involves vulnerability, resistance, and emotional breakthroughs. Research indicates that clients who perceive their therapist as empathic, trustworthy, and collaborative show higher engagement and better outcomes (Swift & Greenberg, 2012). However, sustaining this alliance requires ongoing attunement to the client's changing needs. Therapists must recognize shifts in motivation, emotional readiness, and resistance to growth, adjusting interventions accordingly.

Integrating the Five Models to Maintain the Alliance

- **CBT:** Provides structured feedback and helps clients track progress through measurable goals.
- **Psychodynamic:** Identifies patterns of resistance or transference that may impact the therapeutic relationship.
- **Humanistic:** Reinforces the therapist's authenticity and emotional presence, ensuring unconditional positive regard.
- **Person-Centered:** Encourages client autonomy in guiding therapy, maintaining collaboration.
- **Lifestyle Changes:** Reinforces practical coping strategies that support emotional well-being outside of sessions.

Case Study: Marcus and the Fear of Dependency

Marcus, a 40-year-old engineer, struggles with deep-seated fears of relying on others due to childhood neglect. Initially, he engages in therapy but starts missing sessions when deeper emotional work begins.

Recognizing early signs of client resistance is essential to maintaining engagement. Research suggests that resistance often manifests through behaviors such as session cancellations, superficial discussions, or avoidance of difficult topics (Muran et al., 2005). These patterns may indicate underlying emotional conflicts, such as fears of dependency or vulnerability. Addressing these signs proactively by acknowledging shifts in engagement and inviting client reflection can help sustain the therapeutic alliance and prevent disengagement (Norcross, Krebs, & Prochaska, 2011).

Integrated Approach:

1. **CBT:** The therapist uses self-monitoring tools to track Marcus's anxiety levels and therapy attendance patterns.
2. **Psychodynamic:** Exploration reveals that Marcus equates dependency with weakness, leading to avoidance of deeper emotional work.
3. **Humanistic:** The therapist reassures Marcus that seeking support is not a weakness, validating his experiences.
4. **Person-Centered:** Marcus openly discusses his hesitations, ensuring he feels in control of his therapy process.
5. **Lifestyle Changes:** The therapist encourages stress-reducing activities, journaling, and self-care to help Marcus regulate emotions between sessions.

By integrating these approaches, the therapist helps Marcus confront his fears of dependency while maintaining a strong therapeutic alliance. Over time, Marcus becomes more comfortable with emotional vulnerability, allowing him to remain engaged in therapy and explore deeper aspects of his trauma. Studies confirm that therapists who maintain emotional attunement and flexibility, adjusting interventions based on the client's evolving needs, achieve better long-term outcomes (Wampold & Imel, 2015).

As the therapeutic alliance strengthens, helping clients reflect on their progress and setbacks fosters deeper engagement and resilience.

Helping Clients Reflect on Progress and Setbacks

Therapy is not a linear process. Clients experience breakthroughs and regressions, moments of clarity, and periods of emotional resistance. Research on psychotherapy outcomes has shown that progress often follows a pattern of fluctuating change, with setbacks being a normal part of the therapeutic process (A. M. Hayes et al., 2007). Normalizing these fluctuations prevents discouragement and fosters resilience, helping clients remain engaged in therapy (Wampold & Imel, 2015).

Encouraging clients to reflect on both progress and setbacks allows them to recognize their growth and deepen their self-awareness. Studies suggest that structured self-reflection promotes meaningful therapeutic change, as it enhances clients' ability to recognize cognitive and behavioral shifts over time (Kazantzis et al., 2010). Additionally, integrating multiple therapeutic approaches can help clients process their experiences from different perspectives, reinforcing their sense of progress.

Integrating the Five Models

- **CBT:** Uses structured reflection exercises to track changes in thinking patterns and behaviors.
- **Psychodynamic:** Explores unconscious blocks or resistance that may cause stagnation.
- **Humanistic:** Provides validation and encouragement, reinforcing self-acceptance.

- **Person-Centered:** Encourages client-led discussions on progress, reinforcing autonomy.
- **Lifestyle Changes:** Supports reflection through journaling, mindfulness, and self-assessment tools.

Although therapists can provide structured methods to track change, it is equally important to invite clients to define progress in their own terms. Some clients may measure success through symptom reduction, while others may focus on improved relationships, greater self-compassion, or increased confidence in handling life's challenges. Asking questions such as, *"How would you describe growth in your own life?"* or *"What feels different for you since beginning therapy?"* helps ensure therapy remains aligned with clients' personal values and goals.

Case Study: Aisha's Frustration with Progress

Aisha, a 28-year-old law student, sought therapy to manage academic stress and self-doubt. Initially, she responded well to therapy, implementing cognitive and lifestyle strategies that improved her confidence and focus. However, after a particularly stressful exam period, she found herself slipping back into patterns of negative thinking. Frustrated and discouraged, Aisha questioned whether therapy was truly helping her or if she was simply incapable of sustaining change.

Relapses into old thought patterns are common in therapy, particularly when external stressors amplify underlying fears and self-criticism (Wampold & Imel, 2015). Aisha's experience highlights the nonlinear nature of progress, where setbacks do not erase previous gains but instead provide opportunities for deeper insight and reinforcement of coping strategies.

Integrated Approach:

1. **CBT:** The therapist helps Aisha review her thought records, showing evidence of improvement despite setbacks.
2. **Psychodynamic:** Exploration reveals that Aisha's high expectations stem from childhood pressure to succeed, contributing to self-criticism.
3. **Humanistic:** The therapist validates Aisha's frustration while reminding her that healing is a process, not an endpoint.
4. **Person-Centered:** Aisha defines what progress means to her, ensuring therapy aligns with her values.
5. **Lifestyle Changes:** The therapist helps Aisha establish a self-care plan, including sleep hygiene, study breaks, and social support.

Aisha's journey illustrates that progress in therapy is not linear—moments of struggle do not erase past achievements. By recognizing setbacks as learning opportunities rather than failures, Aisha develops a more resilient mindset. Through an integrated approach, she not only strengthens her ability to challenge negative thoughts and self-criticism, but she also redefines success in a way that fosters self-acceptance rather than pressure. As therapy continues, Aisha gains confidence in her capacity to navigate challenges with self-awareness and self-compassion, gaining tools for long-term emotional well-being. Longitudinal studies indicate that clients who actively reflect on their progress in therapy are more likely to sustain gains and remain motivated (Michie et al., 2009).

Beyond reflecting on progress, strengthening self-efficacy and resilience ensures that clients can navigate future challenges independently.

Strengthening Self-Efficacy and Long-Term Resilience

The ultimate goal of therapy is to equip clients with the tools and confidence to manage future challenges independently. Research supports that clients who develop strong self-efficacy are less likely to relapse into maladaptive patterns (Bandura, 1997). Therapists play a crucial role in fostering resilience by ensuring that clients internalize therapeutic techniques, recognize their strengths, and develop sustainable coping strategies.

Integrating the Five Models

- **CBT:** Reinforces self-efficacy by practicing coping strategies until they become second nature.
- **Psychodynamic:** Helps clients gain insight into how past patterns may re-emerge, preparing them to navigate challenges.
- **Humanistic:** Encourages a growth mindset, helping clients recognize their potential.
- **Person-Centered:** Ensures that clients leave therapy feeling empowered and in control of their emotional well-being.
- **Lifestyle Changes:** Supports resilience through healthy routines, stress management, and self-care practices.

A key component of self-efficacy is preparing for potential setbacks. Research on self-efficacy theory suggests that individuals who anticipate challenges and develop strategies in advance are more likely to maintain progress and adapt to difficulties (Bandura, 1997). Helping clients identify early warning signs of distress, such as increased self-criticism or avoidance behaviors, allows them to intervene before challenges escalate. Recognizing these warning signs is a critical aspect of relapse prevention, as studies indicate that early detection of distress signals can significantly reduce the likelihood of regression (Marlatt & Donovan, 2005).

Developing an individualized relapse-prevention plan ensures that clients can apply coping strategies outside of therapy. Cognitive behavioral therapy (CBT) and dialectical behavior therapy (DBT) emphasize the importance of structured plans that outline specific coping mechanisms, emotional regulation techniques, and support systems to prevent setbacks (Linehan, 1993; Witkiewitz & Marlatt,

2004). By proactively identifying triggers and strategies, clients strengthen their resilience and ability to navigate challenges independently, reinforcing their long-term self-efficacy.

Case Study: Jonah's Transition Out of Therapy

Jonah, a 32-year-old musician, has successfully managed his social anxiety and is preparing to transition out of therapy. While he recognizes his progress, he expresses a lingering fear of managing on his own without the structured support of therapy sessions. This uncertainty is common as clients approach the end of therapy, as they may question their ability to sustain their progress without professional guidance (Norcross, Krebs, & Prochaska, 2011).

The transition out of therapy is a critical phase that requires careful reinforcement of coping strategies, emotional processing, and autonomy-building to ensure long-term success. Research suggests that therapeutic gains are best maintained when clients have a structured plan for continued self-reflection and support (Kazantzis et al., 2010). By integrating multiple approaches, Jonah can build confidence in his ability to navigate future challenges independently while maintaining the insights he has gained throughout therapy.

Integrated Approach:

- **CBT:** The therapist reviews coping techniques Jonah has learned, ensuring he feels confident in applying them.
- **Psychodynamic:** Jonah explores how fear of independence stems from early attachment wounds, helping him reframe his emotions.
- **Humanistic:** The therapist celebrates Jonah's growth, reinforcing his ability to handle challenges.
- **Person-Centered:** Jonah decides when and how to taper sessions, ensuring a gradual, client-led transition.

- **Lifestyle Changes:** The therapist helps Jonah develop a mindfulness routine, maintain healthy social habits, and continue self-reflection.

Jonah's transition out of therapy highlights the importance of reinforcing self-efficacy and autonomy in clients who are nearing the end of treatment. While fear of managing independently is natural, a structured approach that integrates multiple therapeutic models can help clients feel empowered in their ability to sustain progress. Through CBT strategies, psychodynamic insight, humanistic encouragement, and lifestyle adjustments, Jonah builds confidence in his capacity to navigate life's challenges without relying on therapy as a crutch.

As therapy concludes, Jonah recognizes that while support systems remain valuable, his growth is self-sustaining, a realization that transforms his fear of independence into a newfound sense of self-trust. By maintaining mindfulness practices, social engagement, and self-reflection, Jonah ensures that therapy's impact extends beyond the session, allowing him to embrace his next chapter with confidence and resilience. Clients who develop a strong sense of self-efficacy and resilience in therapy are less likely to relapse and more likely to adapt to future stressors effectively (Bandura, 1997; Norcross & Wampold, 2011a).

While client growth is essential, therapists also face challenges in integrating multiple approaches effectively.

Common Therapist Challenges in Integration

Integrating multiple therapeutic models offers a dynamic and flexible approach to treatment, allowing therapists to tailor interventions to each client's unique needs. Research suggests that integrative psychotherapy enhances treatment outcomes by drawing on the strengths of different modalities while maintaining a client-centered focus (Norcross & Goldfried, 2019; Barnett et al., 2007; Rupert & Dorociak, 2019). However, while integration allows for greater adaptability, it also presents unique challenges for therapists, requiring clinical intuition, flexibility, and a deep understanding of multiple frameworks.

One primary challenge is knowing when to transition between models. Therapists must balance structure and responsiveness, ensuring that changes in approach align with client engagement and therapeutic goals (Wampold & Imel, 2015). Additionally, therapists may encounter client resistance if an individual strongly favors one modality over another. Research on the therapeutic alliance suggests that validating client preferences and collaboratively introducing new approaches improves engagement and trust (Lambert & Barley, 2001).

Another key concern is maintaining professional boundaries when incorporating lifestyle interventions. While behavioral and mental health strategies fall within a therapist's scope, providing medical or nutritional advice may exceed ethical guidelines (Barnett et al., 2007). Therapists practicing integrative care must be mindful of staying within their professional role while still addressing holistic well-being.

Finally, the cognitive and emotional demands of managing multiple therapeutic models can contribute to therapist burnout. Balancing various approaches requires ongoing self-reflection, supervision, and structured frameworks to prevent emotional exhaustion (Rupert & Dorociak, 2019). Engaging in peer consultation and self-care practices has been shown to reduce burnout and enhance therapist effectiveness (Skovholt & Trotter-Mathison, 2016).

By proactively addressing these challenges, therapists can successfully integrate multiple approaches while ensuring ethical practice, maintaining client engagement, and safeguarding their own well-being.

Below are some common concerns therapists face when implementing an integrated approach, along with practical solutions:

1. How do I know when to switch between therapy models?

Solution: Observe client engagement and responsiveness, normalize integration as part of the process, and maintain a common thread when transitioning approaches to ensure continuity in the therapeutic relationship.

2. What if my client prefers one method and resists others?

Solution: Validate the client's preferences, introduce complementary approaches gradually, and frame integration as a strength rather than a limitation, showing how multiple techniques can work together to enhance progress.

3. How do I integrate lifestyle changes while staying within my scope?

Solution: Focus on behavior and mental well-being rather than providing medical advice. Encourage clients to consult physicians for medical concerns while supporting them in making psychologically-informed lifestyle adjustments.

4. How do I prevent therapist burnout when integrating multiple models?

Solution: Develop a session framework that provides both flexibility and structure, avoid over-personalization of client struggles, and engage in supervision and peer consultation to maintain professional balance and self-care.

Conclusion

Sustaining the therapeutic alliance requires ongoing trust-building, attunement, and adaptability. Helping clients reflect on progress fosters self-awareness and motivation, preventing discouragement during setbacks. Strengthening self-efficacy ensures that clients leave therapy with the confidence to navigate future stressors independently. By integrating CBT, Psychodynamic, Humanistic, Person-Centered, and Lifestyle Change models, therapists create a balanced, holistic approach that promotes long-term growth and resilience.

CHAPTER 10:

Managing Challenges in Therapy

Introduction

Therapy is an evolving process that presents challenges for both clients and therapists. Although progress often emerges through deep self-reflection and skill-building, moments of resistance, transference, countertransference, and therapeutic impasses can slow or even halt progress. These moments, though difficult, provide valuable opportunities for insight and growth when handled with the right approach.

In Chapter 9, we explored how a strong therapeutic alliance fosters resilience and engagement. However, even in trusting therapeutic relationships, clients encounter obstacles that may temporarily hinder progress. This chapter examines how to address these challenges effectively while maintaining the therapeutic alliance and helping clients sustain growth.

This chapter explores common challenges in therapy, the role of transference and countertransference, and strategies for maintaining momentum during therapeutic impasses.

Understanding and Managing Resistance in Therapy

Resistance is a natural defense mechanism that arises when clients feel vulnerable, exposed, or fearful of change. While resistance is sometimes viewed as an obstacle to progress, it often serves a protective function, signaling deep-rooted fears, past traumas, or internal conflicts that require careful navigation. Research suggests that effective therapists do not try to eliminate resistance but rather explore it with curiosity and patience (Beutler et al., 2002).

Integrating the Five Models to Manage Resistance

- **CBT:** Helps clients recognize avoidance behaviors and cognitive distortions that contribute to resistance.
- **Psychodynamic:** Explores unconscious fears or relational patterns that fuel resistance, helping clients make meaningful connections.
- **Humanistic:** Creates an empathetic and nonjudgmental space, reducing the client's need to defend against emotional discomfort.
- **Person-Centered:** Gives clients control over their therapeutic journey, reducing the fear of being pushed too quickly into uncomfortable territory.
- **Lifestyle Changes:** Encourages small behavioral shifts outside of therapy, helping clients see change as manageable rather than overwhelming.

Strategies for Addressing Resistance

Therapists can gently explore resistance without confronting it in a way that might push the client further into avoidance. Effective approaches include:

- **Normalizing resistance** by acknowledging that change is difficult and that therapy can bring up strong emotions (W. R. Miller & Rollnick, 2013).

- **Using Socratic questioning (CBT)** to help clients examine their fears about progress:
    - *"What is the worst that could happen if you allowed yourself to move forward?"* (J. S. Beck, 2011).
- **Exploring underlying emotions (Psychodynamic)** rather than focusing solely on the behavior:
    - *"I notice that each time we discuss vulnerability, you shift the topic. What do you think is making that difficult?"* (Freud, 1915; Shedler, 2010).
- **Encouraging self-compassion (Humanistic)** by helping clients understand that resistance is not failure but a part of growth (Neff, 2011; Rogers, 1961).
- **Breaking down change into small, achievable steps (Lifestyle Changes)** to reduce the overwhelming nature of progress (Prochaska & DiClemente, 1983).

Therapists who engage resistance rather than fight it create an environment where clients feel safe enough to explore the root causes of their fears. By validating resistance as a natural part of change and using an integrative approach that combines cognitive, emotional, and behavioral strategies, therapists can help clients move toward meaningful progress. This process fosters a sense of autonomy, self-awareness, and emotional resilience, ultimately reinforcing the client's ability to engage in change at their own pace. Studies show that when therapists respond to resistance with empathy rather than confrontation, clients experience greater emotional safety and are more likely to engage in change (Norcross & Lambert, 2019b).

While resistance is a common challenge, transference and countertransference also play significant roles in shaping the therapeutic relationship.

Transference and Countertransference: Navigating Emotional Reactions

Transference occurs when clients unconsciously project feelings, expectations, and relational patterns from past experiences onto their therapist. These projections can be positive (idealization, dependence) or negative (mistrust, anger). Countertransference, on the other hand, refers to the therapist's emotional reactions to the client, which may stem from personal experiences or the dynamics of the therapeutic relationship (Gelso & Hayes, 2007).

Recognizing countertransference is crucial for maintaining professional boundaries and ensuring that therapist reactions do not interfere with client progress. Self-awareness, supervision, and consultation with peers can help therapists navigate these reactions effectively (Norcross & Lambert, 2019b).

Integrating the Five Models to Address Transference and Countertransference

- **CBT:** Helps clients recognize distorted perceptions and how they affect their relationship with the therapist.
- **Psychodynamic:** Explores how past experiences shape present relational expectations, allowing clients to gain deeper insight.
- **Humanistic:** Encourages emotional honesty, helping the therapist and client engage in open discussions about their reactions.
- **Person-Centered:** Ensures that discussions about transference are client-led, allowing them to explore their feelings at their own pace.
- **Lifestyle Changes:** Provides external grounding techniques (mindfulness, journaling) to help clients process strong emotions.

Managing Transference and Countertransference

Therapists must recognize when transference or countertransference is shaping the therapeutic relationship in a way that impacts progress. Strategies include:

- **Identifying patterns early** by noticing when emotional reactions seem disproportionate to the situation (Gelso & Hayes, 2007).
- **Encouraging reflection (CBT)** by asking, "*Does this reaction remind you of something or someone from your past?*" (J. S. Beck, 2011).
- **Using self-awareness (Psychodynamic)** to recognize how countertransference may be influencing therapist responses (Freud, 1912; Gabbard, 2001).
- **Validating the client's experience (Humanistic)** while maintaining professional boundaries (Rogers, 1961).
- **Reframing the experience as an opportunity for growth (Person-Centered)** rather than a disruption (Yalom, 2002).

When handled effectively, transference and countertransference provide deep insights into unresolved emotions and relational patterns. By remaining attuned to these dynamics, therapists can transform them into valuable therapeutic tools. Through careful exploration and boundary-setting, clients gain a greater understanding of their past experiences and how these influence their present relationships, fostering deeper self-awareness and emotional growth. Therapists who are trained in recognizing and managing countertransference tend to maintain stronger therapeutic alliances and achieve better treatment outcomes (Gelso & Hayes, 2007).

At times, clients may feel stuck in therapy. Understanding how to navigate therapeutic impasses is essential for maintaining progress.

Strategies for Maintaining Momentum During Therapeutic Impasses

Therapeutic impasses occur when clients feel stuck, disengaged, or emotionally blocked, leading to stagnation in therapy. These moments can be frustrating for both the client and the therapist, but they often indicate that an important breakthrough is on the horizon (Wachtel, 2011). The key is helping clients move through the impasse without feeling forced or pressured.

Integrating the Five Models to Overcome Impasses

- **CBT:** Uses structured goal-setting and problem-solving to re-engage clients.
- **Psychodynamic:** Explores underlying conflicts that may be causing avoidance, such as fear of success or self-sabotage.
- **Humanistic:** Encourages patience and self-acceptance, helping clients feel less frustrated with their perceived lack of progress.
- **Person-Centered:** Respects the client's pace, allowing them to guide discussions about what feels stuck.
- **Lifestyle Changes:** Encourages new activities and behavioral shifts outside of therapy that can provide fresh perspectives.

Practical Approaches to Breaking Through Impasses

- **Revisiting the client's original goals (CBT)** to remind them of their progress and reinforce the connection between effort and change (J. S. Beck, 2011).
- **Exploring deeper fears (Psychodynamic)** by asking, "*What do you think is stopping you from moving forward?*" to uncover unconscious conflicts that may be creating resistance (Freud, 1915; Shedler, 2010).

- **Encouraging emotional expression (Humanistic)** without judgment or pressure, fostering a safe space for processing emotions (Rogers, 1961).
- **Asking the client to define their own stuck points (Person-Centered)** to avoid assumptions and empower them in the therapeutic process (Yalom, 2002).
- **Suggesting a temporary shift in focus (Lifestyle Changes)** such as journaling, creative expression, or physical activity to help clients gain new insights and reconnect with their intrinsic motivation (Pennebaker, 1997b; Prochaska & DiClemente, 1983).

Momentum in therapy is not about relentless forward movement but about helping clients navigate internal resistance with patience and self-compassion. By integrating cognitive, emotional, and behavioral approaches, therapists can support clients in breaking through impasses while respecting their unique pace of change. Encouraging flexibility in thought and action allows clients to redefine progress as a dynamic process rather than a linear path, fostering resilience and deeper self-awareness.

Case Study: Rachel's Stagnation in Therapy

Rachel, a 30-year-old graphic designer, entered therapy for depression and low self-esteem. Initially, she made progress in challenging negative self-talk (CBT) and exploring childhood experiences that shaped her self-perception (psychodynamic). However, over time, she became detached in sessions, responding with short answers and avoiding deeper topics.

Integrated Approach:

- **CBT:** The therapist revisited Rachel's therapy goals, reminding her of past progress and areas she had expressed wanting to explore further.

- **Psychodynamic:** The therapist gently inquired if disengagement felt familiar in other areas of her life, uncovering a pattern of avoidance when feeling vulnerable.
- **Humanistic:** The therapist validated Rachel's experience: "*It makes sense that opening up feels difficult right now. You're not alone in this.*"
- **Person-Centered:** Rachel was encouraged to explore her hesitations at her own pace rather than feeling pressured.
- **Lifestyle Changes:** The therapist suggested creative outlets, such as journaling and art, to help Rachel engage with her emotions nonverbally.

Over time, Rachel recognized that her reluctance to engage stemmed from a fear of vulnerability. By normalizing these emotions and providing structured yet compassionate support, the therapist helped her re-engage in therapy. Therapists who use integrative approaches to address impasses, rather than relying on a single method, are more successful in helping clients regain engagement (Wachtel, 2011).

To navigate the emotional intensity of difficult sessions, therapists must cultivate strategies that help them stay fully present and attuned to their clients.

Practical Therapist Strategies for Staying Present During Difficult Sessions

Working with resistant or emotionally intense clients can be exhausting for therapists. To maintain presence and emotional regulation while managing resistance, transference, or impasses, therapists can employ the following strategies:

- **Mindfulness techniques**: Practicing mindfulness before and after difficult sessions helps therapists maintain a balanced emotional state and reduce reactivity (Kabat-Zinn, 1990; Siegel, 2010).

- **Deep breathing exercises**: Taking a moment to focus on breath can help reset emotional regulation during challenging moments, promoting physiological and psychological calmness (Porges, 2011).
- **Self-reflection**: Journaling about countertransference reactions helps identify personal triggers and unconscious biases, enhancing self-awareness and therapeutic effectiveness (Gelso & Hayes, 2007).
- **Peer consultation**: Engaging in regular supervision provides valuable insights and emotional support, helping therapists manage difficult cases while maintaining professional boundaries (Bernard & Goodyear, 2019).

By integrating these strategies, therapists can enhance their ability to remain present and engaged, even in challenging therapeutic encounters. Maintaining self-awareness and emotional regulation not only supports the therapist's well-being but also creates a more attuned and effective therapeutic experience for the client. A therapist's ability to stay present in difficult moments reinforces the safety and trust essential for meaningful therapeutic work.

Conclusion

Managing challenges in therapy requires an integrative, flexible approach that acknowledges resistance, transference, countertransference, and therapeutic impasses as natural aspects of growth. Rather than eliminating resistance, effective therapists engage with it compassionately to explore its deeper meaning. Transference and countertransference, when properly understood, provide insight into unresolved emotional wounds and relational history. Therapeutic impasses should be seen as opportunities for deeper self-awareness, requiring patience and tailored interventions to maintain progress.

CHAPTER 11:

Closure & Termination in Therapy Using the Yanni Integration Approach (YIA)

Introduction

Termination in therapy is a critical phase, marking the culmination of a client's therapeutic journey. Using the Yanni Integration Approach (YIA), termination is not viewed as an abrupt ending but rather as a transition into the independent application of therapeutic gains. A well-managed termination ensures that clients feel prepared, resilient, and confident in sustaining their progress.

As explored in Chapter 10, therapy often involves navigating resistance, breaking through impasses, and managing complex emotional dynamics such as transference and countertransference. Once these challenges have been addressed, the focus shifts to ensuring that clients can maintain their progress independently. The transition out of therapy is a crucial period that requires careful planning and reinforcement of the strategies that have been cultivated throughout treatment.

Although termination signifies the end of regular sessions, it does not mean the end of a client's growth. A thoughtfully structured termination process empowers clients to internalize what they've learned and apply it effectively in their daily lives.

Research highlights that a gradual, well-planned termination fosters long-term stability and reduces the likelihood of relapse (Norcross, Zimmerman, et al., 2011).

This chapter explores the process of recognizing readiness for termination, addressing emotional responses, consolidating growth, and ensuring lasting therapeutic benefits through a structured, integrative approach.

The first step in preparing for termination is assessing whether the client is truly ready to transition out of therapy.

Recognizing Readiness for Termination

Determining when a client is ready to conclude therapy is a nuanced process that requires careful assessment and collaboration. Termination is not merely the cessation of sessions but a transition toward self-sufficiency, where the client internalizes therapeutic insights and confidently applies them outside of therapy. The Yanni Integration Approach (YIA) incorporates principles from cognitive behavioral therapy (CBT), humanistic therapy, person-centered therapy, psychodynamic therapy, and lifestyle changes to ensure a well-rounded evaluation of readiness.

Indicators of Readiness

- **Sustained Progress:** Clients demonstrate improved emotional regulation, reduced symptom severity, and consistent coping strategies (Beutler & Harwood, 2000).
- **Increased Autonomy:** Clients show confidence in handling challenges without heavy reliance on therapy (Rogers, 1951).
- **Resolution of Core Issues:** Psychodynamic themes, such as unresolved trauma or relational conflicts, have been sufficiently processed (Shedler, 2010).

- **Ability to Self-Regulate:** Clients exhibit greater self-awareness and adaptive responses to stressors (Linehan, 1993).
- **Adoption of Sustainable Lifestyle Habits:** Clients integrate sleep hygiene, physical activity, healthy nutrition, and mindfulness practices as part of long-term self-care (Ratey, 2008).
- **Confidence in Applying Skills Independently:** Clients express confidence in utilizing the coping strategies they have learned, even when new challenges arise (Weisz & Kazdin, 2017).

Recognizing readiness for termination is not about achieving perfection but about ensuring that clients have the resilience and tools to navigate life's challenges on their own. A key milestone in this process is the shift from guided reflection in therapy to self-directed reflection, where clients trust their ability to process emotions without external validation. By reaching this stage, clients not only complete therapy but embark on a lifelong journey of growth, equipped with the confidence and skills to sustain their well-being independently.

Once readiness is established, termination should occur gradually, allowing clients to transition smoothly while maintaining autonomy.

Gradual Transition and Testing Independence

Ending therapy should not feel like an abrupt break but rather a carefully guided transition that empowers clients to sustain their progress. The Yanni Integration Approach (YIA) emphasizes a step-down method, where clients gradually reduce session frequency while strengthening their independence. This structured approach allows for real-world application of therapeutic skills with ongoing support, fostering confidence in their ability to manage challenges on their own.

Strategies for a Gradual Transition

- **Tapering Sessions:** Gradually moving from weekly to biweekly or monthly sessions allows clients to apply skills with increased autonomy (Norcross, Zimmerman, et al., 2011).
- **Practicing Independence:** Clients navigate real-world situations without immediate therapist intervention, reinforcing self-trust.
- **Revisiting Previous Challenges:** Reviewing past difficulties and how they were successfully managed strengthens resilience (Ellis, 2001).
- **Maintaining a Healthy Lifestyle:** Reinforcing the role of daily routines, exercise, balanced nutrition, and social support in sustaining mental well-being.
- **Role-Playing Future Challenges:** Clients practice handling potential stressors in session to boost their confidence in real-world application (Prochaska & DiClemente, 1983).

A gradual transition not only reduces the anxiety associated with termination but also solidifies the client's belief in their own ability to sustain progress. By creating opportunities to test independence within a supportive framework, therapists help clients recognize that therapy is not an external solution but a process that has equipped them with lifelong tools. Ultimately, this approach transforms termination into a milestone of empowerment rather than an end, ensuring that clients continue to thrive well beyond the therapy room.

Case Study: David's Transition Out of Therapy

David, a 40-year-old client, initially sought therapy for anxiety and self-doubt that impacted his professional and personal life. Through the Yanni Integration Approach (YIA), his therapy focused on five key areas, cognitive behavioral therapy

(CBT), humanistic therapy, person-centered therapy, psychodynamic therapy, and lifestyle changes, ensuring a holistic transition out of therapy.

- **Cognitive Behavioral Therapy (CBT):** David identified and challenged negative thought patterns contributing to his anxiety. He developed a structured plan to reframe unhelpful thinking and apply coping strategies in real-world situations, reinforcing his confidence in problem-solving.
- **Humanistic Therapy:** David's journey emphasized self-acceptance and emotional growth. His therapist validated his progress and encouraged self-compassion, helping him recognize that occasional doubts were natural rather than signs of failure.
- **Person-Centered Therapy:** As termination approached, David took an active role in determining his readiness. Sessions were spaced out, allowing him to test his ability to manage challenges independently while still maintaining a safety net of support.
- **Psychodynamic Therapy:** During therapy, David explored underlying themes of self-doubt stemming from past experiences. As termination neared, he recognized how early life patterns had influenced his anxiety, allowing him to develop a deeper sense of self-awareness and break free from old narratives.
- **Lifestyle Changes:** To maintain his progress, David integrated daily mindfulness practices, journaling, and regular exercise into his routine. These habits provided ongoing emotional stability, reinforcing his ability to manage stress outside of therapy.

As termination approached, David experienced a brief resurgence of anxiety, fearing that ending therapy might undo his progress. Recognizing this, his therapist helped him reframe these emotions as a natural response to change. By revisiting the tools he had acquired and acknowledging his ability to self-regulate, David was able to view the transition as a milestone of growth rather than a loss.

David's case exemplifies how a structured, integrative approach fosters long-term resilience. By blending cognitive, emotional, and behavioral strategies, he successfully transitioned out of therapy with the confidence to sustain his well-being independently.

With therapy winding down, it is crucial to consolidate progress and equip clients with tools for long-term success.

Consolidating Growth and Tools for Long-Term Success

The true measure of therapeutic success is not just the progress made during sessions but the client's ability to sustain growth long after therapy concludes. Before termination, it is essential to equip clients with the skills, strategies, and confidence needed to navigate future challenges independently. The Yanni Integration Approach (YIA) ensures that this transition is intentional and empowering, reinforcing long-term resilience rather than fostering dependency on therapy.

- **Therapeutic Toolkit:** Clients create a personalized set of strategies, including mindfulness exercises, reframing techniques, and emotional regulation skills (S. C. Hayes et al., 2011).
- **Journaling & Self-Reflection:** Encouraging continued introspection fosters ongoing personal growth (Pennebaker, 1997a).
- **Maintenance Plan:** Developing a structured plan for handling stressors and recognizing potential relapse signs ensures long-term stability (Prochaska & DiClemente, 1983).
- **Integrating Lifestyle Modifications:** Encouraging continued adherence to healthy habits, including proper nutrition, exercise, and structured routines to support mental health (Ratey, 2008).
- **Encouraging Future Support Networks:** Clients identify key relationships and resources they can turn to for continued emotional support (Weisz & Kazdin, 2017).

As clients transition out of therapy, they should also explore how their identity has evolved throughout the process. Many individuals shift from seeing themselves as someone who needs therapy to recognizing themselves as a person who possesses resilience and emotional competence (Pennebaker, 1997a). This transformation is a testament to the power of therapy, not as a crutch but as a process that fosters self-trust and emotional independence.

The end of therapy is not an end to growth; it is the beginning of a new chapter, one where clients trust their ability to face life's complexities with the strength and insight they have developed. By internalizing the skills gained in therapy and embracing their newfound independence, clients step forward with a renewed sense of identity, knowing they are not leaving therapy behind but carrying its lessons with them.

As therapy concludes, addressing the emotional responses associated with termination helps clients navigate the transition with confidence.

Managing Emotional Responses to Termination

The conclusion of therapy can be an emotionally complex experience for both clients and therapists. While some clients may feel relief and a sense of accomplishment, others may experience anxiety, sadness, or uncertainty about their ability to maintain progress independently. Addressing these emotions proactively ensures a smoother transition and reinforces therapy as a process that empowers rather than abandons.

Client Reactions to Termination

- **Processing Feelings of Loss:** For some clients, therapy has served as a secure base, making the transition to independence feel unsettling. Feelings of abandonment or self-doubt may arise, particularly for individuals with histories of attachment difficulties (Freud, 1917). Normalizing these emotions and reframing them as natural responses to change can help clients embrace termination as a marker of growth rather than a loss.

- **Reframing Termination:** Viewing therapy completion as a graduation rather than an ending reinforces the client's success and self-sufficiency. This perspective shift allows clients to recognize their resilience and the skills they have developed, fostering confidence in their ability to navigate life's challenges independently (Norcross, Zimmerman, et al., 2011).

Therapist Self-Reflection

The termination process also carries emotional significance for therapists, particularly in long-term therapeutic relationships. It is essential for therapists to acknowledge and process their own reactions to avoid unconscious attachment to clients that might interfere with a healthy transition.

- **Recognizing Countertransference**: Therapists may develop strong bonds with clients and experience emotions such as sadness, pride, or even anxiety about a client's ability to maintain progress. Awareness of these responses allows therapists to remain objective and ensure that their attachment does not unconsciously influence the termination process (Gelso & Woodhouse, 2001).
- **Utilizing Supervision and Peer Consultation**: Engaging in professional reflection through supervision or peer discussions provides therapists with the space to process their emotions while maintaining professionalism. This practice helps prevent personal biases from affecting client care and reinforces ethical termination practices (Bernard & Goodyear, 2019).

Emotional responses to termination are an expected and meaningful part of the therapeutic journey. By validating and addressing these emotions, both clients and therapists can ensure that the transition out of therapy is experienced as an empowering step forward rather than an abrupt or distressing end. A thoughtful termination process allows clients to reflect on their progress, solidify their confidence in their coping abilities, and embrace their future with greater emotional resilience.

Although therapy officially ends, post-therapy support options help reinforce long-term progress.

Follow-Up and Post-Therapy Support

The end of formal therapy does not mean the end of growth. While clients transition out of regular sessions, the Yanni Integration Approach (YIA) recognizes that maintaining therapeutic gains requires continued reinforcement and adaptive strategies. Post-therapy support helps clients sustain their progress, navigate new challenges, and remain confident in their ability to apply learned skills independently.

Post-Therapy Strategies

- **Booster Sessions:** Periodic check-ins provide an opportunity to reinforce progress, troubleshoot emerging challenges, and ensure that clients remain on track with their coping strategies (Weisz & Kazdin, 2017).
- **Identifying When to Return to Therapy:** Clients learn to recognize signs that indicate a need for additional support, such as recurrent distress, overwhelming stress, or significant life transitions. Viewing therapy as a resource rather than a last resort helps remove stigma and encourages proactive mental health care.
- **Providing Resources:** Recommending books, support groups, mindfulness practices, and self-guided therapeutic tools enables clients to continue personal development outside of therapy. Having access to structured resources fosters ongoing learning and emotional resilience.

- **Lifestyle Continuation Plan:** Encouraging clients to sustain the lifestyle changes implemented during therapy, such as healthy routines, regular physical activity, balanced nutrition, and mindfulness, ensures long-term well-being and emotional stability.

Successful termination is not about severing ties but about empowering clients to trust in their ability to navigate life independently while knowing that support remains available when needed. By integrating post-therapy strategies, therapists provide a bridge between structured treatment and sustained self-reliance. This approach reinforces that therapy is not just an intervention for crisis but a foundation for lifelong growth, resilience, and self-awareness.

Handling Unexpected Termination

While much of this chapter focuses on planned terminations, therapy does not always conclude in a structured or anticipated way. Unexpected terminations are common and can occur for various reasons, including financial constraints, life transitions, or avoidance of difficult emotional work. When a client leaves therapy abruptly, it is crucial to provide as much closure as possible and ensure they have the tools and resources to continue their growth independently.

Best Practices for Unexpected Termination

- **Provide Closure Even If Brief:** If a client discontinues therapy suddenly, therapists can attempt a final session, even if brief, to summarize progress, reinforce key takeaways, and offer external resources (Barnett & Coffman, 2015).
- **Offer Alternative Support Options:** Suggesting lower-cost therapy alternatives, online support groups, or self-help resources can help clients

maintain their therapeutic journey in a more accessible way (Bhatia & Gelso, 2017).

- **Normalize the Client's Decision:** Clients should feel that they can return to therapy in the future without guilt or judgment. Framing therapy as a flexible resource rather than a rigid commitment fosters a sense of agency in seeking support when needed (Kress & Marie, 2019).

Even when termination is unplanned, the therapist's role is to ensure that the client leaves therapy with a sense of empowerment rather than abandonment. By providing validation, reinforcing progress, and offering alternative pathways for continued growth, therapists can help clients maintain a positive connection to the therapeutic process. The goal of therapy is not just structured treatment but the cultivation of resilience and self-sufficiency, ensuring that clients feel supported, even if their journey takes an unexpected turn.

Conclusion

Termination in YIA is not an endpoint but a transition into greater autonomy. By integrating CBT, humanistic, person-centered, psychodynamic, and lifestyle principles, YIA ensures that clients leave therapy equipped with the tools to manage future challenges independently. A well-managed termination process reinforces therapeutic gains, ensuring long-term success beyond the therapy room.

CHAPTER 12:

Diversity and Cultural Considerations in the Yanni Integration Approach (YIA)

Introduction

Therapy is not a one-size-fits-all process. Clients come from diverse cultural, racial, socioeconomic, gender, and neurodiverse backgrounds, all of which shape their mental health experiences. The Yanni Integration Approach (YIA) embraces this diversity by ensuring that therapeutic models, including cognitive behavioral therapy (CBT), humanistic therapy, person-centered therapy, psychodynamic therapy, and lifestyle approaches, are adapted in a culturally relevant and inclusive manner.

Just as Chapter 11 emphasized the importance of individualized termination and post-therapy support, Chapter 12 expands this perspective by exploring how therapy itself must be personalized to meet the needs of clients from all backgrounds. The way clients engage in therapy, perceive mental health, and respond to interventions is deeply influenced by their cultural context, lived experiences, and systemic barriers. Therapists must approach each client with cultural humility, acknowledging their own biases and privileges while adapting treatment in a way that fosters accessibility, equity, and trust.

This chapter examines how YIA integrates cultural awareness into therapeutic practice, ensuring that interventions remain flexible, relevant, and effective for diverse populations. By understanding the role of culture in mental health, therapists can create a space where clients feel truly seen, respected, and supported.

Before examining how YIA can be tailored to diverse populations, it is essential to understand why cultural considerations matter in therapy.

Why Diversity Matters in Therapy

Culture, race, ethnicity, socioeconomic status, gender identity, sexual orientation, and neurodiversity all influence an individual's mental health, coping mechanisms, and access to care (Williams et al., 2018). These factors shape how individuals perceive and seek mental health treatment, as well as the challenges they face in receiving appropriate care. Systemic influences, such as discrimination, historical trauma, and economic barriers, must be acknowledged in therapy to ensure that treatment is both equitable and effective (Alvidrez et al., 2008).

Key Considerations in Culturally Responsive Therapy

- **Systemic Barriers to Mental Health Access:** Economic disparities, healthcare inequities, and stigma can prevent marginalized individuals from seeking or continuing therapy. Research indicates that racial and ethnic minority groups are less likely to receive mental health treatment due to financial barriers, lack of culturally competent providers, and fear of discrimination (Bailey et al., 2019). A culturally responsive approach requires therapists to address these barriers by advocating for accessible resources and acknowledging the impact of systemic oppression on mental health.
- **Intersectionality:** Clients often experience overlapping forms of discrimination and oppression, influencing their mental health, coping

mechanisms, and response to treatment (Crenshaw, 1989). Understanding intersectionality allows therapists to provide nuanced care that considers the complexities of a client's lived experiences.

- **Avoiding a "Colorblind" Approach:** While some therapists may believe that ignoring cultural differences promotes equality, this "colorblind" approach can invalidate a client's lived experiences. Effective therapy acknowledges and integrates cultural identity into treatment, creating a space where clients feel seen and understood (Sue & Sue, 2016).

Diversity in therapy is not just about awareness, it is about action. Recognizing the profound influence of culture and systemic factors on mental health allows therapists to create more inclusive and effective treatment plans. By embracing cultural humility, challenging biases, and adapting interventions to meet the unique needs of each client, therapists foster an environment where healing is accessible to all. Ensuring that therapy remains responsive to diversity strengthens the therapeutic alliance and empowers clients to navigate their mental health within the realities of their personal and cultural identities.

With these factors in mind, YIA integrates cultural considerations into each of its five therapeutic models to ensure inclusivity.

Adapting the YIA Framework to Diverse Clients

Therapy is most effective when it acknowledges and integrates the cultural identities of clients. The Yanni Integration Approach (YIA) provides a flexible framework that can be adapted to meet the needs of diverse populations by recognizing how cultural experiences shape cognition, emotions, behaviors, and coping mechanisms. Rather than applying a one-size-fits-all model, YIA emphasizes the importance of cultural humility, responsiveness, and the inclusion of culturally relevant interventions to enhance therapeutic outcomes. Each component of YIA can be modified to better serve clients from different backgrounds:

- **CBT & Cultural Considerations:** Cognitive distortions often stem from cultural beliefs and societal narratives. YIA encourages therapists to recognize these influences and tailor interventions accordingly, ensuring that thought-restructuring techniques respect and integrate a client's cultural worldview (Helms, 1995).
- **Person-Centered & Humanistic Therapy:** Creating a safe, affirming space where clients feel heard and valued within their cultural context is essential. A client's cultural background shapes their identity and self-perception, making it crucial for therapists to foster an atmosphere of validation and respect (Comas-Díaz, 2012).
- **Psychodynamic Therapy & Cultural Legacy:** Intergenerational trauma and systemic oppression influence unconscious patterns and relational dynamics. By exploring the cultural history and inherited narratives of a client, therapists can help clients understand how past experiences continue to shape their present emotional world (Sue & Sue, 2016).
- **Lifestyle & Cultural Relevance:** Mental health is deeply connected to cultural practices and traditions. Recognizing the role of family structures, spirituality, nutrition, community, and traditional healing practices allows for a more holistic and personalized therapeutic approach (Ponterotto et al., 1995).

Adapting the YIA framework to diverse clients is not just about cultural competence, it is about cultural attunement and humility. Therapists must actively listen, validate, and integrate the strengths of a client's cultural background into treatment rather than imposing Westernized models of healing. By embracing cultural diversity within the YIA framework, therapy becomes more inclusive, meaningful, and effective, ensuring that clients feel truly understood and empowered in their healing journey.

Case Study: Maria, a First-Generation Immigrant with Anxiety

Maria, a 27-year-old woman from Mexico, experiences intense anxiety stemming from work and family pressures. While she aspires to personal and professional independence, she struggles with guilt due to familial expectations that she financially support her parents and siblings. These conflicting demands create emotional distress, leaving Maria feeling torn between her ambitions and her cultural values of familial obligation.

Integrated Approach:

- **CBT Modification:** Rather than focusing solely on cognitive distortions, the therapist integrates culturally relevant strategies, such as using Mexican proverbs and storytelling to help Maria reframe limiting beliefs. Additionally, strengths-based interventions highlight her resilience and the community support she can draw upon.
- **Humanistic & Person-Centered Techniques:** The therapist validates Maria's internal conflict and acknowledges the legitimacy of both her desire for independence and her deep sense of familial responsibility. By providing a nonjudgmental space, Maria is encouraged to explore her values and define success on her own terms.
- **Psychodynamic Exploration:** Through deeper reflection, Maria uncovers intergenerational narratives that have shaped her anxiety, including family stories of sacrifice and obligation. Understanding these inherited expectations allows her to process the emotional weight of her role and begin separating her personal identity from family-imposed pressures.
- **Lifestyle Adjustments:** Rather than relying on Western mindfulness practices, Maria incorporates faith-based meditation and family storytelling as grounding techniques. These culturally aligned practices help her manage stress while staying connected to her heritage.

Maria's case highlights the importance of adapting therapy to align with a client's cultural background. By integrating culturally responsive interventions, the therapist helps Maria navigate her anxiety in a way that honors both her personal aspirations and her family values. Over time, Maria develops greater confidence in asserting boundaries while maintaining strong family ties, recognizing that self-growth and cultural loyalty can coexist. Her therapy journey underscores the power of culturally attuned approaches in fostering meaningful, sustainable healing.

While adapting therapy to cultural backgrounds is essential, therapists must also engage in self-reflection to ensure they are addressing personal biases and practicing with cultural humility.

Therapist Bias & Cultural Humility

Culturally responsive therapy requires more than knowledge of different backgrounds—it demands an ongoing commitment to self-awareness and adaptability. Recognizing and addressing personal biases is essential to ensuring therapy remains an inclusive and affirming space for all clients (Sue & Sue, 2016). While cultural competence suggests that therapists can attain a fixed level of expertise, cultural humility emphasizes a lifelong process of learning, reflection, and self-correction (Helms, 1995). By embracing humility, therapists foster deeper therapeutic connections and create environments where clients feel truly seen and understood.

Strategies for Practicing Cultural Humility

- **Self-Reflection:** Therapists should regularly examine their assumptions and beliefs regarding race, gender, cultural identity, and privilege to identify potential biases.
  Reflection Question: What unconscious biases might I bring into the therapy room?

- **Seeking Supervision and Training:** Engaging in consultation with professionals from diverse backgrounds enhances cultural awareness, challenges blind spots, and strengthens multicultural competency (Comas-Díaz, 2012).
- **Acknowledging Power Dynamics:** Therapists must recognize the privilege and authority they hold in the therapeutic relationship and strive to create a collaborative, client-led space where clients feel empowered in their healing journey.

Cultural humility is not a skill to be mastered but a continuous practice of self-examination and growth. By committing to ongoing reflection, openness, and adaptability, therapists ensure that their work remains responsive to the diverse and evolving needs of their clients. This approach fosters trust, strengthens the therapeutic alliance, and ultimately allows for a deeper, more authentic healing process.

Despite a commitment to cultural humility, therapists may still experience discomfort or resistance when discussing cultural issues. Acknowledging and addressing this resistance is essential for fostering open, effective conversations in therapy.

Addressing Therapist Resistance to Cultural Conversations

Discussions about race, privilege, and systemic oppression can feel challenging for some therapists, leading to avoidance due to discomfort or fear of saying the wrong thing. However, avoiding these topics can create distance in the therapeutic relationship and leave clients feeling unseen. Research shows that clients value therapists who approach cultural conversations with humility, openness, and a genuine willingness to learn (Williams et al., 2018). Engaging in these discussions fosters trust, deepens therapeutic connections, and ensures that therapy remains a space where all aspects of a client's identity are acknowledged and validated (Sue & Sue, 2016). Therapists who actively engage in cultural discussions also reduce the risk of unintentionally reinforcing systemic biases and power imbalances within the therapeutic setting (Comas-Díaz, 2012).

Best Practices for Engaging in Cultural Conversations

- **Acknowledge Uncertainty:** Rather than avoiding cultural topics, therapists can admit when they are unfamiliar with a client's lived experience while expressing openness to learning. Research indicates that acknowledging limitations fosters stronger client-therapist rapport (Tummala-Narra, 2016). *Example Statement: "I want to understand your experiences better. If I ever say something that doesn't resonate, I encourage you to let me know."*
- **Encourage Client-Led Discussions:** Allowing clients to introduce cultural topics in their own time respects their autonomy while validating their lived experiences (Helms, 1995). Creating a safe and supportive space for these discussions improves therapeutic engagement and outcomes (Hays, 2016).
- **Seek Education:** Instead of relying on clients to educate therapists about their identities, therapists should pursue ongoing training in cultural competence and humility through supervision, literature, and professional development (Comas-Díaz, 2012). Studies show that culturally responsive training enhances therapists' ability to navigate difficult conversations and reduce implicit bias (Hook et al., 2013).

Engaging in cultural conversations requires vulnerability, but avoidance only reinforces discomfort and limits therapeutic effectiveness. By approaching these discussions with honesty, openness, and a commitment to growth, therapists create a space where clients feel truly heard. Cultural responsiveness is not about having all the answers—it's about showing up with curiosity, respect, and a willingness to evolve. Research underscores that when therapists engage in culturally attuned discussions, clients report stronger therapeutic alliances, greater trust, and improved therapeutic outcomes (Hays, 2016; Sue & Sue, 2016).

Addressing therapist resistance is key, but true cultural responsiveness requires understanding how intersecting identities shape a client's experience in therapy.

Intersectionality and Its Role in Therapy

Mental health is shaped not just by individual experiences but by the broader social structures in which a person exists. Intersectionality recognizes that identities such as race, gender, disability, socioeconomic status, and sexual orientation do not exist in isolation but interact to influence mental health and access to care (Crenshaw, 1989). Clients from marginalized backgrounds often face overlapping layers of discrimination, privilege, and systemic barriers, making it essential for therapists to acknowledge and integrate these complexities into treatment. Ignoring intersectionality risks oversimplifying a client's experience, while a thoughtful, intersectional approach fosters deeper understanding, validation, and empowerment in therapy.

Addressing Systemic Barriers

- **Understanding Oppression and Privilege:** Clients from marginalized backgrounds may experience chronic stressors such as racial discrimination, gender inequality, or economic hardship. These external pressures impact mental health, self-perception, and coping mechanisms, making it crucial for therapists to recognize the societal factors contributing to a client's distress (Hays, 2016).
- **Validating Lived Experiences:** An intersectional, strengths-based approach ensures that clients are not defined solely by their struggles but are empowered through their resilience and adaptive strategies (Alvidrez et al.,

2008). Therapy should be a space where clients' experiences are acknowledged and affirmed, rather than dismissed or minimized.

- **Advocacy in Therapy:** Therapists can play a role in helping clients navigate institutional barriers, whether by connecting them to culturally competent resources, discussing workplace discrimination, or addressing healthcare disparities. A therapist's role extends beyond the therapy room, validating and advocating for clients' needs can help foster systemic change (Sue & Sue, 2016).

Intersectionality is not just a theoretical framework, it is a necessary lens for understanding and addressing the diverse challenges clients face. By integrating intersectionality into therapy, clinicians move beyond a one-size-fits-all approach and create space for clients to explore the full complexity of their identities. When therapists acknowledge how overlapping systems of power and privilege affect mental health, they foster deeper trust, more meaningful healing, and a truly inclusive therapeutic experience.

Integrating these considerations into practice requires therapists to employ inclusive and adaptable strategies.

Practical Strategies for Inclusive Therapy

Inclusive therapy goes beyond cultural awareness—it requires intentional adaptation of therapeutic techniques to align with a client's unique background, values, and lived experiences. Culturally responsive therapy ensures that interventions are not only accessible but also meaningful, allowing clients to feel seen and understood. Therapists who integrate inclusive strategies foster stronger therapeutic alliances and create an environment where clients feel safe to explore their challenges within the context of their cultural identity.

- **Using Culturally Relevant Language and Metaphors:** Adapting CBT techniques to align with a client's cultural expressions ensures accessibility.

Metaphors, proverbs, or storytelling methods relevant to the client's background can enhance engagement and understanding (Sue & Sue, 2016).

- **Validating Systemic Struggles While Promoting Agency:** Acknowledging the impact of oppression and systemic barriers without reinforcing helplessness helps clients balance external realities with self-efficacy and empowerment (Crenshaw, 1989).
- **Recognizing Cultural Expressions of Distress:** Symptoms of distress may manifest differently across cultures, such as somatic complaints, spiritual crises, or collective family distress. Understanding these variations ensures that symptoms are interpreted accurately rather than pathologized through a Western lens (Ponterotto et al., 1995).
- **Including Family and Community in the Healing Process:** Many cultures emphasize collectivism, where healing is seen as a communal rather than individual process. When appropriate, incorporating family or community values into therapy enhances effectiveness and strengthens support systems (Comas-Díaz, 2012).
- **Modifying Lifestyle Interventions to Fit Cultural Norms:** Recommendations for diet, physical activity, or mindfulness should align with cultural traditions to ensure sustainability. Recognizing the role of spirituality, traditional healing practices, and community rituals allows for holistic, culturally attuned care (Sue & Sue, 2016).

Inclusive therapy is not about making assumptions, it's about creating a flexible and adaptive space where clients' cultural identities are recognized as strengths rather than barriers to healing. By tailoring interventions, validating diverse expressions of distress, and integrating culturally relevant healing practices, therapists can ensure that therapy is both effective and affirming. When cultural responsiveness becomes an active part of therapeutic work, clients are more likely to engage in meaningful growth, fostering long-term resilience and empowerment.

Conclusion

Diversity and inclusivity are essential in therapy. By integrating CBT, humanistic, person-centered, psychodynamic, and lifestyle principles in a culturally aware and adaptable manner, YIA ensures that therapy is personalized, effective, and affirming for all clients. Therapists who embrace cultural humility and intersectionality can foster meaningful, empowering, and transformative therapeutic experiences.

CHAPTER 13:

The Role of Lifestyle Changes

Introduction

As explored in Chapter 12, therapy must be adapted to each client's cultural identity, values, and lived experiences. This same awareness extends to lifestyle interventions, as health behaviors, daily routines, and wellness practices are shaped by cultural norms, socioeconomic factors, and systemic barriers. Simply prescribing Westernized self-care strategies, such as meditation, dietary changes, or structured exercise, without considering a client's background or access to resources, risks alienating clients rather than empowering them. Effective therapy acknowledges these influences and ensures that lifestyle recommendations are both culturally responsive and accessible.

Mental health is deeply interconnected with physical health, daily routines, and engagement in meaningful activities. While therapy focuses on cognitive restructuring, emotional healing, and self-exploration, clients often overlook the impact that lifestyle factors, such as sleep, exercise, nutrition, social engagement, and hobbies, have on their psychological well-being. Research consistently shows that healthy lifestyle habits contribute to improved mood, reduced anxiety, and greater overall resilience (Walsh, 2011).

The Yanni Integration Approach (YIA) recognizes that lifestyle changes are not separate from therapy but an essential component of sustainable mental health. By incorporating cognitive behavioral therapy (CBT), psychodynamic therapy, humanistic therapy, person-centered therapy, and lifestyle changes, therapists can help clients develop realistic, individualized strategies for improving their daily lives.

This chapter explores how lifestyle choices influence mental well-being, the importance of integrating culturally sensitive wellness strategies into therapy, and how therapists can help clients build sustainable habits that support long-term emotional resilience.

Why Routines, Physical Health, and Hobbies Matter for Mental Health

Many clients struggle with mental health symptoms that are exacerbated by lifestyle imbalances. Irregular sleep, poor diet, lack of movement, and disconnection from enjoyable activities all contribute to heightened stress, fatigue, and emotional instability (Harvey et al., 2011). When clients ignore the body's needs, they often reinforce patterns of emotional distress. Therapists must help clients see the connection between their daily habits and their psychological well-being.

The Science Behind Lifestyle and Mental Health

- **Sleep:** Research indicates that sleep deprivation leads to increased anxiety, depression, and cognitive impairment. Establishing consistent sleep routines reduces stress and enhances emotional regulation (Walker, 2017).
- **Exercise:** Physical activity reduces cortisol levels, boosts serotonin and dopamine, and improves resilience against stress and depression. Even small increases in movement enhance mood and energy (Blumenthal et al., 2007).

- **Nutrition:** Nutritional psychiatry studies show that diets high in processed foods contribute to inflammation, which is linked to depression and anxiety. A diet rich in whole foods supports brain function and emotional stability (Jacka et al., 2017).
- **Hobbies and Creativity:** Engaging in creative activities stimulates neural pathways associated with pleasure and meaning, reducing symptoms of depression and increasing cognitive flexibility (Fancourt & Finn, 2019).
- **Social Connections:** Isolation and loneliness exacerbate mental health conditions, while social engagement buffers against stress and enhances well-being (Holt-Lunstad et al., 2015).

Despite understanding these benefits, many clients struggle with motivation, fear of failure, or systemic barriers that limit their access to healthy lifestyle choices. Therapists must acknowledge these challenges and provide strategies for overcoming them in a way that fosters gradual and sustainable change.

While clients often feel powerless over their emotions, lifestyle changes provide a tangible, controllable way to improve mood, energy, and resilience. The key is introducing these changes in a manageable way.

Addressing Common Barriers to Lifestyle Changes

While lifestyle modifications can significantly enhance mental health, many clients encounter psychological, socioeconomic, and behavioral obstacles that hinder their ability to implement and sustain these changes. Simply recommending healthier habits without addressing these barriers risks reinforcing frustration and self-doubt rather than fostering long-term progress. Research highlights that clients who experience structural, emotional, or motivational barriers are less likely to sustain behavioral changes unless these obstacles are directly acknowledged and integrated into therapy (Kandula et al., 2007; Prochaska & DiClemente, 1983). Therapists play a crucial role in helping clients navigate these challenges with realistic, accessible, and emotionally attuned strategies that promote sustainable change.

Psychological Barriers

- **Fear of Failure**: Clients may avoid starting new habits due to previous unsuccessful attempts, leading to self-doubt and avoidance. Motivational interviewing techniques can shift their mindset from self-judgment to self-compassion, encouraging a focus on progress rather than perfection (W. R. Miller & Rollnick, 2013).
- **Negative Emotional Associations**: Food, exercise, and self-care routines may be tied to past trauma, body image struggles, or childhood experiences. Psychodynamic exploration can help clients uncover deeper emotional blocks, allowing for a more compassionate and personalized approach to lifestyle changes (Sue & Sue, 2016).

Socioeconomic Barriers

- **Limited Access to Resources**: Not all clients have equal access to fresh food, safe exercise spaces, or leisure time. Therapists can assist clients in identifying low-cost, community-based alternatives that align with their needs, such as home workouts, accessible nutrition plans, and free mental wellness resources (Kandula et al., 2007).
- **Work and Family Demands**: Many clients struggle to prioritize self-care due to overwhelming schedules and responsibilities. Using behavioral activation strategies from CBT, therapists can help clients integrate small, realistic self-care actions into their daily routines without adding undue stress (N. S. Jacobson et al., 2001).

Behavioral and Motivational Barriers

- **All-or-Nothing Thinking**: Some clients believe that if they cannot fully commit to a change, it is not worth attempting at all. CBT techniques can help reframe rigid thinking patterns, encouraging gradual, sustainable progress rather than perfectionistic expectations (A. T. Beck, 1976).
- **Lack of Immediate Results**: Clients often expect rapid improvements and become discouraged if they do not see immediate benefits. Using humanistic validation, therapists can help clients appreciate the long-term nature of habit formation and recognize small victories as part of a larger transformation (Prochaska & DiClemente, 1983).

Sustainable lifestyle changes require more than motivation, they demand an understanding of the psychological, socioeconomic, and behavioral barriers that clients face (Hagger & Luszczynska, 2014; W. R. Miller & Rollnick, 2013). Research indicates that when therapists actively address these barriers through integrated therapeutic approaches, clients demonstrate greater long-term success in behavior change (Prochaska & DiClemente, 1983; Walsh, 2011). By integrating CBT, psychodynamic, humanistic, and person-centered strategies, therapists can help clients reframe setbacks, develop realistic strategies, and cultivate self-compassion throughout the process. Addressing these challenges not only enhances treatment outcomes but also empowers clients to make lasting, meaningful improvements in their mental and physical well-being.

Therapists can help clients build momentum by incorporating small, actionable steps into therapy sessions, making lifestyle changes more achievable and sustainable.

Incorporating Small, Actionable Steps into Therapy Sessions

Many clients resist lifestyle changes because they seem overwhelming or insignificant compared to deeper emotional struggles. However, research indicates that incremental, achievable modifications increase adherence and long-term success in behavior change (Prochaska & DiClemente, 1983; Walsh, 2011). When therapists integrate small, manageable interventions, clients are more likely to engage, build confidence, and experience positive results. Gradual changes reinforce self-efficacy, allowing clients to take ownership of their well-being rather than feeling pressured to make drastic shifts (Bandura, 1997).

Integrating the Five Models to Support Lifestyle Changes

- **CBT:** Helps clients identify and challenge distorted thought patterns that contribute to poor lifestyle habits, such as "*Exercise won't help me*" or "*I don't have time for self-care.*" By restructuring these beliefs, clients develop a more adaptive mindset toward health and self-improvement (A. T. Beck, 1976).
- **Psychodynamic:** Explores why clients struggle with self-care, uncovering deep-seated emotional blocks related to self-worth, discipline, or family dynamics that may unconsciously shape their resistance to change (Shedler, 2010).
- **Humanistic:** Reinforces the idea that self-care is not a luxury but a fundamental part of self-respect, helping clients reframe lifestyle modifications as acts of self-compassion rather than obligations (Rogers, 1961).
- **Person-Centered:** Encourages clients to set their own realistic goals and make autonomous choices, ensuring that lifestyle changes feel personally meaningful rather than externally imposed (Deci & Ryan, 2000).
- **Lifestyle Changes:** Supports practical experimentation with sleep, movement, nutrition, hobbies, and relaxation techniques in a way that fits the client's individual personality, cultural background, and daily routine (Walsh, 2011).

Sustainable lifestyle change is not about making drastic shifts overnight, it is about consistent, intentional progress. By incorporating small, actionable steps into therapy, clients experience tangible benefits, reinforcing motivation and long-term engagement in healthier habits (W. R. Miller & Rollnick, 2013). When therapists integrate CBT, psychodynamic, humanistic, and person-centered approaches alongside lifestyle interventions, they empower clients to build confidence in their ability to change, leading to lasting improvements in both mental and physical well-being.

Practical Approaches for Introducing Small Steps in Therapy

Clients often resist lifestyle changes because they perceive them as overwhelming or unattainable. Research shows that breaking down behavior change into small, manageable steps increases adherence and long-term success (Prochaska & DiClemente, 1983; W. R. Miller & Rollnick, 2013). When clients experience quick wins through micro-adjustments, they build confidence and motivation, reinforcing their ability to sustain long-term changes (Bandura, 1997). Therapists can play a critical role in helping clients integrate small, achievable habits into their daily routines, making self-care feel accessible rather than burdensome. Therapists can help clients make realistic, incremental lifestyle changes by:

- **Starting with micro-habits:** Encouraging small, low-effort actions makes new behaviors less intimidating. "*Let's aim for 5 minutes of movement rather than an hour at the gym.*"
- **Tying new behaviors to existing routines:** Linking habits to well-established routines increases consistency. "*After you brush your teeth, take a deep breath and set an intention for the day.*"
- **Encouraging nonjudgmental experimentation:** Creating a flexible, trial-based approach allows clients to explore what works best for them without pressure. "*Let's try switching your evening screen time for a book or a podcast and see if your sleep improves.*"
- **Helping clients track progress:** Simple tracking methods, such as reflection journals or habit trackers, help clients stay accountable while recognizing gradual progress.

- **Reframing self-care as self-respect rather than obligation:** Emphasizing that self-care is not about checking off a to-do list but about honoring one's well-being fosters intrinsic motivation and long-term adherence (Deci & Ryan, 2000).

Sustainable change does not happen overnight, it develops through small, consistent steps that reinforce self-efficacy and resilience (Bandura, 1997; Walsh, 2011). By integrating micro-habits, behavioral tracking, and flexible experimentation, therapists can help clients move past resistance and engage in meaningful self-care without feeling pressured or overwhelmed. The goal is not perfection but progress, allowing clients to reframe self-improvement as an empowering, self-directed journey rather than an imposed obligation.

While starting small is important, the ultimate goal is to help clients develop sustainable lifestyle habits that endure beyond therapy.

Supporting Clients in Developing Sustainable Lifestyle Habits

One of the biggest challenges in lifestyle modification is consistency. While clients may begin with strong motivation, research shows that without reinforcement, many struggle to sustain new habits, leading to frustration and relapse into old behaviors (Prochaska & DiClemente, 1983; Baumeister & Tierney, 2011). Sustainability requires a shift from short-term motivation to long-term adaptability, where patience and flexibility replace the expectation of immediate, dramatic results. Therapists play a crucial role in helping clients build sustainable habits by integrating psychological models that promote reinforcement, emotional awareness, self-compassion, autonomy, and adaptability (Walsh, 2011).

Integrating the Five Models for Long-Term Success

- **CBT:** Reinforces habit formation through behavioral reinforcement, helping clients identify patterns of self-sabotage and develop strategies to overcome them (A. T. Beck, 1976).
- **Psychodynamic:** Explores underlying emotional conflicts that interfere with consistency, such as unresolved beliefs like "*I don't deserve to feel good*" or "*If I succeed, I'll have to keep it up*" (Shedler, 2010).
- **Humanistic:** Encourages self-compassion, helping clients recognize that progress is about sustained effort rather than perfection (Neff, 2011).
- **Person-Centered:** Supports clients in determining what works best for them, ensuring that lifestyle changes feel autonomous and meaningful rather than imposed (Deci & Ryan, 2000).
- **Lifestyle Changes:** Focuses on adapting habits to life's changing circumstances rather than promoting rigid, all-or-nothing routines, making sustainability more achievable and less overwhelming (Walsh, 2011).

Long-term success in lifestyle modification is not about willpower alone, it's about creating a foundation of psychological flexibility, self-awareness, and self-compassion (Baumeister & Tierney, 2011; Neff, K., 2011). When therapists integrate CBT, psychodynamic, humanistic, and person-centered approaches alongside lifestyle interventions, they help clients develop realistic, adaptable habits that align with their values and daily lives. By shifting the focus from perfection to persistence, therapy fosters lasting behavioral change that enhances both mental and physical well-being (Walsh, 2011).

Case Study: John's Struggle with Lifestyle Changes

John, a 42-year-old professional, came to therapy overwhelmed by chronic stress and burnout, feeling physically exhausted and emotionally depleted. Despite understanding the benefits of healthier habits, such as exercise, improved sleep, and better nutrition, he struggled to implement these changes, often feeling stuck in cycles of avoidance and frustration. His therapist used an integrative approach to help John reframe his resistance, develop self-compassion, and make sustainable adjustments to his lifestyle.

Applying the Yanni Integration Approach (YIA) to John's Lifestyle Changes

- **CBT**: John identified self-sabotaging thoughts, such as "*I'll never be able to stick to this,*" and reframed them into more achievable, self-compassionate beliefs, reinforcing progress over perfection.
- **Psychodynamic**: Through deeper exploration, John recognized that his childhood experiences with rigid discipline had made him resist structured routines as an adult, associating them with control rather than self-care.
- **Humanistic**: His therapist validated his frustrations and encouraged small wins over all-or-nothing thinking, helping John recognize that incremental progress was still success.
- **Person-Centered**: John set his own self-care goals, choosing an activity he genuinely enjoyed rather than one he felt he "should" do, increasing his intrinsic motivation.
- **Lifestyle Change**: Instead of forcing himself into intense workouts, John started with 5-minute stretching and breathing exercises, gradually increasing as he gained confidence and energy.

John's journey demonstrates that sustainable lifestyle change is not about willpower alone but about reworking deep-seated beliefs, reframing setbacks, and embracing flexibility. By addressing the cognitive, emotional, and behavioral barriers to self-care, John shifted from resisting change to actively engaging in a routine that felt natural and empowering. Over time, these small, intentional steps led to lasting improvements in his stress levels, mood, and overall well-being, proving that true transformation starts with self-compassion and consistency.

To support long-term success, therapists can implement key strategies that help clients maintain these habits over time.

Key Strategies for Helping Clients Maintain Lifestyle Changes

Making lifestyle changes is one step, sustaining them over time is where the real challenge lies. Many clients start strong but struggle with setbacks, rigid expectations, or discouragement when routines are disrupted. Long-term success requires a mindset shift, where habits are seen as adaptable, identity-based, and part of an ongoing process rather than a fixed outcome (Walsh, 2011). Therapists play a crucial role in helping clients develop strategies that reinforce self-efficacy, resilience, and consistency in maintaining healthy behaviors.

- **Encourage flexibility:** Habits should be adaptable to different life circumstances, preventing discouragement when routines change.
- **Use identity-based motivation:** Clients who see themselves as "someone who prioritizes their well-being" are more likely to maintain long-term habits and integrate them into their sense of self (Oyserman, 2009).
- **Introduce self-reflection techniques:** Mindfulness, journaling, and therapy check-ins help clients evaluate what is working, what isn't, and make necessary adjustments (Lally et al., 2010).
- **Celebrate small wins:** Acknowledging even minor successes reinforces positive behavior and prevents discouragement, helping clients stay engaged in the change process.
- **Remind clients that lifestyle change is a process, not an event:** Therapy builds a mindset of progress over perfection, ensuring that clients continue growing beyond their time in therapy (W. R. Miller & Rollnick, 2013).

These strategies are supported by research showing that integrating lifestyle modifications into therapy leads to greater long-term improvements in mood and stress resilience compared to traditional talk therapy alone (Walsh, 2011). Understanding the psychology behind habit formation further reinforces why small, consistent changes are more sustainable than drastic overhauls (Lally et al., 2010).

Conclusion

Small, actionable steps are key to successful habit formation, and therapists can support clients by making changes manageable, reinforcing progress, and addressing emotional blocks to consistency. Sustainable growth requires self-awareness, flexibility, and identity-based motivation, allowing clients to take ownership of their well-being beyond the therapy room. By integrating these factors into therapy while acknowledging cultural, socioeconomic, and emotional barriers, therapists can help clients develop sustainable habits that support long-term growth.

CHAPTER 14:

Evaluating and Refining Your Approach

Introduction

Therapy is an ever-evolving practice, requiring continuous self-reflection, professional development, and adaptability. While therapists develop their unique styles over time, ongoing evaluation and refinement are necessary to maintain effectiveness and uphold ethical standards in clinical work (Norcross & Goldfried, 2019). The ability to adjust strategies, recognize personal biases, and integrate innovative approaches ensures that therapists remain responsive to their clients' evolving needs.

In chapter 13, we explored the role of lifestyle changes in mental health and how behavioral modifications can support emotional well-being. While guiding clients through these transformations, therapists must also engage in their own process of growth and self-improvement.

The Yanni Integration Approach (YIA) emphasizes that therapists must remain active participants in their own professional growth by evaluating their effectiveness, recognizing areas for improvement, and integrating emerging psychological insights into their work. By applying cognitive behavioral therapy (CBT), psychodynamic therapy, humanistic therapy, person-centered therapy, and lifestyle changes, therapists can create a structured yet flexible framework for ongoing learning, professional growth, and ethical responsibility.

This chapter explores strategies for self-reflection, gathering client feedback, integrating new research, and ensuring continuous professional growth, allowing therapists to provide high-quality, evidence-based care.

Self-Reflection and Supervision for Continued Growth

Therapy is a dynamic and evolving practice, requiring therapists to engage in ongoing self-reflection and professional development to maintain effectiveness and ethical integrity. Self-reflection is a core competency that allows therapists to examine their strengths, biases, emotional responses, and areas for improvement, ensuring they remain attuned to both their clients' needs and their own professional growth (Schön, 1983). Without regular self-examination, therapists risk stagnation, blind spots, and ethical drift, which can compromise clinical effectiveness.

While self-reflection fosters internal awareness, supervision and peer consultation provide essential external perspectives that challenge assumptions, refine clinical skills, and enhance ethical decision-making. Supervision is not just for early-career therapists, it is a lifelong resource that supports continuous learning and accountability (Bernard & Goodyear, 2019). By integrating both self-reflection and structured supervision, therapists create a professional feedback loop that ensures adaptability, ethical practice, and long-term clinical effectiveness.

Integrating YIA into Self-Reflection and Supervision

The Yanni Integration Approach (YIA) supports structured, intentional professional development by incorporating cognitive, emotional, relational, and lifestyle-based awareness into self-reflection and supervision. This integration allows therapists to refine their approach in a balanced and evidence-based manner.

- **CBT (Cognitive Behavioral Therapy):** Encourages therapists to identify their own cognitive distortions and automatic reactions in therapy, helping them challenge self-imposed expectations such as *"I should always have the right answer"* or *"If a client doesn't improve, I failed"* (A. T. Beck, 1979).
- **Psychodynamic Therapy:** Examines how countertransference and unconscious biases may influence therapeutic interactions. Reflecting on how past experiences shape emotional responses enables therapists to differentiate personal reactions from professional judgment (Shedler, 2010).
- **Humanistic Therapy:** Reinforces the importance of genuineness, empathy, and self-awareness in maintaining an authentic therapeutic presence. Engaging in reflective dialogue about emotional attunement helps therapists foster stronger client relationships (Rogers, 1961).
- **Person-Centered Therapy:** Encourages therapists to evaluate how well they are honoring client autonomy and whether they are meeting clients where they are rather than imposing structured expectations (Deci & Ryan, 2000).
- **Lifestyle Changes Approach:** Highlights the necessity of therapist self-care and work-life balance. Reflection on personal stress levels, emotional exhaustion, and restorative activities helps prevent burnout and sustain long-term effectiveness (Walsh, 2011).

Practical Approaches for Self-Reflection

Self-reflection is a cornerstone of ongoing professional development, allowing therapists to assess their effectiveness, refine their clinical skills, and ensure ethical integrity (Schön, 1983; Bernard & Goodyear, 2019). Engaging in structured self-reflection practices helps therapists recognize personal biases, emotional triggers, and patterns of countertransference, ultimately improving their ability to provide client-centered care. Research suggests that therapists who engage in intentional reflection and supervision experience greater clinical competence, stronger therapeutic alliances, and lower burnout rates (Hill et al., 2017; Neff, 2011).

To make self-reflection an active and impactful practice, therapists can incorporate the following structured and intentional techniques into their routines:

- Journaling about challenging sessions, identifying emotional responses, patterns of countertransference, and areas for growth. This method encourages deeper processing of professional experiences and enhances self-awareness in therapeutic interactions (Schön, 1983).

Using structured reflection questions, such as:

  - *"What went well in this session? What could have been improved?"*
  - *"Am I maintaining an open, nonjudgmental stance? If not, what influenced my response?"*
  - *"How might my personal values, biases, or assumptions be affecting my clinical work?"*

- Recording and reviewing sessions (with client consent) to assess communication patterns, intervention effectiveness, and areas for refinement. Research suggests that reviewing recorded sessions enhances therapist insight and strengthens therapeutic skills (Rousmaniere, 2016).
- Seeking peer consultation or clinical supervision to gain objective feedback, challenge blind spots, and refine intervention strategies. Supervision helps therapists remain accountable, ethically sound, and adaptable in their evolving practice (Bernard & Goodyear, 2019).
- Practicing mindfulness and self-care routines to regulate emotional responses, reduce professional stress, and maintain long-term sustainability in the field (Neff, 2011).

Self-reflection is not just a passive process, it is an active commitment to professional growth, ethical responsibility, and clinical excellence (Hill et al., 2017). When therapists intentionally engage in structured reflection methods, they cultivate greater self-awareness, stronger therapeutic relationships, and improved client outcomes. By integrating journaling, structured prompts, supervision, session review, and mindfulness, therapists ensure that their professional development remains dynamic, responsive, and rooted in self-awareness. Research consistently supports that therapists who engage in regular self-reflection and external feedback demonstrate higher levels of clinical competence, emotional resilience, and long-term career satisfaction (Schön, 1983; Neff, 2011; Rousmaniere, 2016).

The Role of Supervision

Supervision is a cornerstone of therapist development, ethical accountability, and clinical effectiveness. It provides a structured space for therapists to receive feedback, reflect on challenges, and refine their interventions, ensuring they continue to grow throughout their careers. Supervision is not just a requirement for early-career clinicians, it is an essential component of lifelong professional development (Bernard & Goodyear, 2019).

Engaging in regular supervision, peer consultation, or group discussions allows therapists to gain valuable external perspectives that help them stay objective, challenge blind spots, and refine intervention strategies. Without ongoing professional feedback, therapists risk reinforcing ineffective patterns, developing unchecked biases, or experiencing professional stagnation (Hill et al., 2017).

Key Benefits of Supervision

- **Enhancing Clinical Competence**: Supervision allows therapists to review and refine their interventions, ensuring they are using evidence-based, ethical, and client-centered approaches (Norcross & Goldfried, 2019).
- **Challenging Blind Spots and Cognitive Biases**: Therapists, like all professionals, may develop cognitive biases or countertransference that

impact their work. Supervision helps identify and address these biases, leading to greater self-awareness and therapeutic neutrality (Shedler, 2010).

- **Strengthening Ethical Practice**: Supervision provides a structured forum for ethical discussions, allowing therapists to navigate complex client situations, boundary concerns, and ethical dilemmas with guidance and accountability (Bernard & Goodyear, 2019).
- **Reducing Burnout and Compassion Fatigue**: Studies indicate that therapists who engage in ongoing supervision report lower levels of emotional exhaustion and burnout. The support offered through supervision helps mitigate the stress of clinical work, fostering long-term professional sustainability (Hill et al., 2017).
- **Improving Client Outcomes**: Research has consistently shown that therapists who regularly engage in supervision and self-reflection achieve better client outcomes. Supervision enhances therapist confidence, intervention effectiveness, and therapeutic alliance strength (Norcross & Wampold, 2018).

Types of Supervision and Consultation

Therapists can engage in various forms of supervision depending on their career stage, clinical setting, and professional needs:

- **Individual Supervision**: One-on-one mentorship from an experienced supervisor, allowing for deep case analysis, skill refinement, and personalized feedback.
- **Group Supervision**: A collaborative environment where multiple therapists share case challenges, receive diverse perspectives, and learn from peer experiences.
- **Peer Consultation**: More experienced therapists may engage in peer consultation, where they discuss complex cases, ethical concerns, or practice management issues with colleagues.

- **Deliberate Practice Supervision**: A structured approach focused on enhancing specific therapeutic skills through role-playing, real-time feedback, and targeted training (Rousmaniere, 2016).

Integrating YIA into Supervision and Professional Growth

Supervision is most effective when it aligns with a therapist's therapeutic approach and personal development goals. The Yanni Integration Approach (YIA) offers a structured yet adaptable framework that ensures therapists engage in multi-dimensional supervision that supports cognitive, emotional, relational, and lifestyle-based growth.

- **CBT Focus in Supervision**: Helps therapists recognize and challenge their own cognitive distortions about their effectiveness, competence, or client progress. This fosters self-compassion and adaptability rather than rigid self-criticism (A. T. Beck, 1979).
- **Psychodynamic Perspective**: Encourages exploration of countertransference, unconscious biases, and relational dynamics that emerge in clinical work, enhancing therapist self-awareness and emotional neutrality (Shedler, 2010).
- **Humanistic Integration**: Reinforces the importance of genuineness, empathy, and congruence in supervision, ensuring that therapists remain authentic and emotionally engaged in their work (Rogers, 1961).
- **Person-Centered Approach**: Emphasizes the role of self-directed learning in supervision, encouraging therapists to take ownership of their professional development and reflective practice (Deci & Ryan, 2000).
- **Lifestyle Changes Component**: Recognizes that supervision is not just about clinical skills, but also therapist well-being. Maintaining work-life balance, engaging in self-care, and managing burnout are critical to long-term professional sustainability (Walsh, 2011).

By integrating YIA into supervision, therapists benefit from a holistic developmental model that not only sharpens their clinical skills but also supports emotional resilience, ethical awareness, and self-care.

Supervision is not a sign of inexperience, it is a hallmark of professional excellence. By regularly engaging in individual, group, or peer supervision, therapists enhance their clinical competence, strengthen ethical decision-making, and reduce burnout (Bernard & Goodyear, 2019). Research consistently supports that supervised therapists demonstrate greater self-awareness, improved client outcomes, and long-term career satisfaction (Norcross & Wampold, 2018). As therapy evolves, so too must the therapist, and supervision remains one of the most effective tools for ensuring ongoing professional refinement and growth.

While self-reflection and supervision enhance therapist growth, client feedback provides direct insight into what is working and what may need adjustment.

Gathering Feedback from Clients to Adjust and Improve Your Approach

Therapists often assume they know what is working for a client, but direct client feedback provides critical insights into the effectiveness of therapy and areas for improvement. Research indicates that clients who feel heard, validated, and actively involved in their treatment experience better therapeutic outcomes and greater engagement (Duncan et al., 2010; Norcross & Wampold, 2018). Tracking client perceptions of progress helps therapists refine their approach, strengthen the therapeutic alliance, and ensure that therapy remains responsive to the client's evolving needs (Lambert & Shimokawa, 2011).

While therapist intuition plays a role in guiding sessions, studies show that clinician estimates of client progress often do not align with actual client experiences, emphasizing the need for structured, evidence-based feedback mechanisms (S. D. Miller et al., 2006). Gathering feedback through session check-ins, structured assessment tools, and post-therapy reflection allows therapists to adjust interventions in real-time, improving retention rates and overall treatment effectiveness (Duncan & Reese, 2015).

Integrating the Five Models to Enhance Client Feedback

The Yanni Integration Approach (YIA) incorporates multiple perspectives to ensure feedback is gathered in a structured, relational, and meaningful way:

- **CBT:** Uses structured tools such as client progress tracking, goal-setting worksheets, and self-report assessments to measure change and identify areas needing further attention (Lambert et al., 2001).
- **Psychodynamic:** Encourages exploration of the client's experience within the therapeutic relationship, helping uncover unconscious dynamics or resistances that may be affecting progress (Shedler, 2010).
- **Humanistic:** Creates a safe, nonjudgmental space for open and honest feedback, reinforcing the message that the client's experience and perspective are central to therapy success (Rogers, 1961).
- **Person-Centered:** Empowers clients to take an active role in shaping their therapy experience, ensuring that their needs, goals, and preferences are continuously addressed (Norcross & Goldfried, 2019).
- **Lifestyle Changes:** Uses behavioral tracking methods (e.g., sleep logs, mood tracking, exercise logs) to assess how external life changes impact therapeutic progress and overall well-being (Walsh, 2011).

Methods for Gathering Client Feedback

Therapists can integrate feedback into sessions using the following strategies:

- **Session Check-Ins:** Asking open-ended, reflective questions to invite feedback, such as:
    - *"How do you feel about the direction of our work together?"*
    - *"Is there anything you would like to adjust in our sessions?"*

  - *"What aspects of therapy have been most or least helpful?"*

- **Therapeutic Alliance Measures:** Using standardized tools such as the Session Rating Scale (SRS) or Outcome Rating Scale (ORS) to assess client satisfaction, engagement, and perception of progress (S. D. Miller et al., 2006; Duncan & Reese, 2015).
- **Post-Therapy Reflection:** Encouraging clients to reflect on what has been most helpful in therapy and what could be improved, ensuring insights are carried into future treatment adjustments.
- **Exit Interviews or Follow-Ups:** Gathering long-term feedback from clients who complete therapy provides insight into what aspects of therapy had lasting benefits and how future treatment approaches can be refined (Lambert & Shimokawa, 2011).

Regularly gathering client feedback is not just a best practice, it is an evidence-based method for improving therapy effectiveness, strengthening the therapeutic alliance, and increasing client retention rates (Norcross & Wampold, 2018; Lambert et al., 2001). Studies indicate that therapists who consistently incorporate structured feedback mechanisms into their sessions see significantly better client outcomes compared to those who rely solely on their clinical judgment (Duncan et al., 2010; S. D. Miller et al., 2006). By integrating multiple feedback methods across different therapeutic models, therapists can ensure that therapy remains flexible, responsive, and deeply attuned to the client's evolving needs.

In addition to gathering client feedback, staying informed about emerging research and innovations ensures that therapists continue to refine their approach and provide evidence-based care.

Staying Informed and Adapting to New Research and Innovations

Psychotherapy is an ever-evolving field, requiring therapists to continually adapt to new research, methodologies, and technological advancements to maintain effectiveness. Evidence-based interventions, neuroscience discoveries, and digital mental health tools are reshaping best practices, offering therapists innovative ways to enhance treatment outcomes (Norcross & Wampold, 2018; Duncan et al., 2010). Without ongoing learning, therapists risk relying on outdated models that may not fully address clients' evolving needs.

Staying informed is not just about keeping up with trends, it is about ensuring that therapy remains relevant, effective, and backed by the latest scientific insights. Research consistently shows that therapists who actively engage in ongoing education, training, and research integration report higher professional satisfaction, greater client engagement, and improved treatment outcomes (Wampold & Imel, 2015). By incorporating new research into clinical practice, therapists ensure they are delivering the highest standard of care while fostering their own professional growth.

Integrating the Five Models with New Research and Innovations

The Yanni Integration Approach (YIA) encourages therapists to incorporate cutting-edge research and advancements into their therapeutic framework:

- **CBT:** Adapts to new cognitive-behavioral techniques, including digital mental health tools, AI-driven self-monitoring apps, and virtual reality exposure therapy, which enhance accessibility and engagement (Andersson et al., 2019).
- **Psychodynamic:** Incorporates advances in attachment theory, trauma research, and neurobiology, deepening insight-based work and reinforcing how early experiences shape present behaviors (Fonagy & Target, 2007).

- **Humanistic:** Explores new approaches in mindfulness, somatic therapy, and emotional intelligence training, integrating research on how self-awareness and embodiment enhance therapeutic outcomes (Siegel, 2020).
- **Person-Centered:** Engages with client-driven therapy trends, such as narrative therapy, strengths-based interventions, and culturally responsive counseling, ensuring therapy remains collaborative and affirming (Norcross & Wampold, 2018).
- **Lifestyle Changes:** Integrates updated research on nutrition, exercise, sleep science, and behavioral health, recognizing the strong connection between physical and mental well-being (Walsh, 2011).

By integrating new research into these therapeutic models, therapists can refine their practice to align with the latest evidence while maintaining a flexible, client-centered approach.

Strategies for Staying Informed

To ensure ongoing professional development, therapists can actively engage with new research through various channels:

- **Attending Conferences and Workshops:** Engaging in professional development opportunities exposes therapists to emerging techniques and interdisciplinary insights (Kazdin, 2021).
- **Subscribing to Peer-Reviewed Journals:** Reading journals such as *Psychotherapy*, *Journal of Clinical Psychology*, and *American Psychologist* keeps therapists up to date with scientifically validated interventions.
- **Participating in Online Training and Continuing Education:** Webinars, certification programs, and online courses provide accessible ways to learn new skills and interventions.

- **Collaborating with Research Institutions:** Engaging in research collaborations or clinical trials allows therapists to contribute to and directly apply new findings (Wampold & Imel, 2015).
- **Utilizing Professional Networks and Peer Consultation:** Connecting with colleagues, supervision groups, and online forums fosters knowledge exchange and practical application of new research.

Staying informed about new research and innovations is not just a professional obligation, it is an ethical commitment to providing the highest quality care. As therapy continues to evolve, therapists who embrace evidence-based advancements ensure their practice remains effective, relevant, and client-centered (Norcross & Wampold, 2018; Duncan et al., 2010). Research consistently shows that clinicians who prioritize ongoing learning and research integration experience greater professional fulfillment and improved client outcomes (Wampold & Imel, 2015). By actively engaging with new methodologies, technological advancements, and interdisciplinary findings, therapists enhance their ability to meet clients' needs while maintaining their own professional growth and adaptability.

Conclusion

Therapists must continuously evaluate and refine their approach to maintain effectiveness and ensure the best outcomes for clients. Self-reflection, supervision, and gathering client feedback provide valuable insights into strengths and areas for growth, helping therapists maintain self-awareness and prevent burnout. Staying informed about new research and therapeutic innovations allows therapists to integrate cutting-edge techniques into their work while maintaining ethical standards.

By committing to lifelong learning and self-improvement, therapists can continue to provide high-quality, client-centered care that evolves with the changing landscape of mental health treatment.

CHAPTER 15:

Ethical Considerations in Integration

Introduction

As discussed in Chapter 14, therapists must continually evaluate and refine their practice to ensure effectiveness. However, ongoing professional growth must be guided by ethical principles that protect clients, maintain professional integrity, and ensure that integration remains structured and intentional. Integrative therapy is powerful because it allows for flexibility, but with flexibility comes the responsibility of maintaining ethical transparency, ensuring cultural competence, and staying within one's professional scope (Norcross & Goldfried, 2019).

Blending multiple therapeutic models requires thoughtful application to avoid misrepresentation, boundary violations, or potential harm. The Yanni Integration Approach (YIA) draws from cognitive behavioral therapy (CBT), psychodynamic therapy, humanistic therapy, person-centered therapy, and lifestyle-based Interventions, offering flexibility while ensuring that integration remains transparent, ethical, and client-centered.

Therapists who practice ethically not only uphold professional standards but also enhance client trust, therapeutic engagement, and long-term success in therapy (Barnett, 2019). Ethical integrity fosters a sense of safety in clients, allowing them to fully engage in integrative therapy without fear of misrepresentation or harm.

This chapter will explore the core ethical responsibilities in integrative therapy, including informed consent, maintaining professional boundaries, cultural competence, and evidence-based integration. Additionally, modern challenges such as the ethics of teletherapy and potential therapist biases in integration will be examined to ensure therapists uphold ethical excellence in evolving clinical landscapes.

Why Ethical Considerations Matter in Integrative Therapy

Blending multiple therapeutic models requires ethical awareness, especially when working across diverse client backgrounds, cultural frameworks, and clinical needs. The Yanni Integration Approach (YIA) draws from cognitive behavioral therapy (CBT), psychodynamic therapy, humanistic therapy, person-centered therapy, and lifestyle-based interventions, offering flexibility while ensuring that integration remains transparent, ethical, and client-centered.

Core Ethical Responsibilities in Integrative Therapy

- **Informed Consent:** Clearly explaining the integrative approach and obtaining the client's agreement. Therapists must provide clients with a clear understanding of how different modalities will be used, ensuring transparency in treatment (Pope et al., 2021).
- **Scope of Practice:** Ensuring therapists operate within their professional boundaries, particularly when incorporating lifestyle-based interventions. Practitioners must adhere to state licensure laws and professional guidelines to avoid practicing outside their competence (Knapp et al., 2015).
- **Cultural Competence:** Recognizing that different communities and clients have varied understandings of mental health and therapy. A culturally competent therapist acknowledges and integrates a client's values, beliefs,

and traditions into treatment to enhance therapeutic outcomes (Sue, Rasheed, & Rasheed, 2016).

- **Evidence-Based Decision-Making:** Using research-backed strategies to ethically blend different therapeutic approaches. Ethical integration requires selecting interventions with demonstrated efficacy, ensuring that methods align with established psychological research (Norcross & Wampold, 2011a).
- **Client Autonomy and Beneficence:** Balancing the client's right to self-determination with the therapist's role in guiding treatment. Clients should feel empowered to make choices regarding their therapy while therapists maintain a responsibility to act in their best interests (Beauchamp & Childress, 2019).
- **Confidentiality and Privacy:** Adhering to legal and ethical guidelines concerning client information. Integrative therapy may involve a more holistic approach, but maintaining strict confidentiality remains paramount (American Psychological Association, 2017).

Ethical Challenges and Solutions

Integrative therapy can present ethical dilemmas, such as potential conflicts between models, client expectations, or boundary concerns. To navigate these challenges:

- **Engage in Ongoing Supervision and Peer Consultation:** Consulting with colleagues or supervisors can provide ethical guidance when dilemmas arise (Pope et al., 2021).
- **Stay Informed on Ethical Codes and Legal Standards:** Regularly reviewing the ethical codes of professional organizations, such as the American Psychological Association (APA) and the American Counseling Association (ACA), helps ensure compliance.
- **Maintain Self-Awareness and Reflective Practice:** Therapists should engage in continual self-reflection to recognize biases and ethical blind spots that may impact integrative therapy (Schön, 1983).

Ethical considerations in integrative therapy are not simply regulatory requirements; they are essential to fostering trust, respect, and effectiveness in the therapeutic relationship. The Yanni Integration Approach aims to provide a comprehensive yet ethical framework that upholds client well-being while harnessing the strengths of multiple therapeutic models. By prioritizing ethical mindfulness, therapists can navigate the complexities of integration with integrity, professionalism, and a commitment to client-centered care.

A crucial aspect of maintaining ethical integrity in integrative therapy is ensuring that clients fully understand the therapeutic process, including how different modalities will be combined. This brings us to the fundamental principle of Informed Consent in an Integrative Approach, where transparency, collaboration, and client autonomy take center stage.

Informed Consent in an Integrative Approach

Clients have the right to understand the therapeutic methods being used and how they are combined. Many clients enter therapy expecting a specific approach; for example, a client seeking CBT may be unfamiliar with psychodynamic exploration or lifestyle interventions. Ethical practice requires transparent communication about integration before beginning treatment (Barnett, 2019). Additionally, informed consent is not only an ethical requirement but also a legal obligation in many jurisdictions (American Psychological Association, 2017).

Best Practices for Informed Consent

- Explain the integrative approach at the start of therapy
    - *"In our work together, we will use a combination of approaches tailored to your needs. This may include cognitive restructuring from CBT, insight-building from psychodynamic therapy, and practical lifestyle modifications."*

- Encourage questions and discussion
    - *"What are your thoughts about using different approaches? Are there any methods you feel more comfortable or uncomfortable with?"*
- Obtain explicit client agreement
    - Clients should provide informed consent to integrative therapy just as they would for any single therapeutic model.
- Recognize that informed consent is an ongoing process
    - As therapy evolves, therapists should revisit the discussion on integration, particularly if introducing new techniques or interventions (Knapp et al., 2015).
- Consider cultural sensitivity in consent
    - Some clients may have linguistic or cultural barriers that require additional effort in explaining therapeutic approaches. Offering consent forms in multiple languages or adapting discussions to align with clients' cultural understandings of therapy enhances the informed consent process (Sue, Rasheed, & Rasheed, 2016).

Studies suggest that clients who understand their therapist's approach upfront feel more engaged and report higher satisfaction in treatment (Swift & Greenberg, 2015). Furthermore, Beahrs and Gutheil (2001) emphasized that clear, collaborative consent strengthens the therapeutic alliance and reduces potential misunderstandings.

Beyond informed consent, maintaining ethical boundaries within an integrative framework is crucial, especially when incorporating lifestyle-based interventions.

Scope of Practice: Ethical Boundaries in Lifestyle Interventions

Therapists incorporating lifestyle-based interventions (such as sleep hygiene, exercise, or nutrition) must remain within their professional scope. While these factors can significantly impact mental health, psychotherapy is not a substitute for medical treatment. Recommending specific diets, prescribing supplements, or advising on medication falls outside the ethical and legal boundaries of psychotherapy and into the domain of medical professionals (Zur, 2007). Overstepping these boundaries can not only mislead clients but also expose therapists to legal and ethical liability. However, when applied appropriately, lifestyle-based interventions can enhance therapeutic outcomes by helping clients develop behavioral habits that support mental well-being.

Best Practices for Staying Within Scope

- Use behavioral guidance instead of medical advice
    - Rather than directing clients toward specific medical treatments, therapists should encourage self-awareness and behavioral changes.
      <u>Example:</u> *"Have you noticed how your sleep patterns affect your mood? Would you be open to tracking them?"*
- Refer to primary care providers when necessary
    - If a client presents with concerns related to diet, exercise, or other health-related areas that require medical expertise, a referral to a healthcare professional is warranted.
      <u>Example:</u> *"If you're considering major dietary changes, it would be a good idea to consult your doctor to ensure it aligns with your health needs."*

- Base recommendations on established research
    - When discussing the benefits of lifestyle changes, therapists should rely on peer-reviewed research rather than anecdotal evidence or personal beliefs. This ensures that the guidance provided is both ethical and evidence-based.
      Example: *When suggesting exercise for mental health, cite studies showing its benefits (Blumenthal, Smith, & Hoffman, 2012).*

- Clarify the role of lifestyle interventions in therapy
    - Therapists should frame lifestyle-based interventions as complementary to, rather than a replacement for, psychological treatment. Clients should understand that although improving sleep, exercise, and diet can support mental well-being, these changes should be made in conjunction with, not in place of, therapy.

Therapists who provide evidence-based lifestyle interventions while respecting professional boundaries are more likely to build client trust and reduce liability risks. Research shows that clients respond best when therapists clearly distinguish between psychological support and medical recommendations, reinforcing ethical integrity in practice (Barnett, 2019).

Although staying within ethical boundaries is important, cultural sensitivity is equally essential when integrating diverse therapeutic models.

Cultural Competence in Integrative Therapy

Many traditional therapy models, especially CBT and psychodynamic therapy, were developed in Western contexts, often prioritizing individualism, self-exploration, and direct verbal processing. Applying these models without cultural adaptation can lead to misalignment with a client's worldview, limiting the effectiveness of therapy and potentially alienating clients from diverse backgrounds (Sue, Rasheed, & Rasheed, 2016). Cultural competence in integrative therapy ensures that interventions are not only evidence-based but also relevant and respectful of a client's cultural identity.

Best Practices for Culturally Competent Integration

- Recognize cultural perspectives on mental health
    - Some cultures emphasize collective healing over individual therapy. Integrative approaches should acknowledge and incorporate community-based supports, such as family networks, religious leaders, or traditional healing practices, to align with the client's cultural framework.
    - *Example:* A therapist working with a client from a collectivist culture might involve trusted family members in discussions or explore culturally significant healing rituals as part of the therapeutic process.
- Adapt language and interventions to fit cultural values
    - In some cultures, expressing emotions openly is discouraged, making traditional Western talk therapy less effective. Instead of focusing solely on verbal processing, therapists can use indirect methods like storytelling, proverbs, metaphors, or artistic expression to align with cultural norms (Fernando, 2010).
    - *Example:* If a client is uncomfortable with direct self-disclosure, a therapist might use fables or cultural narratives to explore emotions and coping strategies in a way that feels more natural.
- Avoid imposing Western models

- Instead of assuming all clients benefit from cognitive restructuring (as emphasized in CBT), therapists should explore whether the client resonates with other approaches, such as narrative therapy, mindfulness-based interventions, or indigenous healing traditions.
- *Example:* A client from an Eastern background may find mindfulness and meditation practices more aligned with their cultural beliefs than cognitive restructuring exercises. Therapists should remain flexible and open to integrating culturally relevant methods.

Cultural competence in integrative therapy is not about replacing traditional models but rather ensuring that therapy remains inclusive, flexible, and responsive to a client's cultural context. By acknowledging cultural variations in emotional expression, healing practices, and therapeutic expectations, therapists can foster deeper engagement, trust, and effectiveness in their work. A culturally adaptive approach strengthens the therapeutic alliance and enhances treatment outcomes by honoring the unique worldviews and lived experiences of each client.

Case Study: Riya and the Conflict Between Family and Therapy

Riya, a 26-year-old South Asian woman, sought therapy for anxiety stemming from family expectations regarding marriage, career, and independence. Raised in a collectivist culture that prioritizes family harmony, she found it difficult to reconcile traditional family values with the Western emphasis on individual autonomy often emphasized in therapy. She reported feelings of guilt when making personal decisions that diverged from family expectations, leading to heightened anxiety and self-doubt.

- **CBT:** The therapist initially introduced cognitive restructuring to help Riya identify and challenge automatic negative thoughts about disappointing her family. However, recognizing that direct confrontation of these beliefs might feel unnatural within her cultural framework, the therapist adapted the approach by incorporating cultural proverbs and analogies that resonated with Riya. Additionally, family-inclusive decision-making techniques were explored, allowing Riya to balance her needs with familial expectations without feeling as though she was betraying her values.

- **Psychodynamic Therapy:** Through psychodynamic exploration, Riya and the therapist examined how her early childhood experiences shaped her current anxieties. The therapist helped her uncover unconscious fears related to parental approval and the internalized expectation that self-sacrifice equates to love. This insight helped Riya reframe her emotional responses and recognize patterns that perpetuated her anxiety.
- **Humanistic Therapy:** The therapist created a safe, nonjudgmental space where Riya felt heard and validated. Rather than pushing an agenda of Western-style independence, the therapist acknowledged the depth of her struggle and honored the cultural significance of family loyalty. This validation helped Riya feel seen rather than pathologized for her values.
- **Person-Centered Therapy:** Instead of imposing external definitions of success or progress, the therapist encouraged Riya to define what fulfillment and balance looked like for her. Over time, she was able to develop a more flexible mindset—one that allowed for both personal aspirations and familial respect without feeling entirely torn between the two. By prioritizing Riya's autonomy in shaping her own path, the therapist reinforced her sense of self-agency in a culturally sensitive manner.
- **Lifestyle-Based Interventions:** To help manage Riya's anxiety, the therapist introduced mindfulness and breathing techniques that aligned with her cultural background. Meditation practices that had roots in South Asian traditions were suggested as ways to calm her mind, making these strategies feel more natural and acceptable to her. The therapist also encouraged Riya to engage in community-based support systems, such as talking to an elder or engaging in cultural practices that provided her with a sense of stability and belonging.

Riya's case highlights the importance of cultural competence in therapy. By integrating multiple therapeutic approaches in a way that honored her values, the therapist helped her reduce anxiety without forcing a rigid, Western-centric model of independence. This case demonstrates that ethical, effective therapy is not about erasing cultural frameworks but rather working within them to foster healing and personal growth. Through the Yanni Integration Approach, Riya was able to navigate the complexities of her identity, family expectations, and personal aspirations, ultimately finding a path that felt both authentic and sustainable. Therapists who integrate culturally adapted approaches report higher client retention and satisfaction rates (Sue, Cheng, et al., 2012).

Cultural competence is crucial, but ensuring integration is evidence-based is equally important in ethical therapy.

Ethical Dilemmas for Therapists

Ethical dilemmas are an inevitable part of clinical practice, requiring therapists to navigate difficult decisions while upholding professional integrity. Therapists often face challenges such as balancing personal values with client autonomy, managing the risk of client dependence, and handling dual relationships. These dilemmas are particularly pronounced in integrative therapy, where multiple therapeutic models intersect, requiring careful ethical considerations. Ethical integration demands ongoing self-reflection, consultation, and strict adherence to professional codes of conduct to ensure that therapeutic decisions are in the best interest of the client (Barnett, 2019).

Ethical Dilemmas in Therapy and How to Manage Them

- **Navigating Personal Values Without Imposing Them on Clients**

- Therapists, like all individuals, hold personal beliefs and values shaped by their own experiences. However, ethical practice requires therapists to create a space where clients feel free to explore their own values without feeling judged or influenced. This can be particularly challenging when a client's choices or beliefs conflict with those of the therapist.
- *Example:* A therapist who personally values traditional family structures must ensure they do not impose these beliefs on a client exploring non-traditional relationship dynamics. Instead, the therapist should help the client clarify their own values and decision-making processes.

- **Managing Client Dependence and Fostering Autonomy**

  - Clients who struggle with self-efficacy or significant emotional distress may develop an over-reliance on their therapist. While the therapeutic relationship is meant to provide support, ethical practice requires therapists to empower clients rather than foster dependence.
  - *Example:* A client experiencing chronic anxiety might excessively seek reassurance from their therapist. Instead of reinforcing this pattern, the therapist can use techniques such as CBT to help the client develop independent coping strategies. Encouraging clients to practice self-reflection and problem-solving skills outside of sessions promotes autonomy.

- **Dual Relationships and Boundary Management**

  - In certain contexts, therapists may encounter situations where professional and personal relationships overlap, especially in small communities, cultural groups, or professional networks. Ethical practice requires careful boundary-setting to prevent conflicts of interest.
  - *Example:* A therapist working in a rural community may inevitably interact with a client outside of therapy. In such cases, it is essential to establish clear professional boundaries from the beginning and discuss

potential concerns with the client in a transparent manner. Consulting ethical guidelines and seeking supervision can help navigate these complex situations (Knapp et al., 2015).

- **Confidentiality vs. Duty to Protect**
  - Maintaining confidentiality is a cornerstone of therapy, yet there are circumstances where a therapist may need to break confidentiality to protect a client or others from harm. Understanding legal and ethical requirements regarding mandated reporting, risk assessment, and crisis intervention is crucial.
  - *Example:* A therapist working with a teenager who expresses suicidal ideation must assess risk carefully, balancing confidentiality with the responsibility to intervene and ensure the client's safety. Consulting state laws and ethical guidelines is essential in making an informed decision.

- **Ethical Considerations in Integrative Therapy**
  - Integrative therapy involves blending multiple therapeutic models, which can raise ethical concerns about transparency and evidence-based practice. Therapists must clearly explain their integrative approach to clients, ensuring informed consent and ethical adherence to established therapeutic principles.
  - *Example:* A therapist using both psychodynamic and CBT techniques must clarify how these approaches complement each other, ensuring that clients understand and agree to the integrative process. Providing evidence-based justifications for selected interventions further enhances ethical practice (Norcross & Wampold, 2011a).

Ethical dilemmas in therapy are not always straightforward, and therapists must engage in ongoing reflection, supervision, and professional development to navigate them effectively. By maintaining self-awareness, consulting ethical guidelines, and seeking supervision when needed, therapists can ensure that their decisions remain aligned with the best interests of their clients. Ethical integration in therapy requires balancing flexibility with professional responsibility, allowing therapists to provide effective care while upholding the highest ethical standards.

With the rise of virtual care, therapists must navigate new ethical challenges in teletherapy while maintaining the integrity of an integrative approach.

Addressing Ethical Challenges of Teletherapy in an Integrative Approach

As teletherapy becomes an increasingly common mode of delivering mental health care, therapists must navigate a range of ethical challenges to ensure that digital sessions maintain the same level of professional integrity as in-person therapy. Issues such as confidentiality, cultural adaptations, accessibility, and informed consent require careful consideration to avoid potential risks associated with remote care. Teletherapy has the potential to increase access to mental health services, particularly for clients in underserved areas, but only if ethical standards are upheld (Wampold & Imel, 2015). Research indicates that therapists who implement clear telehealth guidelines experience greater trust and engagement from clients, reinforcing the need for structured ethical practices in virtual therapy (Glueckauf et al., 2018).

Best Practices for Teletherapy Ethics

- **Establish Clear Informed Consent Policies**
    - Clients should fully understand the limitations, risks, and benefits of teletherapy. This includes discussing potential technological disruptions, differences in privacy compared to in-person sessions, and protocols

for emergency situations. Clients must be made aware of how their personal data will be handled and stored, and what steps will be taken to protect confidentiality (American Psychological Association, 2024).
    - *Example:* Therapists should provide a detailed teletherapy consent form that outlines expectations, security measures, and the limitations of virtual care, ensuring that clients make an informed decision about their treatment.

- **Ensure Secure Technology**
    - The use of HIPAA-compliant platforms is essential to safeguard client confidentiality. Non-secure communication methods, such as standard video conferencing tools or text messaging apps, pose risks to data privacy. Therapists should stay updated on best practices for cybersecurity and ensure that both they and their clients are using encrypted, professionally approved platforms (Maheu et al., 2019).
    - *Example:* A therapist conducting virtual sessions should utilize end-to-end encrypted platforms and educate clients on the importance of securing their personal networks and devices when engaging in therapy.

- **Adapt Therapy to Cultural and Digital Literacy Needs**
    - Not all clients have the same level of comfort or familiarity with digital communication. Some may need additional guidance on using teletherapy platforms, while others may experience cultural or linguistic barriers that affect virtual engagement. Therapists should ensure that technology does not become an obstacle to treatment by offering step-by-step assistance and culturally sensitive adaptations (Sue, Cheng, et al., 2012).
    - *Example:* A therapist working with an older client unfamiliar with video conferencing may provide additional instructions on accessing the

platform or offer alternative methods such as phone sessions. Similarly, culturally relevant teletherapy adaptations, such as using visual aids or incorporating traditional healing practices, may enhance client comfort and engagement (Sue, Cheng, et al., 2012).

- **Maintain Professional Boundaries in a Virtual Setting**
    - Teletherapy blurs the lines between professional and personal spaces, as sessions often take place in clients' homes. Therapists must set clear boundaries to maintain professionalism and ethical integrity. This includes discussing appropriate locations for sessions, minimizing distractions, and ensuring that both the therapist and the client maintain privacy during the session (Zur, 2007).
    - *Example:* If a client frequently attends sessions in public spaces where confidentiality cannot be guaranteed, the therapist should discuss the importance of privacy and explore alternative solutions.

- **Develop Contingency Plans for Emergencies**
    - Unlike in-person therapy, teletherapy presents unique challenges when clients experience crises. Therapists must have clear emergency protocols, including knowing the client's location at the start of each session, having emergency contacts readily available, and understanding local crisis intervention resources (Barnett & Kolmes, 2016).
    - *Example:* At the beginning of a teletherapy session, a therapist should confirm the client's current location and discuss steps to take in case of a psychological or medical emergency, ensuring that appropriate interventions can be implemented if needed.

The ethical challenges of teletherapy require therapists to remain vigilant, adaptable, and informed as digital mental health services continue to expand. By prioritizing confidentiality, informed consent, cultural sensitivity, and clear emergency protocols, therapists can ensure that teletherapy maintains the same ethical rigor as in-person care. Ethical teletherapy is not just about meeting legal standards, it is about fostering trust, engagement, and accessibility in a way that upholds the integrity of the therapeutic process.

As therapists navigate the ethical complexities of teletherapy, it is equally important to examine how cultural biases in evidence-based practices can impact the effectiveness and inclusivity of treatment approaches.

Cultural Bias in Evidence-Based Practices

Evidence-based practices (EBPs) are the foundation of modern psychotherapy, offering structured, research-backed approaches to treatment. However, many of these interventions were developed within Western, Eurocentric frameworks, often prioritizing individualism, self-expression, and cognitive-based change models. As a result, they may not fully apply to clients from collectivist cultures or those who hold different conceptualizations of mental health and healing (Sue, Cheng, et al., 2012). The assumption that EBPs are universally applicable can lead to unintended cultural insensitivity, alienating clients whose values, communication styles, and healing practices differ from dominant Western norms (Gone, 2016).

Therapists must critically assess research findings, acknowledging their cultural limitations and ensuring that interventions are applied in ways that respect and align with clients' lived experiences. A failure to do so risks reinforcing systemic biases in mental health care, ultimately reducing treatment engagement and effectiveness for diverse populations (Bernal & Scharrón-del-Río, 2001).

Best Practices for Addressing Bias in Evidence-Based Practices

- **Critically Evaluate Research Findings Before Applying Them Across Cultural Groups**

  - Therapists should consider the cultural context in which a treatment model was developed. Many widely used EBPs, such as cognitive behavioral therapy (CBT), were tested primarily on Western populations, often excluding racial, ethnic, and indigenous groups. Therapists must examine whether a particular intervention has been validated with diverse populations and, if not, modify or supplement it accordingly (G. C. N. Hall, 2001).
  - *Example:* A therapist working with a client from a culture that prioritizes indirect communication might adapt CBT's cognitive restructuring techniques to incorporate storytelling, metaphor, or spiritual references rather than relying solely on rational disputation.

- **Use a Client-Centered Approach to Tailor Interventions Rather Than Applying Rigid Models**

  - Rather than assuming that an EBP is inherently effective, therapists should co-create treatment plans with clients, incorporating cultural knowledge and preferences. The therapeutic relationship should prioritize collaboration, allowing the client's cultural identity to shape the intervention (Rogers-Sirin et al., 2015).
  - *Example:* If a client from a collectivist background feels discomfort with the individual focus of traditional therapy, the therapist might explore incorporating family members or community-based healing practices into the treatment process.

- **Acknowledge That Some Interventions Require Modification to Align With Cultural Values**

  - Some interventions may need structural adjustments to align with cultural beliefs about mental health, healing, and help-seeking. For instance, direct emotional expression—a key aspect of many Western

therapies—may be discouraged in certain cultural contexts. Therapists must adapt their techniques to fit these norms rather than expecting clients to conform to the dominant therapeutic model (Hwang, 2009).
  - *Example:* Exposure therapy for anxiety might be modified for a client from a culture that values emotional restraint by incorporating guided imagery or symbolic actions rather than direct confrontation of feared stimuli.

- **Incorporate Culturally Responsive Assessments and Measures**
  - Many standardized psychological assessments are based on Western diagnostic frameworks, which may not fully capture distress as experienced by individuals from non-Western cultures. Therapists should seek out or develop culturally adapted measures and be cautious in interpreting results that may not align with a client's lived experience (Streltzer, 2016).
  - *Example:* A therapist working with a client from an indigenous background might explore traditional explanations for emotional distress (e.g., spiritual imbalance) rather than immediately applying DSM-based diagnostic criteria.

- **Recognize and Address Power Dynamics in Research and Clinical Practice**
  - The dominance of Western research in defining EBPs reflects broader systemic power imbalances in psychology. Therapists should remain critical of how privilege, colonization, and historical marginalization have shaped mental health discourse and be willing to challenge outdated or exclusionary frameworks (Gone, 2016).
  - *Example:* A therapist working with an immigrant client might acknowledge the historical marginalization of their cultural healing practices and explore ways to integrate these methods into therapy rather than dismissing them as "unscientific."

Cultural bias in evidence-based practices is an ongoing challenge in the mental health field. While EBPs provide valuable frameworks for treatment, they must be applied with cultural humility, flexibility, and an awareness of their limitations. By critically evaluating interventions, adapting treatment plans to fit diverse perspectives, and integrating culturally relevant approaches, therapists can create more inclusive and effective therapeutic experiences. Ethical, client-centered therapy must honor the diversity of human experiences rather than expecting all clients to conform to Western norms of psychological well-being.

As therapists work to address cultural biases in evidence-based practices, it is equally important to ensure that integrative therapy remains grounded in ethical, research-based best practices that enhance client care.

Research-Based Best Practices for Ethical Integration

Ethical integration in therapy is not merely about combining different models; it requires a structured, evidence-based approach to ensure that the blending of theories and techniques enhances, rather than undermines, treatment effectiveness. While integrative therapy offers flexibility and personalization, poorly structured integration can dilute the effectiveness of interventions, create confusion for clients, and even lead to ethical concerns about inconsistent treatment approaches (Wampold & Imel, 2015). Without a strong foundation in research, integration runs the risk of becoming eclecticism without direction, potentially compromising client outcomes (Norcross & Goldfried, 2019).

Research supports the notion that well-structured integration, where each model is purposefully selected based on scientific literature and clinical relevance, leads to better therapeutic outcomes (Leichsenring & Leibing, 2003). Effective integration requires not only theoretical compatibility but also ongoing reflection, supervision, and adherence to ethical guidelines to ensure that interventions remain both effective and appropriate for each client.

Best Practices for Evidence-Based Integration

- **Ground Integration in Scientific Literature**
  - Therapists must ensure that the therapeutic models they integrate are supported by empirical research, particularly when used in combination. Certain approaches complement each other, while others may conflict or reduce treatment efficacy. Research has shown that combining CBT with psychodynamic therapy enhances emotional processing and long-term insight, making it a viable integrative approach when appropriately structured (Leichsenring & Leibing, 2003). Conversely, blending directive and non-directive therapies without a clear framework can create confusion for both the therapist and client (Kazdin, 2008).
  - *Example:* A therapist combining CBT's structured thought restructuring with psychodynamic therapy's focus on unconscious processes should ensure that interventions are sequenced appropriately—using CBT to provide symptom relief while gradually incorporating deeper psychodynamic work for long-term emotional insight.

- **Ensure Each Model Serves a Purpose in Treatment**
  - Ethical integration means that every theoretical approach used in therapy should be intentionally selected to address a specific aspect of the client's needs. Arbitrary mixing of models can create inconsistencies in treatment, reducing effectiveness and causing clients to feel disoriented in therapy (Norcross & Goldfried, 2019). Therapists should clearly explain how each method contributes to the overall treatment plan and ensure coherence in their application.
  - *Example:* A therapist working with trauma may integrate EMDR for reprocessing distressing memories, CBT for restructuring maladaptive thoughts, and humanistic therapy to create a validating, client-centered

space. Each model serves a clear function in addressing different aspects of the client's healing process.

- **Seek Supervision and Peer Consultation**
  - Ethical integration requires therapists to continuously refine their approach, ensuring that they are not blending models in ways that inadvertently cause harm. Regular supervision and peer consultation provide an opportunity to discuss integration methods, receive feedback, and align clinical decisions with ethical best practices (Hill & Knox, 2013). Supervision also helps therapists recognize personal biases that may affect the way they apply integrative techniques.
  - *Example:* A therapist incorporating lifestyle interventions alongside traditional talk therapy may seek consultation to determine whether certain recommendations (e.g., mindfulness practices, exercise regimens) fall within their professional scope or require referrals to other specialists.

- **Maintain Transparency With Clients**
  - Clients should be fully informed about the integrative approach being used and how different models will be applied in their treatment. Research suggests that when clients understand the rationale behind therapeutic interventions, they are more likely to engage with the process and experience greater treatment success (Swift & Greenberg, 2015). Informed consent in integrative therapy should be an ongoing conversation rather than a one-time discussion at intake.
  - *Example:* A therapist might say, *"We're going to incorporate elements of CBT to help manage immediate anxiety symptoms while also exploring deeper patterns from your past through psychodynamic techniques. Does this approach sound comfortable to you?"*

- **Continuously Evaluate and Adapt Integration Methods**
  - Ethical integration requires ongoing assessment of its effectiveness. Therapists should track progress, adjust techniques based on client feedback, and remain open to modifying the treatment plan as needed. Research emphasizes that flexibility in treatment, when applied thoughtfully, leads to better client outcomes (Norcross & Goldfried, 2019). However, this flexibility must remain structured and intentional, ensuring that integration does not become an unstructured mix of interventions.
  - *Example:* If a client initially responds well to CBT but later shows resistance, the therapist might incorporate more person-centered or mindfulness-based strategies while still maintaining the core CBT framework for managing symptoms.

Ethical integration is not simply about using multiple therapeutic approaches, it is about ensuring that each method is selected, applied, and evaluated with scientific rigor and ethical mindfulness. By grounding integration in research, maintaining coherence in treatment, and seeking continuous supervision, therapists can create a structured and ethical approach that enhances client outcomes. The goal of integrative therapy is not to blend approaches haphazardly but to synthesize them in ways that honor both clinical evidence and the individual needs of each client.

Conclusion

Ethical integration in therapy is both a professional obligation and a clinical necessity. The flexibility of integrative therapy allows for personalized treatment tailored to the unique needs of each client, but this adaptability must be grounded in ethical principles that uphold client trust, professional integrity, and the scientific rigor of evidence-based practice. Without a clear ethical framework, integration risks becoming arbitrary or inconsistent, potentially undermining the therapeutic process rather than enhancing it.

The Yanni Integration Approach (YIA) ensures that ethical considerations remain at the forefront by prioritizing informed consent, maintaining professional boundaries, practicing cultural competence, and implementing evidence-based strategies. Ethical integration is not about mixing techniques at random but about creating a structured, intentional, and client-centered approach that maximizes therapeutic outcomes.

As the field of psychotherapy evolves, so too must our ethical considerations. The rise of teletherapy, the increasing recognition of cultural biases in evidence-based practices, and the ongoing expansion of integrative methods demand that therapists remain reflective, engaged, and committed to lifelong learning. By seeking supervision, engaging in peer consultation, and staying informed about evolving ethical standards, therapists can ensure that their integrative practice remains both effective and ethically sound.

Ultimately, ethical integration is a balance between flexibility and responsibility, between innovation and adherence to professional guidelines. When applied with care, integrity, and a commitment to best practices, integrative therapy has the potential to offer clients a deeply personalized and effective treatment experience. By embracing both ethical rigor and clinical creativity, therapists can foster therapeutic relationships built on trust, transparency, and transformative healing.

CHAPTER 16:

The Science of Integrative Therapy: Research Supporting Multimodal Approaches

Introduction

The ethical responsibility of a therapist, as discussed in Chapter 15, is not just about maintaining professional standards, it's about ensuring that the methods used are backed by both ethical reasoning and scientific validation. Integrative therapy, while ethically sound in its client-centered adaptability, must also stand up to empirical scrutiny. This chapter shifts from the ethical considerations of integration to the research that supports its effectiveness, demonstrating why a multimodal approach is not only beneficial but necessary.

Decades of psychological research reveal that while individual therapy models offer unique strengths, they also carry inherent limitations when applied in isolation. No single approach comprehensively addresses the complexity of human struggles. Studies comparing standalone methods to integrative approaches consistently show that combining cognitive, psychodynamic, person-centered, humanistic, and lifestyle-oriented techniques leads to more effective and enduring client outcomes (Norcross & Alexander, 2019).

This chapter will first examine the strengths and limitations of individual therapy models, assessing their contributions and constraints. It will then explore research comparing individual models to integrated approaches, illustrating why multimodal therapy produces superior results. From there, we will build the case for integration, grounding it in empirical evidence and demonstrating how the Yanni Integration Approach (YIA) synthesizes these elements for optimal therapeutic effectiveness. Finally, we will discuss future directions in integrative therapy research, identifying emerging trends and areas where further study can continue refining this approach.

By bridging ethical responsibility with scientific validation, this chapter reinforces why integrative therapy is not just a preference but a research-supported necessity in modern psychotherapy.

The Strengths and Limitations of Individual Therapy Models

The field of psychotherapy has long been shaped by distinct therapeutic models, each offering valuable insights and techniques for addressing mental health concerns. Research consistently demonstrates that cognitive, psychodynamic, person-centered, humanistic, and lifestyle-based interventions can be highly effective within their respective domains. However, no single model sufficiently addresses the complexities of human experience on its own. Each has inherent limitations when used in isolation, making a strong case for an integrative approach.

By examining both the strengths and constraints of these models, we can better understand why a multimodal framework, such as the Yanni Integration Approach (YIA), provides a more adaptable and comprehensive method for therapy.

Cognitive Behavioral Therapy (CBT)

CBT has been extensively studied and is widely regarded as one of the most effective treatments for anxiety, depression, and behavioral disorders (Hofmann et al., 2012; Cuijpers et al., 2014). Its structured approach, which focuses on identifying and restructuring maladaptive thought patterns while implementing behavioral modifications, makes it particularly effective for clients seeking symptom relief.

However, research suggests that CBT alone may be less effective for individuals with deeply rooted emotional trauma, personality disorders, or those who struggle to access their emotions (Leichsenring et al., 2013; Shedler, 2010). Additionally, Longmore and Worrell (2007) argued that while CBT emphasizes cognitive restructuring, it may not sufficiently address the emotional depth of a client's experiences. These findings highlight the importance of supplementing CBT with approaches that emphasize deeper emotional exploration and relational dynamics.

Psychodynamic Therapy

Rooted in Freud's theories, psychodynamic therapy aims to uncover unconscious conflicts that shape present behaviors. Research supports its effectiveness in treating complex trauma, personality disorders, and chronic depression, particularly by fostering insight and self-awareness (Shedler, 2010; Town et al., 2011).

Despite its strengths, psychodynamic therapy can sometimes lack the structured symptom-focused strategies that many clients need for immediate relief. Studies suggest that when used alone, it may not produce symptom reduction as quickly as CBT (Driessen et al., 2015). Leichsenring and Rabung (2011) found that while psychodynamic therapy is highly effective for long-term personality changes, it benefits from integration with more structured methods. By incorporating psychodynamic principles within YIA, therapists can facilitate both deeper psychological exploration and practical symptom management.

Person-Centered Therapy

Developed by Carl Rogers, person-centered therapy emphasizes the therapeutic relationship as the primary vehicle for change. Research confirms that empathy, congruence, and unconditional positive regard significantly contribute to positive therapy outcomes (Elliott et al., 2013; Farber & Doolin, 2011).

However, while this approach is invaluable in fostering a strong therapeutic alliance, it may not provide the structure or directive interventions some clients require to make tangible progress (Norcross & Alexander, 2019). Bohart and Wade (2013) suggested that person-centered therapy alone may not be sufficient for clients with severe mental health conditions, as they often require more structured interventions. When combined with CBT's structured techniques and psychodynamic therapy's depth-oriented insights, person-centered therapy enhances the client's experience within an integrative framework.

Humanistic Therapy

Humanistic therapy focuses on self-actualization and personal growth, helping clients navigate existential distress, low self-esteem, and identity struggles. Studies have found it particularly effective for individuals seeking meaning and personal fulfillment (Schneider & Krug, 2017; Cain, 2010).

However, its non-directive nature can be a limitation for clients who need more concrete strategies to manage symptoms. Research suggests that integrating humanistic approaches with structured interventions, such as those found in CBT or psychodynamic therapy, improves long-term outcomes, particularly for individuals with clinical disorders (Norcross & Alexander, 2019). By incorporating humanistic principles within a broader integrative model, therapists can balance personal growth with structured interventions tailored to the client's needs.

Lifestyle-Based Interventions

Lifestyle interventions—such as sleep regulation, nutrition, and physical activity—have gained increasing recognition as essential components of mental health treatment. Research has shown that exercise significantly reduces symptoms of depression and anxiety (Blumenthal, Smith, & Hoffman, 2012; Rebar et al., 2015), while proper sleep and nutrition contribute to emotional regulation and cognitive function (Firth, Gangwisch, et al., 2020; Lopresti et al., 2013).

Despite their effectiveness, these interventions are often overlooked in traditional therapy models. Walsh (2011) has highlighted the necessity of integrating lifestyle modifications into therapeutic approaches to enhance long-term mental well-being. YIA integrates lifestyle-based strategies into the therapeutic process, ensuring a more holistic and sustainable approach to mental health care.

Each of these models offers valuable tools, but their limitations reveal the need for a more comprehensive approach. A rigid adherence to one model can leave gaps in treatment, whereas integration allows therapists to draw on multiple perspectives, tailoring interventions to each client's unique needs.

The Yanni Integration Approach (YIA) builds upon the strengths of these methods while addressing their shortcomings, creating a balanced, research-supported framework for effective therapy. By integrating cognitive, psychodynamic, person-centered, humanistic, and lifestyle-based strategies, YIA offers a flexible yet structured model that enhances client outcomes. In the next section, we will explore how research comparing individual models to integrated approaches further supports this case for integration.

These strengths and limitations underscore the need to evaluate how individual therapy models perform when used in isolation versus when strategically combined.

Comparing Individual Models to Integrated Approaches

As the field of psychotherapy continues to evolve, mounting evidence supports the idea that integrative therapy models offer superior outcomes compared to single-method approaches. While traditional therapeutic models provide well-researched frameworks for treating mental health disorders, research suggests that their effectiveness is often enhanced when combined. Meta-analyses and longitudinal studies indicate that clients receiving blended interventions experience greater symptom relief, higher engagement, and improved long-term outcomes compared to those receiving treatment from a single modality (Norcross & Alexander, 2019; Wampold & Imel, 2015). The flexibility inherent in integrative therapy allows clinicians to tailor interventions to individual client needs, increasing treatment adherence and depth of therapeutic change (Safran et al., 2011).

By examining the research comparing singular therapy models to integrated approaches, it becomes evident why a multimodal framework, such as the Yanni Integration Approach (YIA), provides a more comprehensive and effective strategy for psychotherapy.

Key Research Findings on Integrative Therapy

Empirical research strongly supports the efficacy of integrative therapy over standalone approaches:

- A meta-analysis by Wampold and Imel, (2015) found that integrative therapy consistently outperformed singular models across various disorders, including mood and anxiety disorders, trauma-related conditions, and interpersonal difficulties.
- Norcross and Alexander (2019) reported that therapists who utilized an integrative framework were more likely to achieve positive treatment outcomes than those relying on a single modality.
- A study by Safran et al. (2011) emphasized that treatment flexibility leads to higher adherence and greater symptom improvement, particularly among clients with complex or comorbid conditions.
- Research comparing pure CBT versus CBT integrated with psychodynamic therapy found that blended approaches facilitated deeper emotional change and increased long-term effectiveness (Leichsenring et al., 2013).
- A study by Castonguay and Beutler (2005) on psychotherapy integration highlighted that customized interventions based on client needs led to better treatment engagement and higher rates of sustained improvement over time.

These findings emphasize that integrating multiple therapeutic approaches not only enhances symptom management but also fosters a more holistic and enduring healing process.

Comparison of Individual Models vs. Integrated Therapy

Therapy Model	Strengths	Limitations	Benefit of Integration
CBT	Effective for symptom management	Less effective for deep emotional issues	Combines with psychodynamic therapy for deeper emotional work
Psychodynamic Therapy	Addresses unconscious patterns	May take longer to see symptom relief	Blends with CBT for structured progress
Person-Centered Therapy	Strengthens therapeutic alliance	Lacks structured symptom relief techniques	Enhances engagement in structured therapy
Humanistic Therapy	Supports self-actualization	Non-directive, may not fit all clients	Provides emotional safety in structured interventions
Lifestyle-Based Interventions	Improves long-term well-being	Often overlooked in traditional therapy	Enhances mind-body connection for sustained progress

The research shows that although traditional therapy models provide essential tools for treatment, their limitations underscore the need for integration. Single-method approaches may be effective in specific contexts, but they often fail to address the full spectrum of a client's psychological, emotional, and behavioral needs. An integrative framework, such as the Yanni Integration Approach (YIA), leverages the strengths of multiple modalities to create a balanced, individualized, and empirically supported approach to therapy.

By blending structured symptom relief techniques (CBT), deep emotional exploration (psychodynamic therapy), relational connection (person-centered therapy), existential growth (humanistic therapy), and lifestyle-based interventions, integrative therapy ensures a more comprehensive and sustainable healing process.

These research findings highlight the importance of translating evidence-based integrative approaches into practical strategies that enhance real-world clinical outcomes.

Applying Research to Clinical Practice

Research consistently supports the effectiveness of integrative therapy, but its success ultimately depends on how it is applied in clinical practice. The Yanni Integration Approach (YIA) provides a framework that allows therapists to tailor interventions based on individual client needs, ensuring that treatment is both evidence-based and adaptable. By combining structured cognitive-behavioral strategies, insight-driven psychodynamic exploration, relational depth from person-centered and humanistic therapy, and holistic lifestyle-based interventions, YIA offers a comprehensive approach that aligns with modern psychotherapy research (Norcross & Goldfried, 2019; Castonguay & Beutler, 2005).

Therapists implementing YIA can apply these research findings by integrating techniques from five core areas of the approach:

- Blending structured interventions (CBT) with insight-based methods (psychodynamic therapy) to ensure both symptom management and deeper emotional processing.

- Building and maintaining a strong therapeutic alliance through person-centered and humanistic approaches, which research shows enhances engagement and treatment outcomes (Elliott et al., 2013).
- Incorporating lifestyle-based modifications to extend the benefits of therapy beyond sessions, recognizing that physical health, social engagement, and daily routines play a significant role in mental well-being (Firth, Gangwisch, et al., 2020).

Example: Integrating Models in Practice

To illustrate how YIA applies these principles in a clinical setting, consider the case of a client struggling with social anxiety:

- **Cognitive behavioral therapy (CBT)** techniques such as cognitive restructuring and gradual exposure can provide immediate symptom relief by challenging negative thought patterns and promoting behavioral change (Hofmann et al., 2012).
- **Psychodynamic therapy** can help the client explore past experiences of rejection or social trauma that contribute to their current anxiety (Leichsenring et al., 2013).
- **Humanistic and person-centered approaches** can foster self-acceptance and a greater sense of self-worth, empowering the client to engage more confidently in social interactions (Rogers, 1951).
- **Lifestyle-based interventions** such as mindfulness training, physical exercise, and structured social exposure can help the client build resilience and confidence in real-world situations (Blumenthal, Smith, & Hoffman, 2012; Rebar et al., 2015).

This multimodal strategy aligns with research demonstrating that an integrative approach not only reduces symptoms but also fosters long-term emotional and behavioral change (Wampold & Imel, 2015). Applying research to clinical practice is essential for ensuring that therapy is both effective and responsive to client needs. The YIA model offers a structured yet flexible approach that allows therapists to combine the best elements of different therapeutic traditions, maximizing the potential for meaningful change. As research continues to validate integrative approaches, clinicians can refine their practice by staying informed about emerging evidence and adapting their interventions accordingly.

Conclusion

The research explored in this chapter underscores a fundamental truth in psychotherapy, no single model fully addresses the complexities of human experiences. While cognitive-behavioral, psychodynamic, person-centered, humanistic, and lifestyle-based interventions each provide valuable tools, their limitations highlight the need for a more comprehensive and adaptable approach. The Yanni Integration Approach (YIA) exemplifies this necessity by weaving together the strengths of these models to create a balanced, client-centered, and research-supported framework for therapy.

The evidence consistently supports integrative therapy as a superior approach, not just in terms of symptom reduction, but also in fostering deeper emotional processing, therapeutic engagement, and long-term well-being (Norcross & Goldfried, 2019; Wampold & Imel, 2015). Studies comparing standalone methods to blended interventions reinforce that multimodal strategies enhance treatment outcomes, increase client adherence, and provide more sustainable mental health improvements (Leichsenring et al., 2013; Safran et al., 2011).

Applying these research findings to clinical practice is both an ethical and practical imperative. Therapists must move beyond rigid adherence to a single model and embrace flexibility, responsiveness, and scientific validation. The YIA framework provides a structured yet adaptable roadmap for achieving this balance, ensuring that clients receive interventions tailored to their unique psychological, emotional, and lifestyle needs.

CHAPTER 17:

Real-World Applications of the Yanni Integration Approach (YIA)

Introduction

Theory without application remains abstract, and research without real-world implementation lacks tangible impact. As discussed in Chapter 16, empirical evidence strongly supports integrative therapy models, demonstrating that multimodal approaches improve client outcomes across diverse populations. The Yanni Integration Approach (YIA) is not just a theoretical framework, it is a dynamic, adaptable method that has been tested and refined through real clinical experiences.

This chapter bridges the gap between research and practice, offering concrete examples of how the YIA transforms therapy into a deeply personalized and effective process. Through case studies spanning various clinical presentations, we explore how blending cognitive behavioral therapy (CBT), psychodynamic therapy, humanistic therapy, person-centered therapy, and lifestyle changes fosters meaningful and lasting progress. These cases highlight not only the effectiveness of YIA but also the ways in which therapists can adapt it to meet the unique needs of each client.

By examining real-world applications, this chapter provides a deeper understanding of how the YIA operates in practice, illustrating the power of an integrated approach to create lasting change.

Research Supporting the Integrated Approach

Therapy is not a one-size-fits-all endeavor. Decades of research have dismantled the notion that a single therapeutic model is universally superior, instead highlighting that treatment effectiveness is deeply tied to how well interventions align with individual client needs (Wampold & Imel, 2015). As human beings, clients bring complex emotional landscapes, unique histories, and diverse psychological needs into the therapy room, needs that cannot always be met by a rigid, singular approach.

The Yanni Integration Approach (YIA) embraces the reality that successful therapy requires flexibility. By weaving together cognitive behavioral therapy (CBT), psychodynamic therapy, humanistic therapy, person-centered therapy, and lifestyle changes, YIA ensures that therapy is both structured and adaptive. This integrative framework allows therapists to provide clients with the symptom management tools they need in the short term while fostering deeper emotional processing for lasting transformation. The effectiveness of this approach is not just theoretical, it is strongly supported by empirical research.

Key Research Findings Supporting an Integrated Model

CBT and Psychodynamic Therapy Combined: A Powerful Partnership

Cognitive behavioral therapy (CBT) is widely recognized for its ability to alleviate acute distress by helping clients reframe negative thoughts and develop coping strategies. However, research suggests that while CBT alone is effective for symptom relief, its benefits are significantly enhanced when combined with psychodynamic therapy, which facilitates deeper emotional work. Studies have shown that clients who receive both CBT and psychodynamic interventions experience more enduring therapeutic gains compared to those treated with CBT alone (Leichsenring, Salzer, et al., 2013). This synergy underscores the importance of integrating structured symptom management with deeper exploration of underlying emotional conflicts.

Humanistic and Person-Centered Approaches: The Role of the Therapeutic Relationship

Beyond structured interventions, the quality of the therapeutic relationship plays a critical role in client outcomes. Research indicates that clients who feel genuinely heard, validated, and empowered in therapy demonstrate greater motivation and engagement in the process (Elliott et al., 2004). Humanistic and person-centered therapies emphasize the therapist's ability to create an environment of empathy, unconditional positive regard, and authenticity, factors that have been shown to enhance therapeutic success across diverse populations. These findings reinforce that technical interventions alone are insufficient; they must be delivered within a framework of trust and emotional safety.

The Impact of Lifestyle Changes on Mental Health

Integrating lifestyle modifications into therapy is another evidence-backed approach that enhances treatment efficacy. Studies confirm that interventions such as regular exercise, improved sleep hygiene, and dietary adjustments significantly reduce symptoms of depression and anxiety, often as effectively as medication in mild to moderate cases (Blumenthal et al., 2007; Walsh, 2011). These findings highlight the importance of addressing mental health holistically, recognizing that psychological well-being is deeply intertwined with physical health and daily habits. By incorporating lifestyle recommendations into therapy, clinicians can equip clients with additional tools to sustain their mental health beyond the therapy room.

Client-Tailored Therapy: The Gold Standard for Success

A growing body of research underscores the importance of tailoring therapy to the unique characteristics of each client. Meta-analyses reveal that therapists who adapt interventions based on client personality, cultural background, and personal preferences achieve significantly higher success rates than those who adhere rigidly to a single model (Norcross & Wampold, 2018). This evidence supports the premise of the YIA, effective therapy is not about choosing one modality over another but rather integrating the right approaches for each individual.

The research is clear, integrating multiple therapeutic approaches leads to better outcomes than adhering to a single modality. The Yanni Integration Approach is built on the foundation of empirical evidence, ensuring that therapy is not only structured and evidence-based but also deeply personalized. By blending CBT's practical strategies with psychodynamic depth, fostering humanistic connection, and incorporating lifestyle modifications, YIA creates a dynamic and responsive framework for healing.

As we move from research to application in the following sections, we will explore real-world cases that demonstrate how the YIA brings these principles to life. These case studies illustrate that when therapy is tailored, flexible, and integrative, clients experience not just symptom relief but profound, lasting change.

Case Studies Demonstrating the Effectiveness of the Integrated Approach

The following detailed case studies illustrate how the YIA model can be applied to a variety of therapeutic contexts. Each case demonstrates how combining multiple therapeutic models results in deeper insights, improved engagement, and long-term client success.

Case Study #1: Managing Generalized Anxiety Disorder with a Multi-Layered Approach

Client Profile

Name: Rachel

Age: 29

Occupation: Marketing Executive

Presenting Concerns: Chronic worry, muscle tension, difficulty sleeping, persistent self-doubt, and a tendency toward perfectionism.

Rachel is a highly driven marketing executive who has struggled with anxiety since adolescence. She describes feeling constantly "on edge," experiencing racing thoughts about work performance, social interactions, and her future. She reports excessive rumination about potential mistakes and fears of failure, which often lead to physical symptoms such as tension headaches and difficulty falling asleep. Despite career success, Rachel feels emotionally exhausted, questioning her self-worth and ability to maintain control over her anxiety.

A structured yet flexible intervention was needed to address both Rachel's immediate symptoms and the deeper emotional patterns reinforcing her anxiety. The Yanni Integration Approach (YIA) was applied, utilizing cognitive behavioral therapy (CBT) for symptom relief, psychodynamic exploration for insight into underlying fears, humanistic support for emotional processing, person-centered techniques for self-empowerment, and lifestyle changes to promote physiological well-being.

Intervention Using the Five Models

- **Cognitive Behavioral Therapy (CBT): Restructuring Thought Patterns and Behavioral Experiments**

CBT was implemented as an initial intervention to provide Rachel with concrete tools for managing her chronic worry. Thought restructuring techniques helped Rachel identify cognitive distortions such as catastrophizing (*"If I mess up a presentation, my entire career will collapse"*) and overgeneralization (*"I always fail under pressure"*). By keeping a thought record, she began recognizing patterns of negative self-talk and gradually replaced automatic anxious thoughts with more balanced perspectives.

Behavioral experiments were introduced to challenge Rachel's perfectionistic tendencies. One key exercise involved intentionally submitting a non-perfect draft of a marketing campaign to her team for feedback. Initially, this triggered significant anxiety, but when she received constructive feedback instead of criticism, she began reassessing her assumptions about perfection and external validation. Over time, exposure to these small challenges reduced her fear of making mistakes and increased her tolerance for uncertainty.

- **Psychodynamic Therapy: Exploring the Roots of Anxiety**

While CBT addressed Rachel's symptoms, psychodynamic therapy helped uncover the deeper emotional conflicts driving her anxiety. Through guided exploration, Rachel traced her need for perfectionism to childhood experiences with her parents, who praised achievement but withheld emotional validation. She recalled feeling immense pressure to excel academically and internalized the belief that mistakes equated to personal failure.

By revisiting these formative experiences, Rachel recognized that her anxiety was not just about work stress but was rooted in a lifelong pattern of seeking approval through performance. This insight allowed her to shift from rigid self-expectations toward self-compassion. Through free association and exploring unconscious fears, Rachel began integrating a more balanced self-concept, one where her worth was not solely defined by success.

- **Humanistic Therapy: Creating Space for Emotional Processing**

A core element of Rachel's treatment was the therapeutic relationship itself. Using a humanistic approach, therapy provided a non-judgmental space where Rachel could openly express her fears without pressure to "fix" them immediately. As she became more comfortable sharing vulnerabilities, she developed greater trust in her ability to process emotions rather than suppress them.

This emotional validation was particularly important for Rachel, who previously avoided discussing anxiety for fear of being seen as weak. Through active listening, empathy, and validation, therapy helped her break the cycle of emotional avoidance, enabling her to engage more deeply with her internal experiences.

- **Person-Centered Therapy: Encouraging Self-Empowerment**

As Rachel progressed in therapy, she was encouraged to take an active role in defining her own therapeutic goals. Instead of focusing solely on reducing anxiety, she set broader intentions, developing self-acceptance, fostering meaningful personal relationships, and prioritizing well-being over external validation.

Through person-centered techniques, Rachel learned to trust her own judgment and values rather than seeking external reassurance. This shift in mindset significantly reduced her need for perfectionism-driven control and allowed her to embrace flexibility in both work and personal life.

- **Lifestyle Changes: Strengthening Mental and Physical Resilience**

Incorporating lifestyle modifications helped Rachel address the physiological aspects of anxiety. A structured sleep hygiene plan was implemented, including setting consistent bedtimes, reducing screen time before sleep, and practicing guided relaxation exercises. Within weeks, she reported improved sleep quality, which significantly reduced daytime fatigue and irritability.

Rachel also integrated mindfulness techniques, such as guided breathing exercises and grounding techniques, to manage acute anxiety symptoms. Additionally, a personalized exercise routine, focusing on yoga and moderate-intensity cardio, helped reduce muscle tension and provided a constructive outlet for stress.

Research supports the efficacy of lifestyle interventions in anxiety management, with studies confirming that regular exercise, improved sleep, and mindfulness practices can significantly decrease anxiety symptoms, often rivaling medication in effectiveness for mild to moderate cases (Blumenthal et al., 2007; Walsh, 2011).

Rachel reported significant reductions in anxiety symptoms, improved emotional regulation, and greater self-confidence in managing stress. She no longer viewed perfection as a prerequisite for success and instead embraced a more balanced perspective on personal and professional growth.

The integration of CBT and psychodynamic therapy was particularly effective: While CBT provided immediate symptom relief, the psychodynamic work allowed for deeper, long-term emotional healing. Research supports this combined approach, showing that clients who receive both CBT and psychodynamic interventions experience greater anxiety reduction and lower relapse rates than those who receive CBT alone (Leichsenring & Steinert, 2017).

By blending structured cognitive strategies with emotional insight, validation, self-empowerment, and holistic wellness, Rachel's therapy experience exemplified the strength of the Yanni Integration Approach. Her transformation was not simply about managing symptoms, it was about building resilience, fostering self-acceptance, and creating a sustainable path to emotional well-being.

Case Study #2: Addressing Depression and Low Self-Esteem in a College Student

Client Profile
Name: Jamal
Age: 22
Occupation: College Senior
Presenting Concerns: Persistent sadness, social withdrawal, feelings of worthlessness, loss of motivation, and difficulty concentrating.

Jamal is a 22-year-old college senior who has struggled with depression for the past two years. He describes feeling disconnected from his peers, unmotivated in his coursework, and overwhelmed by a persistent sense of inadequacy. Despite once being an engaged and social student, he now isolates himself, spending most of his time alone in his dorm. He experiences low energy, difficulty concentrating, and frequent negative self-talk, often questioning his intelligence and worth.

Jamal's depressive symptoms appear to be rooted in longstanding issues with self-esteem. He grew up in a highly competitive environment where academic success was emphasized, but emotional validation was scarce. As a result, he internalized the belief that his worth was tied to achievement, and when faced with academic setbacks, his self-concept deteriorated. Therapy was designed to help Jamal reframe his negative self-perceptions, process unresolved emotional wounds, and rebuild confidence through both psychological and lifestyle-based interventions.

Intervention Using the Five Models

- **Cognitive Behavioral Therapy (CBT): Restructuring Thought Patterns and Behavioral Experiments**

CBT was introduced as an initial intervention to help Jamal identify and restructure his automatic negative thoughts. He frequently engaged in cognitive distortions, such as:

- All-or-nothing thinking: *"If I don't excel, I'm a failure."*
- Personalization: *"If someone doesn't respond to my text, it must mean they don't like me."*
- Mind-reading: *"My classmates probably think I'm awkward and uninteresting."*

Through structured exercises, Jamal tracked these thoughts and evaluated their accuracy. By using cognitive restructuring techniques, he began replacing irrational self-judgments with more balanced perspectives. For instance, he reinterpreted academic struggles as learning opportunities rather than definitive failures.

Behavioral activation was also integrated to combat his withdrawal from social life. Initially, he set small, achievable goals, such as attending club meetings or studying with a classmate. Over time, these small steps reduced his avoidance behaviors and helped rebuild social confidence.

- **Psychodynamic Therapy: Exploring Childhood Origins of Low Self-Worth**

While CBT addressed Jamal's thought patterns, psychodynamic therapy helped uncover the deeper emotional roots of his depression. Through guided reflection, Jamal realized that his feelings of inadequacy stemmed from childhood experiences with emotionally distant parents who prioritized performance over personal expression.

He recalled moments in his childhood when achievements were praised, but emotional struggles were dismissed. Whenever he expressed sadness or frustration, he was told to "push through" or "work harder." As a result, he learned to suppress emotions and equated self-worth with external validation. This pattern continued into adulthood, where any academic setback or social rejection triggered intense feelings of failure.

By revisiting these early experiences, Jamal began to understand his depressive patterns as learned responses rather than inherent flaws. He developed greater self-compassion, recognizing that his worth was not solely defined by achievements. Processing these emotions in therapy helped him shift from self-criticism to self-acceptance.

- **Humanistic Therapy: Fostering Emotional Safety and Encouragement**

A key aspect of Jamal's therapy was providing a space where he felt genuinely seen and understood. Given his history of emotional invalidation, the therapeutic relationship itself became a healing factor. Using a Humanistic approach, the therapist prioritized warmth, encouragement, and nonjudgmental support, allowing Jamal to express his emotions without fear of dismissal.

This approach helped Jamal feel validated in his struggles for the first time. Rather than focusing solely on performance, therapy reinforced that his feelings and experiences were important regardless of achievement. Over time, this emotional safety encouraged him to engage more openly, confront vulnerabilities, and develop healthier ways of expressing himself.

- **Person-Centered Therapy: Encouraging Self-Exploration and Autonomy**

As Jamal gained emotional insight, he was encouraged to take an active role in shaping his therapy goals. Rather than having treatment imposed on him, he explored what truly mattered to him outside of external expectations.

Through self-reflection, Jamal realized he had been pursuing a career path dictated by familial expectations rather than personal passion. Therapy provided him with the space to explore his own interests, leading him to consider alternative career paths that aligned with his strengths and values.

This shift from external validation to self-determination was pivotal in rebuilding his confidence. Instead of seeking approval from others, Jamal began making decisions based on what felt authentic to him.

- **Lifestyle Changes: Strengthening Mental and Physical Well-Being**

Jamal's depression was exacerbated by poor lifestyle habits, including a lack of exercise, irregular eating patterns, and minimal social engagement. To address this, he worked on integrating key lifestyle modifications:

- Exercise: A structured fitness routine helped improve his energy levels and mood. Studies confirm that regular physical activity can be as effective as medication in reducing depressive symptoms (Blumenthal et al., 2007).
- Nutrition: He was encouraged to adopt a more balanced diet, focusing on nutrient-dense foods that support brain health. Research shows that proper nutrition plays a critical role in mental well-being (Walsh, 2011).
- Social engagement: To combat isolation, Jamal gradually reintroduced social activities into his routine. He began reconnecting with old friends and attending campus events, which helped alleviate loneliness and foster a sense of belonging.

These lifestyle changes, combined with psychological interventions, contributed to a holistic recovery process.

By integrating multiple therapeutic models, Jamal experienced significant improvements in both mood and self-esteem. He became more engaged socially, regained motivation for academic work, and developed a healthier self-concept.

Most importantly, he learned to separate his self-worth from external achievements, reducing his vulnerability to depressive episodes in the future.

Jamal's case reinforces research findings that combining CBT with self-exploration and lifestyle modifications results in greater long-term remission from depression than using symptom-focused CBT alone (Cuijpers et al., 2014). By addressing both immediate symptoms and underlying emotional conflicts, the Yanni Integration Approach provided a comprehensive framework for lasting change.

Case Study #3: Processing Childhood Trauma and PTSD in an Adult Client

Client Profile
Name: Maria
Age: 41
Occupation: High School English Teacher
Presenting Concerns: Flashbacks, hypervigilance, emotional numbness, avoidance behaviors, difficulty forming and maintaining trusting relationships.

Maria, a 41-year-old high school English teacher, entered therapy after decades of struggling with the emotional impact of childhood trauma. She grew up in an environment of emotional neglect and verbal abuse, where expressions of vulnerability were met with criticism or rejection. As a result, Maria developed deep-seated trust issues, difficulty regulating emotions, and an instinct to emotionally withdraw in relationships. Although she met the clinical criteria for post-traumatic stress disorder (PTSD), she had never engaged in therapy, fearing that revisiting the past would be overwhelming.

Maria reported frequent nightmares, intrusive flashbacks of emotionally abusive experiences, and a pervasive sense of shame and unworthiness. She avoided conversations, places, and situations that reminded her of her past. Additionally, she struggled with an internalized belief that she was "broken" or "too damaged" to heal.

Her work as a teacher added another layer of complexity to her struggles. While she found meaning in mentoring students, she often felt emotionally drained, particularly when working with children who reminded her of her younger self. The stress of maintaining composure in a classroom setting, coupled with her tendency to suppress emotions, left her feeling exhausted and isolated.

Given her history, a structured yet compassionate approach was necessary—one that would provide both symptom relief and deeper emotional healing while ensuring Maria felt safe throughout the therapeutic process.

The Yanni Integration Approach (YIA) was utilized to help Maria process trauma in a way that was both research-supported and deeply personalized.

Intervention Using the Five Models

- **Cognitive Behavioral Therapy (CBT): Exposure Therapy, Cognitive Restructuring, and Grounding Techniques**

Given Maria's PTSD symptoms, CBT techniques were introduced early in therapy to help her manage distressing thoughts and behaviors. The initial focus was on psychoeducation—helping Maria understand how trauma affects the brain and why her symptoms, such as avoidance and hypervigilance, were normal adaptive responses to past experiences.

Key CBT techniques used:

- **Exposure Therapy:** Maria gradually confronted trauma-related memories and avoided situations in a controlled, supportive environment. Instead of pushing her to recount traumatic events immediately, the therapist guided her through small exposure exercises, such as writing about past experiences in a journal before discussing them in sessions. This gradual approach helped Maria reduce avoidance behaviors while maintaining emotional safety.

- **Cognitive Restructuring:** Maria worked on identifying and challenging core negative beliefs she had internalized from childhood, such as "*I am unlovable*" or "*I will always be hurt in relationships.*" Through reframing exercises, she learned to replace these deeply ingrained thoughts with more balanced and compassionate perspectives.
- **Grounding Techniques:** Given Maria's tendency to dissociate when discussing trauma, grounding exercises were incorporated to keep her present. Techniques like the 5-4-3-2-1 method (identifying five things she could see, four she could touch, etc.) and deep-breathing exercises helped her regulate distress in moments of emotional overwhelm.

- **Psychodynamic Therapy: Addressing Childhood Trauma, Attachment Wounds, and Avoidance Patterns**

While CBT helped Maria manage symptoms, psychodynamic therapy provided the space for deeper emotional work. Through exploring her early childhood experiences, Maria began to see how her relational patterns and self-concept had been shaped by emotional abuse and neglect.

Core psychodynamic interventions used:

- **Unpacking attachment wounds:** Maria was guided to reflect on her early relationships with caregivers, recognizing how inconsistent emotional support led to difficulties trusting others in adulthood. She saw how she had unconsciously recreated these dynamics in friendships and romantic relationships by either withdrawing or forming connections with emotionally unavailable individuals.
- **Addressing avoidance behaviors:** Maria avoided not only memories of her past but also emotions that felt too painful to confront. Therapy helped her understand how avoidance had served as a protective mechanism in

childhood but was now limiting her ability to heal. By acknowledging these patterns, Maria gradually opened up to processing difficult emotions.

- **Symbolic expression of trauma:** Since verbalizing trauma was challenging for Maria, creative approaches such as guided imagery and writing letters to her younger self were used to facilitate emotional expression in a way that felt manageable.

- **Humanistic Therapy: Creating a Safe Therapeutic Environment and Normalizing Trauma Responses**

Building trust in the therapeutic relationship was paramount for Maria's healing. Because she had never experienced a safe space to express her emotions, the therapist prioritized creating an atmosphere of warmth, acceptance, and nonjudgment.

Key Humanistic elements included:

- **Normalizing trauma responses:** Maria often blamed herself for her emotional struggles, believing that she "should be over it by now." Therapy emphasized that PTSD symptoms were not personal failings but natural responses to prolonged childhood adversity (van der Kolk, 2014).
- **Validation and unconditional support:** By fostering an environment where Maria's experiences were validated, therapy helped her dismantle the shame and self-blame that had been instilled in her since childhood.
- **Encouraging self-compassion:** Maria struggled with self-directed anger, often criticizing herself for feeling weak or vulnerable. Therapy helped her shift this perspective by encouraging self-compassion, reframing past coping mechanisms as survival strategies rather than failures.

- **Person-Centered Therapy: Allowing Maria to Guide Trauma Processing at Her Own Pace**

Given Maria's history of emotional invalidation, a person-centered approach ensured that she had full control over her therapeutic journey. Rather than imposing a rigid structure, therapy allowed Maria to determine the pace and focus of discussions.

Strategies used:

- **Self-directed trauma exploration:** Maria was given space to decide when and how much she wanted to disclose about her past, reducing the risk of retraumatization.
- **Client-driven goal-setting:** Rather than pushing for immediate trauma processing, therapy emphasized small, self-defined goals, such as rebuilding self-trust and setting boundaries in relationships.
- **Empowerment through choice:** Maria was encouraged to recognize her own agency in the healing process, reinforcing that she was not powerless in shaping her future.

- **Lifestyle Changes: Incorporating Mind-Body Interventions**

Since trauma often manifests physically, integrating lifestyle modifications helped Maria develop a sense of control over her body and emotions.

- **Yoga and mindfulness:** Research shows that trauma-sensitive yoga helps survivors reconnect with their bodies and regulate nervous system responses (van der Kolk, 2014). Maria practiced gentle yoga to reduce hyperarousal and dissociation.
- **Journaling:** Writing served as a therapeutic outlet for Maria, allowing her to process emotions between sessions. Structured journaling prompts, such as gratitude exercises and reflective entries, helped shift her focus toward self-growth.

- **Relaxation techniques:** Progressive muscle relaxation and guided visualization exercises were introduced to help her manage stress responses and improve sleep quality.

After a year of integrative therapy, Maria reported significant improvements in emotional regulation, self-esteem, and relational boundaries. She no longer viewed herself as "broken" and began forming healthier, more trusting relationships. Flashbacks became less frequent, avoidance behaviors decreased, and she developed a greater capacity to express emotions without fear of rejection.

Most importantly, Maria's self-concept transformed, she moved from seeing herself as a victim of her past to recognizing her resilience and capacity for healing.

Her case aligns with trauma research indicating that a combined therapeutic approach incorporating CBT, emotional processing, and mindfulness techniques is most effective for PTSD recovery (van der Kolk, 2014). By integrating structured interventions with deep emotional work and self-directed healing, Maria's therapy experience exemplified the power of the Yanni Integration Approach in facilitating long-term recovery.

Comparison Table: Single-Model vs. Integrated Therapy Outcomes

Case Study	Challenge	Single-Model Limitation	How Integration Improved Outcomes
Rachel (GAD)	Chronic anxiety, sleep disturbances	CBT alone may not explore underlying self-worth issues	Psychodynamic exploration of childhood experiences, lifestyle changes improved sleep

Jamal (Depression & Low Self-Esteem)	Social withdrawal, lack of motivation	Person-centered therapy alone lacks structured symptom relief	CBT for thought restructuring, lifestyle interventions boosted energy & engagement
Maria (PTSD)	Flashbacks, avoidance, relational distrust	CBT alone may not address attachment trauma	Humanistic support, psychodynamic work, and mindfulness techniques led to healing

Key Lessons

The case studies presented in this chapter illustrate the effectiveness of the Yanni Integration Approach (YIA) across a range of clinical concerns, from anxiety and depression to trauma and PTSD. These cases highlight several key lessons for therapists striving to provide comprehensive, individualized care.

1. Balance Symptom Relief with Deeper Exploration

While immediate symptom relief is crucial for client well-being, lasting change often requires addressing the deeper emotional and psychological patterns that contribute to distress. The case studies reinforce the importance of using a dual-layered approach:

- Cognitive behavioral therapy (CBT) provides structure and symptom management tools, helping clients regulate emotions, challenge maladaptive thought patterns, and engage in behavioral activation.

- Psychodynamic therapy facilitates deeper emotional processing, allowing clients to explore unresolved conflicts, attachment wounds, and core beliefs formed in early life.
- Integration is key: In Maria's case, exposure therapy helped manage PTSD symptoms, but true healing came from exploring childhood attachment wounds that reinforced avoidance patterns. Similarly, Rachel benefited from CBT's thought restructuring but achieved lasting change through psychodynamic work that reshaped her self-perception.

Therapists must assess when a client is ready for deeper emotional work and how to integrate it alongside structured interventions for optimal outcomes.

2. Ensure Client Empowerment and Autonomy

Client engagement is significantly enhanced when therapy fosters a sense of autonomy and personal agency. The case studies illustrate that empowerment is not just an ethical imperative, it is a clinical necessity.

Person-centered therapy plays a vital role by giving clients control over their therapeutic journey. Clients should set goals collaboratively with their therapist, ensuring treatment aligns with their values and readiness for change.

Empowering clients builds confidence: In Jamal's case, he was initially hesitant to explore career aspirations due to familial expectations. By allowing him to define his own goals, therapy helped him reconnect with his intrinsic motivations, improving self-esteem and reducing depressive symptoms.

Trauma-sensitive autonomy: Maria's treatment plan was paced according to her comfort level. Instead of rushing into trauma exposure, therapy allowed her to decide when and how she was ready to process past experiences, reducing the risk of retraumatization.

Clinicians should consistently assess a client's readiness for deeper work, involve them in decision-making, and reinforce their sense of control over their progress.

3. Use Lifestyle Interventions to Support Therapy Outcomes

Therapy does not operate in a vacuum—psychological health is deeply connected to lifestyle factors such as sleep, physical activity, and daily habits. Research increasingly supports the role of lifestyle modifications in enhancing emotional resilience and preventing relapse (Walsh, 2011).

- Sleep hygiene, exercise, and nutrition were critical components in Rachel and Jamal's treatment. Improving sleep consistency significantly reduced Rachel's anxiety, while incorporating physical activity helped Jamal regain energy and motivation.
- Mindfulness-based interventions supported trauma processing for Maria by helping regulate her nervous system and reducing dissociation. Trauma-sensitive yoga allowed her to reconnect with her body in a safe and controlled way.
- The research is clear: Studies confirm that integrating lifestyle changes with traditional psychotherapy leads to better long-term outcomes than therapy alone (Blumenthal et al., 2007; van der Kolk, 2014).

Therapists should assess lifestyle factors early in treatment and integrate simple, client-friendly strategies to support psychological well-being.

4. Adapt Therapy Based on Individual Needs

Each case study demonstrated that no two clients require the same therapeutic approach. Flexibility is not just beneficial, it is essential for clinical success.

- Therapists must adjust interventions based on client personality, cultural background, and presenting concerns (Norcross & Wampold, 2018).

- Blending structured and unstructured approaches: Although some clients, like Rachel, respond well to cognitive restructuring, others, like Maria, need a slower, emotion-focused process before engaging in structured techniques.
- Therapy must evolve over time: As clients make progress, their needs shift. Jamal's therapy initially focused on symptom relief through CBT, but later, his growth required more existential self-exploration.

Effective clinicians do not adhere rigidly to one modality, instead, they tailor interventions dynamically, ensuring therapy remains responsive to each client's evolving needs.

The Yanni Integration Approach (YIA) is more than a collection of techniques, it is a philosophy of therapy that prioritizes adaptability, depth, and holistic healing. These case studies highlight that effective treatment is not about choosing one model over another, but rather understanding how different approaches work together to create meaningful and lasting change.

By balancing symptom relief with deep exploration, fostering client empowerment, integrating lifestyle changes, and adapting therapy to individual needs, clinicians can provide a truly comprehensive and impactful therapeutic experience.

Conclusion

The case studies and research presented in this chapter reinforce a crucial insight, effective therapy is not about adherence to a singular theoretical model, but rather the ability to integrate multiple frameworks to meet the diverse needs of clients. The Yanni Integration Approach (YIA) is more than a structured method; it is a flexible, research-supported framework that allows clinicians to provide both immediate symptom relief and deeper emotional healing.

Through examining real-world applications of the YIA, several critical themes emerge. First, symptom-focused interventions alone are insufficient for lasting change, as seen in Rachel's case, CBT helped manage anxiety, but true transformation came from integrating psychodynamic exploration and lifestyle adjustments. Similarly, in

Jamal's treatment, self-exploration and empowerment were as crucial as cognitive restructuring, illustrating that clients must be actively involved in shaping their therapeutic journey. Maria's case further underscores that trauma recovery is not a linear process, requiring a combination of structured techniques, emotional processing, and self-paced healing to foster resilience.

The research is unequivocal: integrative therapy models consistently lead to better long-term outcomes (Norcross & Wampold, 2018). Studies demonstrate that blending CBT, Psychodynamic Therapy, Humanistic support, and Lifestyle Interventions produces greater reductions in anxiety, depression, and PTSD symptoms than any one modality alone (Blumenthal et al., 2007; van der Kolk, 2014; Cuijpers et al., 2014). More importantly, when therapy is tailored to the individual, factoring in their personal history, cultural background, and unique psychological needs, clients experience not just symptom relief, but deep, sustainable healing.

The YIA challenges clinicians to move beyond rigid adherence to single-method interventions and embrace a more personalized, integrative approach to therapy. This requires:

- **Balancing structure with emotional depth:** Therapists must provide symptom relief while also creating space for deeper emotional work.
- **Empowering clients in the healing process:** Therapy must be collaborative, allowing clients to set their own goals and progress at a pace that feels safe and effective.
- **Addressing mental health holistically:** Emotional well-being is deeply connected to lifestyle factors such as sleep, exercise, nutrition, and social engagement—clinicians should integrate these components into treatment.
- **Remaining adaptable:** Every client is different, and successful therapy requires tailoring interventions based on individual needs, rather than forcing clients into a predefined model.

The success of the YIA lies in its ability to honor the complexity of the human experience, recognizing that healing is not a singular path, but rather a dynamic process that requires both structure and flexibility.

As therapists, we have a responsibility to provide our clients with the most effective, research-backed interventions while ensuring that therapy remains deeply human, compassionate, and individualized. The Yanni Integration Approach serves as a blueprint for bridging scientific rigor with clinical intuition, ensuring that therapy is not just effective, but transformative.

CHAPTER 18:

Therapist Self-Care & Preventing Burnout

Introduction

Therapists dedicate their professional lives to supporting others, often prioritizing their clients' needs over their own well-being. However, working within an integrative framework such as the Yanni Integration Approach (YIA) demands a unique level of cognitive, emotional, and methodological adaptability. The constant shift between therapeutic modalities—balancing the structure of cognitive behavioral therapy (CBT), the depth of psychodynamic exploration, the unconditional positive regard of person-centered therapy, and the holistic lens of lifestyle interventions—requires therapists to be both intellectually agile and emotionally attuned. While this flexibility enhances client outcomes, it also places significant demands on the therapist's mental and emotional reserves.

Burnout is a pervasive challenge in the mental health field, and research consistently highlights its detrimental effects on both therapists and their clients. Figley (2002) introduced the concept of compassion fatigue, emphasizing that prolonged exposure to clients' trauma can lead to emotional exhaustion and decreased empathy. Rupert and Kent (2007) further found that burnout among psychologists is closely linked to high caseloads, emotional investment, and blurred boundaries between personal and professional life. Additionally, Barnett et al. (2007) stressed that burnout not only diminishes therapist effectiveness but also compromises ethical decision-making and client care. Given these risks, it is crucial for therapists practicing YIA to implement self-care strategies that promote sustainability in their work.

Recognizing the early signs of burnout and engaging in proactive self-care is not just about self-preservation, it is an ethical imperative. Therapists who prioritize their well-being are better equipped to sustain meaningful therapeutic relationships, make sound clinical decisions, and model healthy coping strategies for their clients. This chapter explores evidence-based approaches to therapist self-care, emphasizing the importance of professional boundaries (Barnett & Cooper, 2009), reflective supervision (Skovholt & Trotter-Mathison, 2016), and intentional self-renewal (Norcross & VandenBos, 2018). By investing in their own resilience, therapists can ensure the longevity of their practice and continue delivering the high-quality, integrative care that YIA demands.

Chapter 17 demonstrated how the Yanni Integration Approach has been successfully applied in real-world settings, showcasing its ability to enhance client outcomes across diverse populations. However, for this model to be sustainable, therapists must also cultivate their own resilience. Just as clients benefit from a structured, integrative approach, therapists must apply a similar level of intentionality to their own well-being. The effectiveness of YIA is not solely dependent on its theoretical foundation or clinical application, it also hinges on the therapist's capacity to remain engaged, attuned, and mentally refreshed.

Now, we turn our attention inward. How can therapists practicing YIA safeguard their emotional and cognitive well-being? What strategies can prevent burnout while maintaining the depth and effectiveness of integrative practice? This chapter provides actionable insights into sustaining a long, fulfilling career in the field of integrative therapy, ensuring that both clients and therapists thrive.

Recognizing Early Signs of Burnout

Burnout does not occur overnight, it is a gradual process that unfolds as chronic stress, emotional exhaustion, and cognitive overload accumulate. In the field of mental health, where therapists are consistently attuned to the struggles and emotions of their clients, burnout poses a significant risk. Research has shown that burnout not only affects therapists' personal well-being but also has direct consequences on the quality of care provided to clients (Figley, 2002; Rupert & Kent, 2007).

The ability to recognize the early signs of burnout is crucial in preventing its long-term impact. Left unchecked, burnout can lead to emotional depletion, reduced empathy, and ethical lapses, ultimately compromising the therapeutic alliance (Barnett et al., 2007). By identifying the warning signs, such as increased frustration with clients, difficulty concentrating, and avoidance of sessions, therapists can take proactive steps to protect both their own well-being and the integrity of their clinical work. Addressing burnout early is not just an act of self-care; it is a professional responsibility that ensures the continued effectiveness of therapy and the well-being of those receiving it.

Common Symptoms of Burnout in Therapists

Category	Symptoms of Burnout
Emotional Symptoms	Exhaustion, irritability, emotional numbness, increased frustration with clients
Cognitive Symptoms	Difficulty concentrating, decision fatigue, self-doubt about clinical effectiveness
Behavioral Symptoms	Avoiding client sessions, excessive use of distractions, withdrawing from colleagues
Physical Symptoms	Sleep disturbances, headaches, fatigue, gastrointestinal issues
Ethical Implications	Decreased empathy, boundary blurring, decreased responsiveness to client needs

Ignoring the early signs of burnout is not an option for therapists who are committed to sustaining a long and meaningful career in mental health. Burnout does not merely affect the individual therapist, it ripples into client care, leading to diminished empathy, impaired decision-making, and potential ethical concerns (Barnett & Cooper, 2009; Skovholt & Trotter-Mathison, 2016). Recognizing burnout at its onset allows therapists to implement necessary self-care strategies, establish professional boundaries, and seek supervision or peer support to mitigate its effects.

Therapists must view self-care not as a luxury but as an ethical imperative. The ability to provide high-quality, integrative care within the Yanni Integration Approach (YIA) depends on therapists maintaining their emotional, cognitive, and physical well-being. By prioritizing self-awareness and early intervention, therapists can safeguard their professional longevity, uphold their commitment to ethical practice, and continue fostering meaningful therapeutic relationships.

Recognizing the early signs of burnout is the first step in protecting therapist well-being, but equally important is learning how to navigate the demands of an integrative practice, balancing multiple therapeutic approaches without feeling overwhelmed.

Balancing Multiple Approaches Without Feeling Overwhelmed

The art of integrative therapy lies in the therapist's ability to fluidly transition between multiple theoretical models to best serve the client's needs. However, this adaptability comes at a cost, without a structured approach, therapists may experience decision fatigue, cognitive overload, and an ongoing sense of uncertainty about whether they are applying the "right" intervention in any given moment (Norcross & Goldfried, 2019). The Yanni Integration Approach (YIA) is designed to offer a dynamic yet cohesive therapeutic framework, but if not managed effectively, the very flexibility that makes it powerful can also become overwhelming.

Research highlights that therapists who work within integrative frameworks must develop intentional strategies to maintain clarity and prevent burnout (Barkham

& Mellor-Clark, 2003). Establishing a structured approach to integration, such as using a default starting model, documenting decision-making processes, and setting realistic expectations, allows therapists to maintain effectiveness without becoming mentally or emotionally depleted. By striking a balance between structure and adaptability, therapists can optimize their practice while ensuring their own sustainability in the field.

Strategies for Balancing Integration

- **Use a session structure:** Begin with a check-in (person-centered), work on presenting issues (CBT/psychodynamic), and conclude with reflection (humanistic/lifestyle-based).
- **Create a "default" model:** If unsure where to begin, establish a starting point (e.g., CBT for symptom management) and integrate other models as needed.
- **Set realistic expectations:** Not every session needs to incorporate all five models, choosing one or two that fit the moment is enough.
- **Document and review integration choices:** Writing brief reflections on why certain models were used helps refine decision-making and prevent overexertion.

Balancing multiple therapeutic approaches is not about perfecting a seamless integration in every session, but rather about cultivating a rhythm that allows for flexibility without mental exhaustion. Therapists who implement structured frameworks while maintaining room for adaptability can prevent decision fatigue and remain fully engaged in the therapeutic process (Stricker & Gold, 2003). More importantly, learning to trust one's clinical intuition, built on experience and reflective practice, fosters confidence in the integration process rather than creating a sense of pressure to apply every model simultaneously.

Ultimately, the effectiveness of the Yanni Integration Approach depends not only on theoretical knowledge but also on the therapist's ability to regulate their own cognitive and emotional load. By embracing structure without rigidity and integration without overwhelm, therapists can provide high-quality, sustainable care to their clients while safeguarding their own well-being.

Establishing a structured yet flexible approach to integration helps therapists manage cognitive overload, but to sustain emotional resilience in their work, they must also engage in self-reflection and supervision to process the emotional labor inherent in therapy.

Managing Emotional Labor Through Self-Reflection & Supervision

Therapists engage in deep emotional labor with every session, holding space for their clients' struggles while maintaining professional composure and therapeutic presence. However, without intentional strategies for processing these emotions, the cumulative weight of this work can lead to compassion fatigue, emotional exhaustion, and even burnout (Figley, 2002). The integrative nature of the Yanni Integration Approach (YIA) further amplifies this challenge, as therapists must continuously attune to clients' evolving emotional states while flexibly applying multiple therapeutic models. This deep level of engagement, although beneficial to clients, increases the therapist's emotional burden if not properly managed.

Research underscores the importance of self-reflection and supervision as essential tools for emotional regulation in therapy. Regular self-reflection helps therapists identify emotional strain before it escalates (Neff, 2003), while supervision and peer consultation offer critical external support and perspective (Bernard & Goodyear, 2019). Additionally, mindfulness-based practices have been shown to reduce burnout and increase professional fulfillment, providing therapists with a structured method to regulate their own emotional well-being (Shapiro et al., 2007). By incorporating these strategies, therapists can sustain their emotional resilience, ensuring that their ability to help others does not come at the cost of their own mental health.

Key Strategies for Emotional Regulation

- **Scheduled Self-Reflection:** Journaling about difficult sessions can help process emotions before they accumulate.
- **Boundary Setting:** Establishing clear emotional and time boundaries to prevent over-involvement in client struggles.
- **Supervision & Peer Consultation:** Regular discussions with colleagues help normalize therapist struggles and provide alternative perspectives.
- **Mindfulness Practices:** Studies indicate that therapists who engage in mindfulness report lower burnout rates and increased professional satisfaction (Shapiro et al., 2007).

Emotional labor is an unavoidable part of therapy, but it does not have to lead to exhaustion or burnout. The most effective therapists are not those who suppress their emotions but those who actively engage in self-awareness and seek support when needed. Supervision and peer consultation help therapists process difficult cases, normalize challenges, and refine their clinical approach, while self-reflection allows for greater emotional clarity and personal insight (Skovholt & Trotter-Mathison, 2016).

In the context of the YIA model, where deep attunement is key to effective integration, maintaining emotional balance is especially crucial. Without self-reflection and external support, the weight of constant emotional engagement can become overwhelming. However, by adopting structured reflection practices, setting firm emotional boundaries, and embracing mindfulness techniques, therapists can safeguard their well-being while continuing to provide compassionate, high-quality care. Prioritizing these practices ensures that therapists remain not only effective clinicians but also fulfilled and resilient professionals throughout their careers.

Maintaining emotional resilience through self-reflection and supervision is vital, but therapists must also recognize that self-care is not just a personal necessity, it is an ethical responsibility that directly impacts client care and professional integrity.

Ethical Considerations in Therapist Self-Care

Therapist self-care is not merely a personal choice, it is a fundamental ethical responsibility that directly impacts client care. The APA's *Ethical Principles of Psychologists and Code of Conduct* (American Psychological Association, 2017) explicitly states that psychologists must ensure their physical, mental, and emotional well-being to provide competent and effective treatment. When therapists neglect their own self-care, they risk becoming emotionally drained, cognitively impaired, and ethically compromised, leading to reduced clinical effectiveness and potential harm to clients (Barnett et al., 2007).

Unchecked burnout can manifest in a variety of ethical pitfalls, including diminished empathy, boundary violations, and impaired decision-making (Figley, 2002). Emotional over-involvement with clients can blur professional boundaries, while emotional detachment can lead to disengagement, misattunement, or even misdiagnosis (Rupert & Kent, 2007). These risks highlight why self-care is not simply an act of self-preservation, it is an ethical obligation that safeguards both therapists and the clients they serve.

Ethical Risks of Neglecting Self-Care

Therapists who fail to engage in regular self-care practices may unintentionally violate ethical principles, particularly those related to competence (Standard 2.06) and avoiding harm (Standard 3.04) as outlined by the APA Code of Ethics (2017). Key ethical risks include:

- **Decreased Clinical Effectiveness:** Emotional exhaustion can impair therapists' ability to fully engage with clients, reducing the quality of therapy and overall treatment outcomes (Barnett et al., 2007).
- **Boundary Issues:** Burnout can lead to poor professional boundaries, including over-identification with clients' struggles or, conversely, emotional detachment and withdrawal (Norcross & VandenBos, 2018).

- **Compromised Decision-Making:** When therapists are overwhelmed, they may struggle with treatment planning, diagnostic accuracy, and overall case conceptualization, leading to ineffective or even harmful interventions (Rupert & Morgan, 2005).

Given these risks, ethical self-care is not an individual luxury but an imperative for ensuring professional integrity and competent client care.

Research on Therapist Self-Care & Emotional Resilience

Numerous studies emphasize the importance of self-care in sustaining professional effectiveness. Barnett et al., (2007) found that therapists who engage in regular self-care report greater job satisfaction, lower burnout, and improved therapeutic outcomes for their clients. Additionally, Shapiro et al. (2007) demonstrated that mindfulness-based practices significantly reduce therapist stress and enhance emotional resilience, reinforcing that self-care must be a continuous, structured effort rather than an afterthought.

Further research highlights that therapists who participate in peer consultation and supervision experience lower rates of emotional exhaustion and higher professional fulfillment (Skovholt & Trotter-Mathison, 2016). These findings support the view that self-care is not only an ethical responsibility but a key determinant of long-term career sustainability.

Evidence-Based Self-Care Strategies for Therapists

To maintain professional competence and uphold ethical standards, therapists should engage in intentional, structured self-care practices across multiple domains:

Self-Care Category	Examples
Physical Self-Care	Regular exercise, proper sleep, balanced nutrition
Cognitive Self-Care	Reading, engaging in creative activities, setting professional goals
Social Self-Care	Maintaining friendships, attending peer support groups, consulting with colleagues
Professional Development	Supervision, attending trainings, workshops, and case discussions

These strategies help therapists mitigate burnout, sustain emotional resilience, and continue providing ethical, high-quality care to clients.

Therapists are ethically obligated to maintain their own well-being, not only for their sake but for the benefit of their clients. The integration of structured self-care routines into professional life ensures that therapists remain emotionally attuned, ethically responsible, and clinically effective (Norcross & VandenBos, 2018). Without prioritizing well-being, the cumulative stress of clinical work can lead to emotional exhaustion, impaired decision-making, and ethical violations, all of which negatively impact client care (Rupert & Morgan, 2005).

By recognizing self-care as an essential ethical duty rather than an optional luxury, therapists can create sustainable professional practices that foster both personal fulfillment and therapeutic excellence. Implementing evidence-based self-care strategies, such as supervision, peer consultation, mindfulness, and boundary setting, ensures that therapists not only survive in the field but thrive, continuously offering the highest level of ethical and effective care to their clients.

Conclusion

Therapist self-care is not an indulgence, it is a necessity for sustaining long-term effectiveness, ethical practice, and emotional resilience. The Yanni Integration Approach (YIA) offers a dynamic and responsive model for client care, but without intentional self-care, the very flexibility that makes it powerful can also contribute to emotional fatigue and burnout. This chapter has highlighted the importance of recognizing early signs of burnout, developing structured approaches to integration, engaging in self-reflection and supervision, and upholding self-care as an ethical duty.

The research is clear: therapists who invest in their own well-being not only experience greater job satisfaction but also deliver more effective and ethically sound care (Barnett et al., 2007; Shapiro et al., 2007). By setting professional boundaries, engaging in peer support, maintaining physical and emotional wellness, and integrating mindful self-care practices, therapists create a sustainable foundation for both personal and professional growth. These strategies are not secondary to clinical competence, they are essential to it.

For those practicing YIA, the challenge is not simply to balance multiple theoretical models but to ensure that their own emotional and cognitive resources remain intact. Just as therapists encourage clients to cultivate self-awareness, establish healthy boundaries, and engage in restorative practices, they must model these same principles in their own lives. Supervision, consultation, and self-reflection are not signs of weakness but hallmarks of ethical, competent professionals who recognize that the best therapy comes from a place of balance and well-being (Norcross & VandenBos, 2018; Skovholt & Trotter-Mathison, 2016). The sustainability of the YIA model, and any effective therapeutic approach, depends on therapists embracing self-care as a lifelong commitment, not a reactive measure taken only in crisis. By prioritizing their well-being, therapists uphold their ethical responsibility, sustain the depth and quality of their work, and ultimately foster long-term professional fulfillment and client success.

CHAPTER 19:

A Path to Meaningful Change

Introduction

Therapy is not just a profession; it is a lifelong commitment to growth, adaptation, and transformation, for both clients and therapists. In an era of increasing mental health challenges, therapists can no longer afford to rely on rigid, single-modality approaches. Therapists must avoid haphazardly combining different therapeutic models without a clear framework, as an unstructured and inconsistent approach can undermine the therapeutic process and potentially cause harm (Norcross & Goldfried, 2019). The Yanni Integration Approach (YIA) represents a new frontier, one that embraces the complexity of human experience and provides a flexible, research-backed framework that evolves alongside the needs of clients.

The integration of cognitive behavioral therapy (CBT), psychodynamic therapy, humanistic therapy, person-centered therapy, and lifestyle-based interventions is more than just a theoretical concept, it is a proven, effective model that is actively reshaping modern therapy. As seen throughout this book, YIA empowers therapists to provide symptom relief, foster deep emotional healing, and encourage sustainable lifestyle changes that promote long-term well-being. The evidence is clear: integrative therapy consistently outperforms single-method approaches in real-world clinical settings (Norcross & Goldfried, 2019; Wampold & Imel, 2015).

But the true power of YIA lies not only in its methodology but in the therapists who apply it. This chapter serves as a final call to action: to embrace integration as a living, evolving practice, to champion the future of therapy, and to ensure that every client receives personalized, transformative care that meets their unique needs.

Key Takeaways: The Foundations of the Yanni Integration Approach

Through Chapters 1–18, we have explored the essential principles and applications of YIA. Below is a recap of the key takeaways that therapists should carry forward into their practice:

1. **The Necessity of Integration (Chapters 1–3)**

    - No single therapy model addresses the full range of client needs. YIA blends multiple evidence-based models to create a more comprehensive and personalized approach (Norcross & Goldfried, 2019).
    - The first step in successful therapy is therapist preparation, ensuring that practitioners are intentional, adaptable, and self-aware in their interventions.

2. **Building the Therapeutic Alliance (Chapters 4–5)**

    - Research confirms that therapeutic rapport is one of the strongest predictors of client success (Norcross & Lambert, 2019c).
    - Understanding the client's worldview, values, and personal history is crucial for crafting effective interventions (Elliott et al., 2004).

3. **Applying YIA in Clinical Practice (Chapters 6–10)**

    - A structured session flow helps therapists seamlessly integrate multiple models while remaining responsive to clients' evolving needs (Wampold & Imel, 2015).
    - YIA ensures symptom relief and deep exploration through a multimodal approach (Leichsenring et al., 2013).
    - Collaboration between therapist and client fosters engagement, goal-setting, and shared responsibility for progress (Swift & Greenberg, 2012).

4. **Beyond Traditional Therapy: Lifestyle & Cultural Awareness (Chapters 11–13)**

    - Lifestyle factors, including sleep, nutrition, movement, and social connections, are fundamental to mental health and must be integrated into treatment (Walsh, 2011).
    - Cultural competence is essential; therapy must be adapted to each client's background, belief systems, and experiences (Sue, Rasheed, & Rasheed, 2016).

5. **Professional Growth & Ethical Integrity (Chapters 14–18)**

    - Therapists must engage in ongoing self-reflection, supervision, and professional development to maintain effectiveness and prevent burnout (Barnett & Cooper, 2009).
    - Ethical integration requires transparency, informed consent, and evidence-based practice to ensure client safety and trust (Beauchamp & Childress, 2019).
    - Therapist well-being is critical to effective therapy. Sustainable practice requires boundaries, self-care, and professional support networks (Figley, 2002; Skovholt & Trotter-Mathison, 2016).

These principles solidify YIA's role as a transformative, client-centered approach that is built for the evolving demands of mental health treatment.

Expanding YIA: The Future of Therapy

The mental health field is at a crossroads. The limitations of single-modality therapy are becoming increasingly evident, and the demand for more adaptive, personalized approaches has never been higher. The Yanni Integration Approach is positioned to become a standard in mental health treatment, but its future depends on continued research, advocacy, and clinical implementation.

1. **Empirical Research on YIA**

    - Future randomized controlled trials (RCTs) and longitudinal studies must assess YIA's impact across diverse populations and clinical settings (Norcross & Wampold, 2011b).
    - Meta-analyses comparing YIA to standalone modalities can validate its superiority in long-term symptom reduction and client satisfaction.

2. **Training and Supervision in YIA**

    - Specialized training programs and certifications should be developed to help therapists gain expertise in multimodal integration (Barnett & Cooper, 2009).
    - Supervision models should focus on ethical, effective blending of therapeutic approaches to support clinical decision-making (Kazdin, 2021).

3. **Technology and the Evolution of Therapy**

    - Digital tools, teletherapy platforms, and AI-assisted interventions will continue to shape the future of psychotherapy.

- Future research should explore how YIA can be effectively implemented in teletherapy and hybrid models.

The success of YIA in psychotherapy depends on continued validation, refinement, and adaptation to meet the evolving needs of clients, clinicians, and mental health professionals.

Final Thoughts on YIA

Therapy is, at its core, a relationship-based and human-centered endeavor. The Yanni Integration Approach bridges the gap between structured intervention and deep emotional exploration, ensuring that each client receives a therapy experience tailored to their unique needs.

The history of psychotherapy demonstrates a continual shift from rigid, single-model approaches to more adaptable, client-centered frameworks. Just as the rise of third-wave therapies (e.g., acceptance and commitment therapy) emphasized flexibility, YIA represents the next step in ensuring that therapy remains dynamic, personalized, and evidence-based.

The key to long-term success in therapy, both for clients and therapists, is flexibility, authenticity, and the willingness to grow. By integrating evidence-based techniques with personal insight, cultural awareness, and a commitment to lifelong learning, therapists can create a truly transformative space for healing and self-discovery.

As you move forward in your practice, I encourage you to:

- Stay curious.
- Remain adaptable.
- Trust the process.
- Continue growing.

The future of therapy is in your hands.

The work is just beginning.

The future of psychotherapy will be shaped by those willing to engage in rigorous study, open dialogue, and innovative practice. Let's lead the way.

CHAPTER 20:

Therapist Toolkit for the Yanni Integration Approach (YIA)

Introduction

Therapists implementing the Yanni Integration Approach (YIA) must navigate the complexities of blending multiple therapeutic models in real-time. While many therapists integrate multiple models, doing so without a structured framework can lead to fragmentation, overwhelm, or ineffective outcomes. YIA ensures that integration is intentional, research-backed, and clinically adaptable, allowing therapists to transition smoothly while maintaining a coherent therapeutic process. Unlike some eclectic approaches that lack a structured framework, YIA provides a scaffolded, strategic method for multimodal therapy.

One of the defining aspects of YIA is its ability to balance structured intervention with therapeutic flexibility. It does not rely on rigid protocols or a one-size-fits-all approach but instead provides a clear yet adaptable method for integrating multiple evidence-based models. Additionally, YIA distinguishes itself by incorporating lifestyle interventions, recognizing that mental health is deeply connected to factors such as sleep, nutrition, movement, and social engagement. This unique combination of structured flexibility and holistic awareness makes YIA an essential advancement in integrative therapy.

This therapist toolkit provides quick-reference guides, decision trees, and self-care strategies to support the efficient and sustainable use of YIA in clinical practice. These tools are designed to enhance decision-making, intervention flexibility, and therapist well-being in integrative practice. By offering structured guidance on integrating therapy models, transitioning between approaches within a session, and preventing burnout, this toolkit ensures that therapists can confidently implement YIA while maintaining their well-being.

Quick-Reference Guide for YIA

The following guide provides practical techniques from each therapeutic model, along with when and how to use them within YIA.

Cognitive Behavioral Therapy (CBT) Techniques

When to Use:

- Clients experiencing anxiety, depression, or maladaptive thought patterns
- When structured problem-solving is needed
- When clients benefit from observable, trackable progress

Quick Tools:

- **Cognitive Restructuring** – Identifying and replacing maladaptive thoughts (A. T. Beck, 1976)
- **Thought Records** – Challenging negative automatic thoughts (A. T. Beck, 1976)

- **Behavioral Activation** – Increasing engagement in positive activities (N. S. Jacobson et al., 1996)
- **Exposure Therapy** – Gradual exposure to anxiety triggers (Hofmann & Smits, 2008)

Psychodynamic Therapy Techniques

When to Use:

- Clients with deep-seated relational issues, past trauma, or unresolved emotions
- When exploring attachment patterns, defense mechanisms, and unconscious conflicts
- When CBT techniques feel too surface-level for the client's distress

Quick Tools:

- **Free Association** – Uncovering unconscious material (Freud, 1915)
- **Exploration of Transference** – Identifying relationship patterns (Luborsky, 1984)
- **Defense Mechanism Analysis** – Recognizing avoidance strategies (Vaillant, 1992)
- **Core Conflictual Relationship Theme (CCRT)** – Identifying repeating interpersonal struggles (Luborsky & Crits-Christoph, 1998)

Person-Centered and Humanistic Techniques

When to Use:

- Clients who need validation, autonomy, and self-acceptance

- When clients benefit from a non-directive approach
- When empathy and trust-building are key therapeutic goals

Quick Tools:

- **Unconditional Positive Regard** – Accepting the client without judgment (Rogers, 1957)
- **Reflective Listening** – Helping clients feel truly heard (Elliott et al., 2004)
- **Congruence and Authenticity** – Therapist openness fosters client honesty
- **Existential Exploration** – Addressing meaning, purpose, and identity (Schneider & Krug, 2017)

Lifestyle Interventions and Mental Health

When to Use:

- Clients struggling with stress, sleep, diet, or exercise-related mental health issues
- To increase emotional regulation through holistic changes

Quick Tools:

- **Sleep Hygiene Coaching** – Establishing bedtime routines to improve mood (Harvey et al., 2011)
- **Exercise and Mental Health** – Promoting movement as a treatment for anxiety (Blumenthal et al., 2007)
- **Nutrition and Mood** – Encouraging balanced eating for emotional stability (Firth, Solmi, et al., 2020)
- **Mindfulness-Based Stress Reduction (MBSR)** – Reducing stress and enhancing emotional resilience (Kabat-Zinn, 1990)

Decision Tree: When to Switch Models During a Session

Why Model Switching Matters in YIA

One of the biggest strengths of the Yanni Integration Approach is the ability to adapt therapy models dynamically within a session. However, knowing when and how to transition is critical. A rigid adherence to one model may lead to client disengagement, while unstructured switching can create confusion or inconsistency. This decision tree framework ensures smooth integration and transition of models based on client responses.

Step 1: Assess Client Engagement

- If the client is engaged and making progress, stay with the current approach and deepen the exploration.
- If the client is frustrated, resistant, or disengaged, consider shifting approaches based on their current emotional state and needs.
- If the client is emotionally overwhelmed or shutting down, pause and provide grounding techniques such as deep breathing and mindfulness. Shift toward person-centered validation to create emotional safety.

Step 2: Match the Intervention to the Client's Emotional State

- Clients struggling with negative thought patterns may benefit from CBT-based cognitive restructuring techniques.
- Clients expressing deep-seated emotional pain may need psychodynamic exploration of past experiences and relational patterns.
- Clients struggling with existential or identity concerns may benefit from humanistic and person-centered approaches focused on self-acceptance.
- Clients feeling stuck and needing direction may benefit from structured lifestyle interventions.

- Clients experiencing trauma-related symptoms may require a blended approach, combining CBT for grounding, psychodynamic therapy for deeper exploration, and person-centered therapy for emotional support.
- Clients intellectualizing or dissociating may benefit from mindfulness-based techniques or somatic interventions before engaging in deeper cognitive or emotional exploration (van der Kolk, 2014).

Therapist Self-Care: Preventing Burnout in Integrative Therapy

Integrating multiple models requires high cognitive engagement and emotional labor. Without proper self-care, therapists risk burnout, compassion fatigue, and decision fatigue (Norcross & VandenBos, 2018).

Therapist Self-Check: Weekly Reflection Guide

At the end of each week, ask yourself:

- Am I feeling emotionally drained after sessions?
- Have I maintained clear boundaries between work and personal life?
- Have I engaged in peer consultation or supervision to process challenging cases?
- Have I taken at least one meaningful self-care action (e.g., mindfulness, exercise, creative activity)?

If more than two of these answers indicate strain, consider adjusting workload, increasing peer support, or revisiting self-care routines (Shapiro et al., 2007).

Quick Self-Care Strategies

- **Micro-Mindfulness Breaks** – Brief breathing exercises between sessions (Kabat-Zinn, 1990).
- **Movement and Stretching** – Incorporating brief movement breaks to prevent physical stagnation.
- **Digital Detox** – Limiting screen time after work hours to reduce mental overload.

Therapists who engage in intentional self-care report lower burnout rates and improved therapeutic presence (Shapiro et al., 2007).

Relaxation and Grounding Techniques for Stress and Anxiety Management

The following relaxation and grounding techniques can be practiced almost anywhere and can help reduce stress, anxiety, and tension. By bringing awareness to the body and the present moment, these strategies can help anchor you when feeling overwhelmed. Try them out and see which works best for you.

1. Progressive Muscle Relaxation (PMR)

Progressive muscle relaxation (PMR) helps release physical tension by systematically tensing and relaxing different muscle groups. This practice has been shown to reduce anxiety, improve sleep, and promote overall relaxation (E. Jacobson, 1938; Bernstein & Borkovec, 1973).

- Find a comfortable position, either seated or lying down.
- Take slow, deep breaths, bringing awareness to your body.

- Focus on one muscle group at a time while keeping the rest of your body relaxed:

  - **Forehead:** Squeeze the muscles in your forehead for 15 seconds, then slowly release over 30 seconds, noticing the sensation of relaxation.
  - **Jaw:** Clench your jaw for 15 seconds, then gradually release, feeling the tension dissipate.
  - **Neck & Shoulders:** Raise your shoulders toward your ears and hold for 15 seconds, then release.
  - **Arms & Hands:** Make fists and pull them toward your chest, holding for 15 seconds before releasing.
  - **Legs & Feet:** Tense your thigh and calf muscles for 15 seconds, then gently release.

- Continue breathing slowly as you scan your body, noticing how each area feels more at ease.

2. Diaphragmatic Breathing (Deep Breathing)

Diaphragmatic breathing, also called deep breathing, activates the parasympathetic nervous system, reducing stress and lowering cortisol levels (Jerath et al., 2006). It is particularly effective when feeling overwhelmed, as it shifts focus to the breath and away from racing thoughts.

- Sit with a straight back, feet flat on the floor, and shoulders relaxed.
- Close your eyes if comfortable.
- Place one hand on your stomach and the other on your chest.
- Inhale deeply through your nose, filling your belly with air like a balloon.
- Exhale slowly through your mouth as if blowing through a straw.
- Focus on lengthening your exhalation, which enhances relaxation.

- Repeat for several minutes, maintaining a steady, controlled breath.

3. The Relaxation Response

Dr. Herbert Benson (1975) developed the "relaxation response," a simple technique for inducing a state of deep relaxation. This practice counteracts the stress response, promoting mental clarity and emotional regulation.

- Find a quiet space and sit or lie down in a comfortable position.
- If desired, play soft music or nature sounds.
- Breathe naturally and focus on a word or phrase (e.g., "peace," "calm") as you exhale.
- If your mind wanders, gently bring your attention back to your breath and chosen phrase.
- Continue for 10–20 minutes, allowing your mind and body to settle into relaxation.

4. The 5-4-3-2-1 Sensory Grounding Technique

This technique engages the five senses to bring awareness back to the present moment.

- **5:** Look around and name five things you see.
- **4:** Touch four objects around you and notice their texture.
- **3:** Identify three things you hear, such as distant sounds or your breath.
- **2:** Recognize two things you can smell (or take a deep breath of fresh air).
- **1:** Acknowledge one thing you can taste (gum, tea, or simply the inside of your mouth).

This method can help break the cycle of anxious or intrusive thoughts by focusing on immediate sensory input (Briere & Scott, 2014).

5. Cold Water Therapy (Temperature-Based Grounding)

Temperature changes can activate the vagus nerve, reducing stress and calming the nervous system (Porges, 2011).

- **Cold Water Splash:** Splash cold water on your face to stimulate the diving reflex, which slows the heart rate and promotes relaxation.
- **Ice Cube Hold:** Hold an ice cube in your hand or place it on your wrist to redirect focus from distressing thoughts to physical sensation.
- **Cold Drink:** Slowly sip a cold drink, paying close attention to the temperature and sensation.

6. The Grounding Object Technique

Using a small object as a tactile grounding tool can help manage anxiety.

- Carry a smooth stone, fidget item, or another small object in your pocket.
- When feeling anxious, focus on the texture, weight, and temperature of the object.
- This practice can serve as a discreet, portable grounding method.

7. Movement-Based Grounding (Walking Meditation)

Physical movement can help regulate emotions and relieve stress (Ratey, 2008).

- Stand up and take slow, intentional steps, focusing on the sensation of your feet touching the ground.
- Notice how your body moves as you walk; how your legs feel, how your arms swing naturally.

- Engage your senses by listening to the sounds around you or feeling the temperature of the air.
- If outdoors, observe nature: the movement of leaves, the sound of birds, or the texture of the ground beneath you.

Walking meditation combines mindfulness and movement to help reconnect with the present moment.

8. Box Breathing (Tactical Breathing)

Used by Navy SEALs for stress management, box breathing can rapidly restore calm (Grossman & Christensen, 2008).

- Inhale deeply through your nose for 4 seconds.
- Hold your breath for 4 seconds.
- Exhale slowly through your mouth for 4 seconds.
- Hold your breath again for 4 seconds before repeating the cycle.

This technique enhances focus and reduces physiological arousal in high-stress situations.

These relaxation and grounding techniques offer practical tools for managing stress and anxiety in real-time. With consistency, they can become essential coping strategies for emotional regulation.

Final Thoughts

Mastering the Yanni Integration Approach is an ongoing journey. By using this toolkit, therapists are not just blending techniques, they are creating a transformative therapeutic experience for their clients. Stay flexible, refine your approach, and prioritize your own well-being. The future of therapy is integrative, adaptive, and client-centered, and therapists at the forefront of this movement need to be mindful to take care of themselves as well.

Index of Key Terms and Definitions

This index provides definitions for key concepts discussed in *A Therapist's Guide to Integrative Therapy*.

A

- **Active Listening** – A communication technique in which the therapist fully concentrates, understands, and responds to the client in an empathetic and validating manner.
- **Adaptability in Therapy** – The therapist's ability to flexibly respond to the client's changing needs by shifting between therapeutic approaches within the YIA framework.
- **Alliance-Building** – The process of establishing trust and collaboration between therapist and client, essential for effective therapy.
- **Anxiety** – A mental health condition characterized by excessive worry, nervousness, or fear, which can interfere with daily functioning; often treated using CBT, lifestyle changes, and psychodynamic insight.
- **Assessment** – The process of gathering information about a client's psychological, emotional, and behavioral state to inform diagnosis and treatment planning.
- **Attachment Theory** – A psychological framework explaining how early relationships with caregivers shape an individual's patterns of relating to others in adulthood.

- **Attunement** – The therapist's ability to be deeply present with and responsive to the client's emotional and relational state; essential for effective integrative practice.
- **Authenticity in Therapy** – The quality of being genuine and transparent as a therapist, allowing for a more open and trusting therapeutic relationship.
- **Autonomy in Therapy** – The principle that clients have the right to make decisions about their own therapeutic process, emphasizing self-determination and empowerment.

B

- **Behavioral Activation** – A CBT technique used to help clients engage in meaningful activities to combat depression and avoidance behaviors.
- **Biopsychosocial Model** – A holistic perspective in mental health care that considers biological, psychological, and social factors in assessment and treatment.
- **Boundaries in Therapy** – Ethical and professional limits that maintain a healthy therapist-client relationship, ensuring clear roles and preventing dual relationships.
- **Burnout** – A state of physical, emotional, and mental exhaustion caused by prolonged stress or overwork, often experienced by helping professionals.
- **Burnout Prevention** – Strategies used by therapists to avoid emotional exhaustion and maintain effectiveness, including self-care, supervision, and workload management.
- **Brief Intervention** – A focused therapeutic approach often used within YIA to address a specific symptom or behavior in a short period of time.
- **Body Awareness** – An aspect of integrative therapy that encourages clients to connect with physical sensations as a path to emotional insight and regulation.

- **Body-Based Interventions** – Techniques that incorporate physical sensations or movement, such as grounding or mindfulness, to support emotional regulation and trauma recovery.
- **Breathing Techniques** – Structured practices such as diaphragmatic or box breathing that help regulate stress responses and support emotional regulation.

C

- **Case Conceptualization** – A therapist's formulation of a client's presenting concerns, drawing on psychological theories to inform treatment planning and guide interventions.
- **Case Formulation** – A structured approach to understanding a client's presenting issues, history, and treatment plan using multiple therapeutic models.
- **CBT (Cognitive Behavioral Therapy)** – A structured, evidence-based therapy model that focuses on identifying and changing negative thought patterns and behaviors.
- **Client-Centered Therapy** – An approach developed by Carl Rogers that prioritizes the client's experiences, autonomy, and self-direction in therapy.
- **Cognitive Distortions** – Inaccurate or exaggerated thought patterns that negatively affect a person's perception of themselves and their experiences; often addressed using CBT.
- **Cognitive Restructuring** – A core CBT technique that involves identifying and challenging distorted thought patterns to improve emotional well-being.
- **Collaboration in Therapy** – A treatment approach where the therapist and client work together to set goals and strategies, reinforcing client empowerment.

- **Compassion Fatigue** – The emotional and physical exhaustion that results from prolonged exposure to client suffering; common among mental health professionals.
- **Congruence** – A therapist's authenticity and alignment between internal feelings and external communication, central to humanistic therapy.
- **Consultation** – Professional peer engagement in which therapists seek feedback, insight, or support to enhance their clinical work.
- **Core Conflictual Relationship Theme (CCRT)** – A psychodynamic method for identifying repeated patterns in a client's relationships to understand unconscious motivations and conflicts.
- **Countertransference** – The therapist's emotional reactions to a client, which may be influenced by the therapist's own past experiences and unresolved conflicts.
- **Cultural Competency** – The ability to understand, respect, and adapt therapy to the diverse cultural backgrounds and values of clients.

D

- **Decision Fatigue** – Mental exhaustion that impairs judgment and responsiveness due to the accumulation of too many decisions; often a risk in integrative therapy.
- **Defense Mechanisms** – Unconscious strategies used to protect oneself from anxiety or emotional discomfort; explored in psychodynamic therapy.
- **Depth-Oriented Work** – Therapeutic exploration that focuses on underlying emotions, memories, and unconscious patterns to promote lasting change.
- **Depression** – A mental health disorder characterized by persistent sadness, loss of interest in activities, and changes in sleep, appetite, and energy levels.
- **Decision-Making in Therapy** – The process therapists use to determine the most appropriate intervention strategies based on client needs and therapy goals.

- **Diagnostic Assessment** – The process of evaluating a client's symptoms to determine a clinical diagnosis and inform treatment planning.
- **Diaphragmatic Breathing** – A relaxation technique that involves deep breathing to activate the parasympathetic nervous system and reduce stress.
- **Dual Relationships** – Situations in which a therapist has more than one relationship with a client (e.g., professional and personal); may pose ethical risks.

E

- **Eclectic Therapy** – An approach where therapists draw techniques from different therapeutic models without a unified framework; differs from YIA's structured integration.
- **Emotional Processing** – The act of understanding, managing, and integrating emotions in therapy to promote healing and resilience.
- **Emotional Regulation** – The ability to manage and respond to emotional experiences in adaptive ways; a common goal across all YIA modalities.
- **Empathy in Therapy** – The therapist's ability to understand and share in the emotions of the client, fostering trust and emotional safety.
- **Ethics in Therapy** – Professional guidelines that ensure therapists maintain client confidentiality, avoid conflicts of interest, and provide responsible care.
- **Evidence-Based Practice** – The use of scientifically supported interventions and research-informed treatment approaches in psychotherapy.
- **Existential Exploration** – A humanistic technique focusing on questions of meaning, purpose, identity, and mortality in therapy.
- **Exposure Therapy** – A CBT-based intervention used to help clients confront and reduce fear responses by gradually exposing them to anxiety-provoking situations.

F

- **Feedback in Therapy** – The process of receiving and incorporating client feedback to improve therapeutic effectiveness and engagement.
- **First Impressions in Therapy** – The initial moments of a session that establish trust, rapport, and therapeutic expectations.
- **Flexibility in Therapy Models** – The ability to shift between different therapeutic approaches based on client needs.
- **Formulation** – A hypothesis about a client's psychological difficulties that informs treatment planning, often used in CBT and psychodynamic approaches.
- **Free Association** – A psychodynamic method where clients verbalize thoughts without censorship, allowing unconscious material to emerge.
- **Functional Impairment** – Difficulties in daily functioning due to psychological distress, often a target for intervention in integrative therapy.

G

- **Goal-Setting** – The collaborative process of defining therapeutic objectives to guide client progress.
- **Grounding Techniques** – Methods used to anchor clients in the present moment during periods of distress or dissociation, including sensory-based and mindfulness exercises.
- **Group Supervision** – A form of professional support where therapists consult with peers to enhance clinical skills, prevent burnout, and promote ethical practice.
- **Guided Discovery** – A CBT technique in which therapists help clients examine and re-evaluate unhelpful beliefs through questioning and exploration.

H

- **Holding Environment** – A psychodynamic concept referring to the therapeutic space as emotionally safe, allowing for vulnerability and healing.
- **Holistic Mental Health** – An approach that addresses mental, emotional, physical, and social aspects of well-being; central to the YIA model.
- **Humanistic Therapy** – A therapy model that emphasizes personal growth, self-actualization, and the therapeutic relationship as central to healing.
- **Hypothesis Testing in CBT** – A technique where clients test the validity of their beliefs through behavioral experiments and real-world evidence.

I

- **Impasses in Therapy** – Moments where progress stalls, often requiring shifts in therapeutic strategies.
- **Informed Consent** – The ethical process of ensuring clients understand the nature, risks, and benefits of therapy before treatment begins.
- **Insight-Oriented Therapy** – A modality that focuses on increasing clients' understanding of the roots of their emotional distress; often used in psychodynamic work.
- **Integration** – The blending of multiple therapeutic models into a cohesive, intentional treatment approach tailored to the client's needs; foundational to the Yanni Integration Approach (YIA).
- **Integrative Therapy Models** – Approaches that combine multiple therapeutic methods to enhance client outcomes.
- **Intentionality in Therapy** – The deliberate and thoughtful use of techniques, interventions, and therapist presence to meet therapeutic goals.
- **Interpretation (Psychodynamic)** – A technique where the therapist offers insight into unconscious motives or conflicts based on patterns observed in therapy.

- **Intervention Strategies** – Specific therapeutic techniques used to facilitate client growth and symptom reduction.

J

- **Journaling** – A therapeutic tool used to enhance self-reflection, process emotions, and track progress; commonly applied in CBT and lifestyle-based interventions.
- **Judgment-Free Space** – A core aspect of person-centered and humanistic therapy, where clients feel accepted without criticism, promoting trust and openness.

K

- **Key Session Steps** – Structured components within a therapy session that guide flow and integration, including check-ins, goal setting, interventions, and closure.
- **Knowledge of Models** – Therapist understanding of therapeutic modalities (e.g., CBT, psychodynamic, person-centered) essential for effective integration under YIA.

L

- **Lifestyle Interventions** – Behavioral changes related to sleep, exercise, diet, and stress management that support mental health.
- **Listening Skills** – Core therapist abilities that include active listening, reflective responses, and empathetic attunement, vital in all YIA modalities.

- **Locus of Control** – A psychological concept describing whether individuals perceive control over events as internal (self-driven) or external; often explored in CBT.
- **Longevity in Practice** – A therapist's sustained effectiveness and well-being over time, supported by self-care, supervision, and ethical practice.
- **Logic of Integration** – The rationale for blending therapeutic models to address client needs holistically and responsively, central to YIA methodology.
- **Long-Term Client Progress** – Sustained improvements in client well-being over time.

M

- **Mental Health and Lifestyle** – The relationship between daily habits and psychological well-being.
- **Mindfulness** – A practice of focused, nonjudgmental awareness of the present moment; often used in stress reduction, emotion regulation, and grounding techniques within YIA.
- **Mindfulness Techniques** – Practices that enhance present-moment awareness and emotional regulation.
- **Modalities of Therapy** – Distinct theoretical frameworks such as CBT, psychodynamic, person-centered, and humanistic approaches used in integrative practice.
- **Model Switching** – The intentional transition between therapeutic approaches during a session to meet client needs; a core feature of YIA flexibility.
- **Multicultural Competence** – Therapist's ability to understand and respect cultural differences, essential for delivering inclusive and effective therapy.
- **Motivational Interviewing** – A client-centered technique used to enhance intrinsic motivation for change, often incorporated into YIA sessions.

- **Mentalization** – The capacity to understand the mental states of oneself and others; frequently addressed in psychodynamic components of therapy.
- **Meaning-Making** – The therapeutic process of helping clients understand life events, relationships, and identity, commonly supported by existential and humanistic interventions.

N

- **Narrative Techniques** – Interventions that help clients construct coherent stories about their lives, supporting identity development and healing.
- **Neurobiological Regulation** – The management of physiological responses to stress through interventions like deep breathing, mindfulness, and grounding.
- **Nonjudgmental Stance** – A therapeutic attitude emphasizing acceptance and curiosity rather than criticism, especially vital in person-centered therapy.
- **Needs-Based Therapy** – Tailoring interventions to meet the specific and evolving psychological needs of the client; a hallmark of YIA integration.
- **Neutrality in Therapy** – The therapist's role in maintaining an unbiased, nonjudgmental stance.

O

- **Outcome Measures** – Tools used to assess therapeutic progress and effectiveness.
- **Overidentification** – A countertransference reaction where the therapist relates too closely with the client, potentially impairing objectivity and clinical boundaries.
- **Observational Skills** – The therapist's ability to detect subtle nonverbal cues, body language, and emotional shifts to guide responsive interventions.

- **Open-Ended Questions** – Non-directive inquiries that encourage clients to explore their thoughts and feelings freely, essential in person-centered and psychodynamic work.
- **Organically Integrated Therapy** – A style of blending modalities based on client needs and clinical intuition, rather than pre-set routines or rigid models.

P

- **Peer Consultation** – Regular meetings with professional colleagues for case discussion, support, and maintaining clinical effectiveness and ethical practice.
- **Personal Growth** – An objective of therapy focused on enhancing self-awareness, self-acceptance, and life satisfaction beyond symptom relief.
- **Person-Centered Therapy** – A non-directive therapy approach that empowers clients to take the lead in their healing.
- **Process-Oriented Therapy** – An approach that emphasizes the evolving dynamics of the therapeutic relationship and moment-to-moment emotional experiences.
- **Professional Boundaries** – Clear limits that define appropriate interactions between therapist and client, protecting the integrity of the therapeutic process.
- **Professional Development** – The ongoing process of learning and skill-building in psychotherapy.
- **Progress Monitoring** – Ongoing evaluation of therapeutic goals and outcomes to inform and adapt treatment over time.
- **Psychoeducation** – The process of teaching clients about psychological concepts, symptoms, or treatment strategies to empower and engage them in therapy.
- **Psychodynamic Therapy** – A therapeutic approach that explores unconscious conflicts, attachment patterns, and early life experiences.

Q

- **Qualitative Change** – Subjective improvements in a client's emotional awareness, relationship patterns, or sense of meaning, often observed in psychodynamic and humanistic work.
- **Questioning Techniques** – The strategic use of questions in therapy (e.g., Socratic questioning, reflective questions) to deepen insight and challenge unhelpful thinking.
- **Quiet Presence** – A therapist's intentional use of silence or minimal verbal interaction to create space for reflection, emotion, or deeper connection.

R

- **Reflection in Therapy** – The process of self-examination and insight development.
- **Reflective Listening** – A technique in which the therapist mirrors the client's feelings and thoughts to foster understanding, validation, and connection.
- **Reframing** – A cognitive strategy used in CBT and integrative work to help clients view situations from a new, more adaptive perspective.
- **Relational Patterns** – Recurrent interpersonal dynamics clients experience in relationships; often explored in psychodynamic and interpersonal therapies.
- **Relaxation Techniques** – Methods such as deep breathing, progressive muscle relaxation, or mindfulness used to manage anxiety and promote emotional regulation.
- **Repair in Therapy** – The process of addressing and resolving ruptures or misunderstandings in the therapeutic relationship to rebuild trust.
- **Repetition Compulsion** – A psychodynamic concept where clients unconsciously reenact past relational patterns; often worked through in integrative therapy.

- **Resilience** – A client's ability to recover from adversity; often a goal of therapeutic interventions and lifestyle-based strategies in YIA.
- **Resistance** – Unconscious or conscious client behaviors that hinder therapeutic progress, such as avoidance, denial, or minimization; often addressed in psychodynamic therapy.
- **Risk Management** – Strategies to prevent ethical and legal issues in therapy.
- **Role of the Therapist** – The therapist's function as facilitator, guide, or collaborator in the client's healing journey; adapted flexibly within the YIA model.

S

- **Safety in Therapy** – The emotional and psychological environment in which clients feel secure enough to be vulnerable and engage in the therapeutic process.
- **Schema** – Deeply held cognitive frameworks or beliefs that influence how individuals perceive themselves, others, and the world; often addressed in CBT and integrative approaches.
- **Self-Awareness** – A therapist's or client's conscious knowledge of their own emotions, thoughts, and behaviors; essential in reflective practice and emotional regulation.
- **Self-Care** – Activities and habits therapists engage in to maintain their mental, emotional, and physical well-being; crucial for preventing burnout.
- **Self-Compassion** – The practice of treating oneself with kindness during times of suffering; promoted in mindfulness-based and humanistic therapy.
- **Self-Disclosure** – When therapists share personal experiences or feelings with clients for therapeutic benefit; used judiciously within the YIA model.
- **Session Structure** – The framework guiding the flow of a therapy session (e.g., check-in, intervention, reflection) to support clarity and integration.

- **Somatic Awareness** – Attention to bodily sensations; often used in grounding or trauma-informed approaches to enhance mind-body integration.
- **Strength-Based Approaches** – A therapeutic perspective that focuses on a client's existing strengths and resilience to facilitate change.
- **Supervision** – A professional relationship in which therapists consult with colleagues or mentors to reflect on and improve clinical work.
- **Symptom Relief** – The reduction of distressing psychological symptoms such as anxiety or depression, often the initial goal in therapy.

T

- **Therapist-Client Relationship** – The professional bond between therapist and client, built on trust, empathy, and collaboration, which is essential for successful outcomes.
- **Therapeutic Alliance** – The cooperative and trusting relationship between therapist and client; considered one of the strongest predictors of successful therapy outcomes.
- **Therapist Burnout** – A state of emotional, mental, and physical exhaustion resulting from chronic work-related stress; addressed through self-care and boundary-setting.
- **Therapist Flexibility** – The ability to shift therapeutic approaches and interventions in response to client needs; central to the YIA model.
- **Therapeutic Goals** – Collaborative objectives established by the therapist and client to guide the direction and focus of therapy.
- **Therapist Neutrality** – Maintaining a nonjudgmental, balanced stance to support client exploration without imposing personal biases.
- **Thought Records** – A CBT tool used to track and challenge automatic negative thoughts, helping clients reframe cognitive distortions.

- **Trauma-Informed Care** – An approach that recognizes the prevalence and impact of trauma, ensuring that therapy is conducted with safety, sensitivity, and empowerment.
- **Therapeutic Boundaries** – Ethical and professional guidelines that define the limits of the therapist-client relationship to maintain safety and professionalism.
- **Transference** – A psychodynamic concept where clients project feelings or expectations from past relationships onto the therapist; often explored in integrative work.
- **Trauma-Focused Therapy** – A specialized approach that helps clients process and heal from past traumatic experiences using evidence-based techniques.
- **Treatment Planning** – The process of outlining therapeutic goals, interventions, and timelines based on client needs and evidence-based practices.
- **Trust-Building** – The deliberate effort to foster emotional safety and openness in therapy, beginning with empathy, consistency, and validation.

U

- **Unconditional Positive Regard** – A core concept from person-centered therapy where the therapist accepts the client without judgment, fostering trust and self-acceptance.
- **Understanding Client Worldview** – The practice of recognizing and respecting a client's cultural, social, and personal perspective; essential in culturally competent therapy.
- **Use of Self in Therapy** – The therapist's intentional use of their personality, insights, and experiences to enhance therapeutic engagement and connection.

V

- **Validation** – Affirming and acknowledging a client's feelings, thoughts, or experiences as understandable, helping build safety and emotional connection in therapy.
- **Vicarious Trauma** – Emotional residue experienced by therapists after working with clients who have experienced trauma; can lead to compassion fatigue if not addressed.
- **Visualization Techniques** – Guided imagery exercises used to reduce anxiety, increase relaxation, or enhance insight during sessions.

W

- **Wellness and Therapy** – The interconnectedness of mental health with physical well-being, lifestyle habits, and self-care practices.
- **Walking Meditation** – A form of mindfulness practice involving slow, intentional movement to increase present-moment awareness and emotional regulation.
- **Well-Being in Therapy** – The broader goal of therapy that extends beyond symptom relief to include lifestyle changes, emotional growth, and life satisfaction.
- **Working Alliance** – The collaborative and purposeful connection between therapist and client, consisting of agreed-upon goals, tasks, and a positive bond.

Y

- **Yanni Integration Approach (YIA)** – A multimodal therapeutic framework that integrates CBT, psychodynamic, person-centered, humanistic, and lifestyle interventions to create personalized, evidence-informed treatment plans.

Z

- **Zones of Regulation** – While not always explicitly named, this refers to recognizing emotional states and developing tools for managing them; often applied within behavioral and integrative therapy contexts.

References

Ackerman, S. J., & Hilsenroth, M. J. (2003). A review of therapist characteristics and techniques positively impacting the therapeutic alliance. *Clinical Psychology Review, 23*(1), 1–33. https://doi.org/10.1016/S0272-7358(02)00146-0

Alvidrez, J., Snowden, L. R., & Kaiser, D. M. (2008). The experience of stigma among Black mental health consumers. *Journal of Health Care for the Poor and Underserved, 19(3),* 874–893. https://doi.org/10.1353/hpu.0.0058

American Psychiatric Association. (2013). *Diagnostic and Statistical Manual of Mental Disorders* (5th ed.). APA Publishing. https://doi.org/10.1176/appi.books.9780890425596

American Psychological Association. (2017). *Ethical principles of psychologists and code of conduct* (2002, amended effective June 1, 2010, and January 1, 2017). https://www.apa.org/ethics/code

American Psychological Association. (2024). ***Proposed revision of guidelines for the practice of telepsychology.*** https://www.apa.org/practice/guidelines/telepsychology-revisions.pdf

Andersson, G., Titov, N., Dear, B. F., Rozental, A., & Carlbring, P. (2019). Internet-delivered psychological treatments: From innovation to implementation. *World Psychiatry, 18*(1), 20–28. https://doi.org/10.1002/wps.20610

Bailey, R. K., Mokonogho, J., & Kumar, A. (2019). Racial and ethnic differences in depression: Current perspectives. ***Neuropsychiatric Disease and Treatment,*** *15,* 603–609. https://doi.org/10.2147/NDT.S128584

Bandura, A. (1997). *Self-efficacy: The exercise of control.* W. H. Freeman.

Barkham, M., & Mellor-Clark, J. (2003). Bridging evidence-based practice and practice-based evidence: Developing a rigorous and relevant knowledge for the psychological therapies. *Clinical Psychology & Psychotherapy, 10*(6), 319–327. https://doi.org/10.1002/cpp.379

Barnett, J. E. (2011). Psychotherapist self-disclosure: Ethical and clinical considerations. *Psychotherapy, 48*(4), 315–321. https://doi.org/10.1037/a0026056

Barnett, J. E. (2019). The ethical practice of psychotherapy: Clearly within our reach. *Psychotherapy, 56*(4), 431–440. https://dx.doi.org/10.1037/pst0000272

Barnett, J. E., Baker, E. K., Elman, N. S., & Schoener, G. R. (2007). In pursuit of wellness: The self-care imperative. *Professional Psychology: Research and Practice, 38*(6), 603–612. https://doi.org/10.1037/0735-7028.38.6.603

Barnett, J. E., & Coffman, C. (2015). Termination and abandonment: A proactive approach to ethical practice. [Web article]. Retrieved from: www.societyforpsychotherapy.org/termination-and-abandonment-a-proactive-approach-to-ethical-practice

Barnett, J. E., & Cooper, N. (2009). Creating a culture of self-care. Clinical Psychology: Science and Practice, 16(1), 16–20. https://psycnet.apa.org/doi/10.1111/j.1468-2850.2009.01138.x

Barnett, J. E., & Kolmes, K. (2016). The practice of tele-mental health: Ethical, legal, and clinical issues for practitioners. *Practice Innovations, 1*(1), 53–66. https://doi.org/10.1037/pri0000014

Baumeister, R. F., & Tierney, J. (2011). *Willpower: Rediscovering the greatest human strength.* Penguin Publishing Group.

Beahrs, J. O., & Gutheil, T. G. (2001). Informed consent in psychotherapy. *American Journal of Psychiatry, 158*(1), 4–10. https://doi.org/10.1176/appi.ajp.158.1.4

Beauchamp, T. L., & Childress, J. F. (2019). *Principles of biomedical ethics* (8th ed.). Oxford University Press.

Beck, A. T. (1976). *Cognitive therapy and the emotional disorders.* International Universities Press.

Beck, A. T. (1979). *Cognitive therapy of depression.* Guilford Press.

Beck, J. S. (2011). *Cognitive behavior therapy: Basics and beyond* (2nd ed.). Guilford Press.

Benson, H. (1975). *The relaxation response.* William Morrow.

Bernal, G., & Scharrón-del-Río, M. R. (2001). Are empirically supported treatments valid for ethnic minorities? Toward an alternative approach for treatment research. *Cultural Diversity and Ethnic Minority Psychology, 7*(4), 328–342. https://doi.org/10.1037/1099-9809.7.4.328

Bernard, J. M., & Goodyear, R. K. (2019). *Fundamentals of clinical supervision* (6th ed.). Pearson.

Bernstein, D. A., & Borkovec, T. D. (1973). *Progressive relaxation training: A manual for the helping professions*. Research Press.

Beutler, L. E., & Harwood, T. M. (2000). *Prescriptive psychotherapy: A practical guide to systematic treatment selection*. Oxford University Press. https://doi.org/10.1093/med:psych/9780195136692.001.0001

Beutler, L. E., Moleiro, C., & Talebi, H. (2002). Resistance in psychotherapy: What conclusions are supported by research? *Journal of Clinical Psychology, 58*(2), 207–217. https://doi.org/10.1002/jclp.1144

Bhatia, A., & Gelso, C. J. (2017). The termination phase: Therapists' perspective on the therapeutic relationship and outcome. *Psychotherapy, 54*(1), 76–87. https://doi.org/10.1037/pst0000100

Blumenthal, J. A., Babyak, M. A., Doraiswamy, P. M., Watkins, L., Hoffman, B. M., Barbour, K. A., Herman, S., Craighead, W. E., Brosse, A. L., Waugh, R., & Sherwood, A. (2007). Exercise and pharmacotherapy in the treatment of major depressive disorder. *Psychosomatic Medicine, 69*(7), 587–596. https://doi.org/10.1097/PSY.0b013e318148c19a

Blumenthal, J. A., Smith, P. J., & Hoffman, B. M. (2012). Is exercise a viable treatment for depression? *ACSM's Health & Fitness Journal, 16*(4), 14–21. https://doi.org/10.1249/01.FIT.0000416000.09526.eb

Bohart, A. C., & Wade, A. G. (2013). The client in psychotherapy. In M. J. Lambert (Ed.), *Bergin and Garfield's handbook of psychotherapy and behavior change* (6th ed., pp. 219–257). Wiley.

Bordin, E. S. (1979). The generalizability of the psychoanalytic concept of the working alliance. *Psychotherapy: Theory, Research & Practice, 16*(3), 252–260. https://doi.org/10.1037/h0085885

Briere, J., & Scott, C. (2014). *Principles of trauma therapy: A guide to symptoms, evaluation, and treatment* (2nd ed.). Sage Publications.

Cain, D. J. (2010). *Person-centered psychotherapies*. American Psychological Association. https://doi.org/10.1037/17330-000

Carek, P. J., Laibstain, S. E., & Carek, S. M. (2011). Exercise for the treatment of depression and anxiety. *International Journal of Psychiatry in Medicine, 41*(1), 15–28. https://doi.org/10.2190/PM.41.1.c

Castonguay, L. G., & Beutler, L. E. (Eds.). (2005). *Principles of therapeutic change that work*. Oxford University Press. https://doi.org/10.1093/med:psych/9780195156843.001.0001

Comas-Díaz, L. (2012). *Multicultural care: A clinician's guide to cultural competence*. American Psychological Association. https://doi.org/10.1037/13491-000

Crenshaw, K. (1989). Demarginalizing the Intersection of Race and Sex: A Black Feminist Critique of Antidiscrimination Doctrine, Feminist Theory and Antiracist Politics. *University of Chicago Legal Forum*: Vol. 1989, Article 8.

Cuijpers, P., Karyotaki, E., Weitz, E., Andersson, G., Hollon, S. D., & van Straten, A. (2014). The effects of psychotherapies for major depression in adults on remission, recovery, and improvement: A meta-analysis. *Journal of Affective Disorders, 159*, 118–126. https://doi.org/10.1016/j.jad.2014.02.026

Deci, E. L., & Ryan, R. M. (2000). The "what" and "why" of goal pursuits: Human needs and the self-determination of behavior. *Psychological Inquiry, 11*(4), 227–268. https://doi.org/10.1207/S15327965PLI1104_01

Dobson, K. S. (Ed.). (2010). *Handbook of cognitive-behavioral therapies* (3rd ed.). Guilford Press.

Driessen, E., Hegelmaier, L., Abbass, A. A., Barber, J. P., Dekker, J. J., & Van, H. P. (2015). The efficacy of short-term psychodynamic therapy for depression: A meta-analysis update. *Clinical Psychology Review, 42*, 1–15. https://doi.org/10.1016/j.cpr.2015.07.004

Duncan, B. L., Miller, S. D., Wampold, B. E., & Hubble, M. A. (Eds.). (2010). *The heart and soul of change: Delivering what works in therapy* (2nd ed.). American Psychological Association.

Duncan, B. L., & Reese, R. J. (2015). The Partners for Change Outcome Management System: A review of the evidence and impact. *Psychotherapy, 52*(4), 391–401. https://doi.org/10.1037/pst0000026

Eells, T. D. (2015). *Psychotherapy case formulation*. American Psychological Association. https://doi.org/10.1037/14667-000

Ehlers, A., Clark, D. M., Hackmann, A., McManus, F., & Fennell, M. (2005). Cognitive therapy for PTSD: Development and evaluation. *Behaviour Research and Therapy, 43*(4), 413–431. https://doi.org/10.1016/j.brat.2004.03.006

Elliott, R., Bohart, A. C., Watson, J. C., & Greenberg, L. S. (2011). Empathy. In J. C. Norcross (Ed.), *Psychotherapy relationships that work: Evidence-based responsiveness* (2nd ed., pp. 132–152). Oxford University Press.

Elliott, R., Watson, J. C., Goldman, R. N., & Greenberg, L. S. (2004). *Learning emotion-focused therapy: The process-experiential approach to change.* American Psychological Association.

Elliott, R., Watson, J. C., Greenberg, L. S., Timulak, L., & Freire, E. (2013). Research on humanistic-experiential psychotherapies. In M. J. Lambert (Ed.), *Bergin & Garfield's handbook of psychotherapy and behavior change* (6th ed., pp. 495–538). Wiley.

Ellis, A. (2001). *Overcoming destructive beliefs, feelings, and behaviors: New directions for rational emotive behavior therapy.* Globe Pequot Publishing.

Fancourt, D., & Finn, S. (2019). *What is the evidence on the role of the arts in improving health and well-being? A scoping review.* WHO Regional Office for Europe (Health Evidence Network (HEN) synthesis report 67).

Farber, B. A., & Doolin, E. M. (2011). Positive regard. *Psychotherapy, 48*(1), 58–64. https://doi.org/10.1037/a0022141

Fernando, S. (2010). *Mental health, race, and culture* (3rd ed.). Palgrave Macmillan.

Figley, C. R. (2002). Compassion fatigue: Psychotherapists' chronic lack of self-care. *Journal of Clinical Psychology, 58*(11), 1433–1441. https://doi.org/10.1002/jclp.10090

Firth, J., Gangwisch, J. E., Borisini, A., Wootton, R. E., & Mayer, E. A. (2020). Food and mood: How do diet and nutrition affect mental wellbeing? *BMJ, 369*, m2382. https://doi.org/10.1136/bmj.m2382

Firth, J., Solmi, M., Wootton, R. E., Vancampfort, D., Schuch, F. B., Hoare, E., Gilbody, S., Torous, J., Teasdale, S. B., Jackson, S. E., Smith, L., Eaton, M.,

Jacka, F., Veronese, N., Marx, W., Ashdown-Franks, G., Siskind, D., Sarris, J., Rosenbaum, S., Carvalho, A. F., & Stubbs, B. (2020). The efficacy of lifestyle interventions in improving mental health outcomes: A review. *World Psychiatry, 19*(3), 360–380. https://doi.org/10.1002/wps.20773

Foa, E. B., Hembree, E. A., & Rothbaum, B. O. (2007). *Prolonged exposure therapy for PTSD: Emotional processing of traumatic experiences.* Oxford University Press. https://doi.org/10.1093/med:psych/9780195308501.001.0001

Fonagy, P., & Target, M. (2007). The rooting of the mind in the body: New links between attachment theory and psychoanalysis. *Journal of the American Psychoanalytic Association, 55*(2), 411–456. https://doi.org/10.1177/00030651070550020501

Fonagy, P., Gergely, G., Jurist, E. L., & Target, M. (2002). *Affect regulation, mentalization, and the development of the self.* Routledge. https://doi.org/10.4324/9780429471643

Freud, S. (1911). Formulations on the two principles of mental functioning. In J. Strachey (Ed. & Trans.), *The standard edition of the complete psychological works of Sigmund Freud* (Vol. 12, pp. 213–226). Hogarth Press.

Freud, S. (1912). Recommendations to physicians practicing psychoanalysis. In J. Strachey (Ed. & Trans.), *The standard edition of the complete psychological works of Sigmund Freud* (Vol. 12, pp. 109–120). Hogarth Press.

Freud, S. (1915). The unconscious. In J. Strachey (Ed. & Trans.), *The standard edition of the complete psychological works of Sigmund Freud* (Vol. 14, pp. 159–204). Hogarth Press.

Freud, S. (1917). Mourning and melancholia. In J. Strachey (Ed. & Trans.), *The standard edition of the complete psychological works of Sigmund Freud* (Vol. 14, pp. 243–258). Hogarth Press.

Gabbard, G. O. (2001). A contemporary psychoanalytic model of countertransference. *Journal of Clinical Psychology, 57*(8), 983–991. https://doi.org/10.1002/jclp.1065

Gabbard, G. O. (2014). *Psychodynamic psychiatry in clinical practice* (5th ed.). American Psychiatric Publishing.

Gelso, C. J., & Hayes, J. A. (2007). *Countertransference and the therapist's inner experience: Perils and possibilities.* Lawrence Erlbaum Associates.

Gelso, C. J., & Woodhouse, S. S. (2001). The termination of psychotherapy: What research tells us about the process of ending treatment. In G. S. Tryon (Ed.), ***Counseling based on process research: Applying what we know*** (pp. 344–369). Allyn and Bacon.

Geurtzen, N., Keijsers, G. P. J., Karremans, J. C., Tiemens, B. G., & Hutschemaekers, G. J. M. (2020). Patients' perceived lack of goal clarity in psychological treatments: Scale development and negative correlates. *Clinical Psychology & Psychotherapy, 27*(6), 915–924. https://doi.org/10.1002/cpp.2479

Gilbert, P., & Simos, G. (2022). *Compassion-focused therapy: Clinical practice and applications.* Routledge. https://doi.org/10.4324/9781003035879

Glueckauf, R. L., Maheu, M. M., Drude, K. P., Wells, B. A., Wang, Y., Gustafson, D. J., & Nelson, E. L. (2018). Survey of psychologists' telebehavioral health practices: Technology use, ethical issues, and training needs. P***rofessional Psychology: Research and Practice, 49(3)***, 205–219. https://doi.org/10.1037/pro0000188

Goldfried, M. R., Burckell, L. A., & Eubanks-Carter, C. (2003). Therapist self-disclosure in cognitive-behavioral therapy. *Journal of Clinical Psychology, 59*(5), 555–568. https://doi.org/10.1002/jclp.10159

Gone, J. P. (2016). Alternative knowledges and the future of community psychology: Provocations from an American Indian healing tradition. *American Journal of Community Psychology, 58*(3–4), 314–321. https://doi.org/10.1002/ajcp.12046

Grossman, D., & Christensen, L. (2008). *On combat: The psychology and physiology of deadly conflict in war and in peace.* Warrior Science Publications.

Hagger, M. S., & Luszczynska, A. (2014). Implementation intention and action planning interventions in health contexts: State of the research and proposals for the way forward. *Applied Psychology: Health and Well-Being, 6*(1), 1–47. https://doi.org/10.1111/aphw.12017

Hall, G. C. N. (2001). Psychotherapy research with ethnic minorities: Empirical, ethical, and conceptual issues. *Journal of Consulting and Clinical Psychology, 69*(3), 502–510. https://doi.org/10.1037/0022-006X.69.3.502

Hall, J. A., Harrigan, J. A., & Rosenthal, R. (1995). Nonverbal behavior in clinician-patient interaction. *Applied & Preventive Psychology, 4*(1), 21–37. https://doi.org/10.1016/S0962-1849(05)80049-6

Harvey, A. G., Murray, G., Chandler, R. A., & Soehner, A. M. (2011). Sleep disturbance as transdiagnostic: Consideration of neurobiological mechanisms. *Clinical Psychology Review, 31*(2), 225–235. https://doi.org/10.1016/j.cpr.2010.04.003

Harvey, A. G., Watkins, E., Mansell, W., & Shafran, R. (2004). *Cognitive behavioral processes across psychological disorders: A transdiagnostic approach to research and treatment.* Oxford University Press. https://doi.org/10.1093/med:psych/9780198528883.001.0001

Hayes, A. M., Laurenceau, J. P., Feldman, G. C., Strauss, J. L., & Cardaciotto, L. A. (2007). Change is not always linear: The study of nonlinear and discontinuous patterns of change in psychotherapy. *Clinical Psychology Review, 27*(6), 715–723. https://doi.org/10.1016/j.cpr.2007.01.008

Hayes, S. C., Strosahl, K. D., & Wilson, K. G. (2011). Acceptance and commitment therapy: The process and practice of mindful change. Guilford Press.

Hays, P. A. (2016). *Addressing cultural complexities in practice: Assessment, diagnosis, and therapy* (3rd ed.). American Psychological Association. https://doi.org/10.1037/14801-000

Helms, J. E. (1995). An update of Helm's white and people of color racial identity models. In J. G. Ponterotto, J. M. Casas, L. A. Suzuki, & C. M. Alexander (Eds.), *Handbook of multicultural counseling* (pp. 181–198). Sage Publications.

Hill, C. E., & Knox, S. (2001). Self-disclosure. *Psychotherapy: Theory, Research, Practice, Training, 38*(4), 413–417. https://doi.org/10.1037/0033-3204.38.4.413

Hill, C. E., & Knox, S. (2013). Training and supervision in psychotherapy. In M. J. Lambert (Ed.), *Bergin and Garfield's handbook of psychotherapy and behavior change* (6th ed.). Wiley.

Hill, C. E., Spiegel, S. B., Hoffman, M. A., Kivlighan, D. M., & Gelso, C. J. (2017). Therapist expertise in psychotherapy revisited. *The Counseling Psychologist, 45*(1), 7–53. https://doi.org/10.1177/0011000016641192

Hofmann, S. G., & Smits, J. A. J. (2008). Cognitive-behavioral therapy for adult anxiety disorders: A meta-analysis of randomized placebo-controlled trials. *The Journal of Clinical Psychiatry, 69*(4), 621–632. https://doi.org/10.4088/jcp.v69n0415

Hofmann, S. G., Asnaani, A., Vonk, I. J. J., Sawyer, A. T., & Fang, A. (2012). The efficacy of cognitive behavioral therapy: A review of meta-analyses. *Cognitive Therapy and Research, 36*(5), 427–440. https://doi.org/10.1007/s10608-012-9476-1

Holt-Lunstad, J., Smith, T. B., Baker, M., Harris, T., & Stephenson, D. (2015). Loneliness and social isolation as risk factors for mortality: A meta-analytic review. *Perspectives on Psychological Science, 10*(2), 227–237. https://doi.org/10.1177/1745691614568352

Hook, J. N., Davis, D. E., Owen, J., Worthington, E. L., Jr., & Utsey, S. O. (2013). Cultural humility: Measuring openness to culturally diverse clients. *Journal of Counseling Psychology, 60*(3), 353–366. https://doi.org/10.1037/a0032595

Horvath, A. O., & Bedi, R. P. (2002). The alliance. In J. C. Norcross (Ed.), *Psychotherapy relationships that work: Therapist contributions and responsiveness to patients* (pp. 37–69). Oxford University Press.

Hwang, W.-C. (2009). The formative method for adapting psychotherapy (FMAP): A community-based developmental approach to culturally adapting therapy. *Professional* Psychology*: Research and Practice, 40*(4), 369–377. https://doi.org/10.1037/a0016240

Jacka, F. N., O'Neil, A., Opie, M., Itsiopoulos, C., Cotton, M., Mohebbi, A., Castle, M., Dash, C., Mihalopoulos, M., & Berk, M. (2017). A randomised controlled trial of dietary improvement for adults with major depression, the "SMILES" trial. *BMC Medicine, 15(1)*, 23. https://doi.org/10.1186/s12916-017-0791-y

Jacobson, E. (1938). *Progressive relaxation*. University of Chicago Press.

Jacobson, N. S., Dobson, K. S., Truax, P. A., Addis, M. E., Koerner, K., Gollan, J. K., Gortner, E., & Prince, S. E. (1996). A component analysis of cognitive-behavioral treatment for depression. *Journal of Consulting and Clinical Psychology, 64*(2), 295–304. https://doi.org/10.1037/0022-006X.64.2.295

Jacobson, N. S., Martell, C. R., & Dimidjian, S. (2001). Behavioral activation treatment for depression: Returning to contextual roots. *Clinical Psychology:* Science *and Practice, 8*(3), 255–270. https://doi.org/10.1093/clipsy.8.3.255

Jerath, R., Edry, J. W., Barnes, V. A., & Jerath, V. (2006). Physiology of long pranayamic breathing: Neural respiratory elements may provide a mechanism that explains how slow deep breathing shifts autonomic nervous system. *Medical Hypotheses, 67*(3), 566–571. https://doi.org/10.1016/j.mehy.2006.02.042

Kabat-Zinn, J. (1990). *Full catastrophe living: Using the wisdom of your body and mind to face stress, pain, and illness*. Delacorte.

Kalin, N. H. (2020). The critical relationship between anxiety and depression. *American Journal of Psychiatry, 177*(5), 365–367. https://doi.org/10.1176/appi.ajp.2020.20030305

Kandula, N. R., Lauderdale, D. S., & Baker, D. W. (2007). Differences in self-reported health among Asians, Latinos, and non-Hispanic whites: the role of language and nativity. *Annals of Epidemiology, 17*(3), 191–198. https://doi.org/10.1016/j.annepidem.2006.10.005

Kazantzis, N., Whittington, C., & Dattilio, F. (2010). Meta-analysis of homework effects in cognitive and behavioral therapy: A replication and extension. *Clinical Psychology: Science and Practice, 17*(2), 144–156. https://doi.org/10.1111/j.1468-2850.2010.01204.x

Kazdin, A. E. (2008). Evidence-based treatment and practice: New opportunities to bridge clinical research and practice, enhance the knowledge base, and improve patient care. *American Psychologist, 63*(3), 146–159. https://doi.org/10.1037/0003-066X.63.3.146

Kazdin, A. E. (2021). *Research design in clinical psychology* (5th ed.). Cambridge University Press.

Kernberg, O. F. (1975). Borderline conditions and pathological narcissism. Jason Aronson.

Kessler, R. C., Berglund, P., Demler, O., Jin, R., Merikangas, K. R., & Walters, E. E. (2005). Lifetime prevalence and age-of-onset distributions of DSM-IV disorders in the National Comorbidity Survey Replication. *Archives of General Psychiatry, 62*(6), 593–602. https://doi.org/10.1001/archpsyc.62.6.593

Knapp, S., Gottlieb, M. C., Berman, J., & Handelsman, M. M. (2015). *Ethical dilemmas in psychotherapy: Positive approaches to decision making.* American Psychological Association.

Kress, V. E., & Marie, M. (2019). Counseling termination and new beginnings. *Counseling Today, 62*(4), 40–44.

Lally, P., Van Jaarsveld, C. H. M., Potts, H. W. W., & Wardle, J. (2010). How are habits formed: Modelling habit formation in the real world. *European Journal of Social Psychology, 40*(6), 998–1009. https://doi.org/10.1002/ejsp.674

Lambert, M. J., & Barley, D. E. (2001). Research summary on the therapeutic relationship and psychotherapy outcome. *Psychotherapy: Theory, Research, Practice, Training, 38*(4), 357–361. https://doi.org/10.1037/0033-3204.38.4.357

Lambert, M. J., & Shimokawa, K. (2011). Collecting client feedback. In J. C. Norcross (Ed.), *Psychotherapy relationships that work* (2nd ed., pp. 203–223). Oxford University Press.

Lambert, M. J., Hansen, N. B., & Finch, A. E. (2001). Patient-focused research: Using patient outcome data to enhance treatment effects. ***Journal of Consulting and Clinical Psychology, 69(2)***, 159–172. https://doi.org/10.1037/0022-006X.69.2.159

Leichsenring, F., Abbass, A., Luyten, P., Hilsenroth, M. J., & Rabung, S. (2013). The emerging evidence for long-term psychodynamic therapy. *Psychodynamic Psychiatry, 41*(3), 361–384. https://doi.org/10.1521/pdps.2013.41.3.361

Leichsenring, F., & Leibing, E. (2003). The effectiveness of psychodynamic therapy and cognitive behavior therapy in the treatment of personality disorders: A meta-analysis. *The American Journal of Psychiatry, 160(7)*, 1223–1232. https://doi.org/10.1176/appi.ajp.160.7.1223

Leichsenring, F., & Rabung, S. (2011). Long-term psychodynamic psychotherapy in complex mental disorders: Update of a meta-analysis. *British Journal of Psychiatry, 199*(1), 15–22. https://doi.org/10.1192/bjp.bp.110.082776

Leichsenring, F., Salzer, S., Beutel, M. E., Herpertz, S., Hiller, W., Hoyer, J., & Leibing, E. (2013). Psychodynamic therapy and cognitive-behavioral therapy in social anxiety disorder: A multicenter randomized controlled trial. *American Journal of Psychiatry, 170*(7), 759–767. https://doi.org/10.1176/appi.ajp.2013.12081125

Leichsenring, F., & Steinert, C. (2017). Is cognitive behavioral therapy the gold standard for psychotherapy? The need for plurality in treatment and research. *JAMA, 318,* 1323–1324. https://doi.org/10.1001/jama.2017.13737

Levenson, H. (1995). *Time-limited dynamic psychotherapy: A guide to clinical practice.* Basic Books.

Linehan, M. (1993). *Cognitive-behavioral treatment of borderline personality disorder.* Guilford Press.

Locke, E. A., & Latham, G. P. (2002). Building a practically useful theory of goal setting and task motivation: A 35-year odyssey. *American Psychologist, 57*(9), 705–717. https://doi.org/10.1037/0003-066X.57.9.705

Longmore, R. J., & Worrell, M. (2007). Do we need to challenge thoughts in cognitive therapy? *Clinical Psychology Review, 27*(2), 173–187. https://doi.org/10.1016/j.cpr.2006.08.001

Lopresti, A. L., Hood, S. D., & Drummond, P. D. (2013). A review of lifestyle factors that contribute to important pathways associated with major depression: Diet, sleep and exercise. *Journal of Affective Disorders, 148*(1), 12–27. https://doi.org/10.1016/j.jad.2013.01.014

Luborsky, L. (1984). *Principles of psychoanalytic psychotherapy: A manual for supportive-expressive treatment.* Basic Books.

Luborsky, L., & Crits-Christoph, P. (1998). *Understanding transference: The core conflictual relationship theme method* (2nd ed.). American Psychological Association.

Maheu, M. M., Drude, K. P., Merrill, C. A., Callan, J. E., & Hilty, D. M. (2019). *Telebehavioral health: Foundations in theory and practice for graduate learners.* Cognella Academic Publishing.

Marlatt, G. A., & Donovan, D. M. (Eds.). (2005). *Relapse prevention: Maintenance strategies in the treatment of addictive behaviors* (2nd ed.). Guilford Press.

Maslow, A. H. (1943). A theory of human motivation. *Psychological Review, 50*(4), 370–396. https://doi.org/10.1037/h0054346

Maslow, A. H. (1968). *Toward a psychology of being* (2nd ed.). Van Nostrand Reinhold.

McLaughlin, K. A., Weissman, D., & Bitrán, D. (2019). Childhood adversity and neural development: A systematic review. ***Annual Review of Developmental Psychology**, 1, 277*–312. https://doi.org/10.1146/annurev-devpsych-121318-084950

Mearns, D., Thorne, B., & McLeod, J. (2013). *Person-centered counselling in action* (4th ed.). Sage Publications.

Michie, S., Abraham, C., Whittington, C., McAteer, J., & Gupta, S. (2009). Effective techniques in healthy eating and physical activity interventions: A meta-regression. *Health Psychology: Official Journal of the Division of Health Psychology, American Psychological Association, 28*(6), 690–701. https://doi.org/10.1037/a0016136

Miller, S. D., Duncan, B. L., Brown, J., Sorrell, R., & Chalk, M. B. (2006). Using formal client feedback to improve retention and outcomes. *Journal of Brief Therapy, 5*(1), 5–22.

Miller, W. R., & Rollnick, S. (2013). *Motivational interviewing: Helping people change* (3rd ed.). Guilford Press.

Muran, J. C., Safran, J. D., Samstag, L. W., & Winston, A. (2005). Evaluating an alliance-focused treatment for personality disorders. *Psychotherapy: Theory, Research, Practice, Training, 42*(4), 532–545. https://doi.org/10.1037/0033-3204.42.4.532

Naeem, F. (2012). *Adaptation of cognitive behaviour therapy for depression in Pakistan: A methodology for adapting cognitive behavior therapy in non-western cultures.* Lambert Academic Publishing.

Neff, K. D. (2003). The development and validation of a scale to measure self-compassion. *Self and Identity, 2*(3), 223–250. https://doi.org/10.1080/15298860309027

Neff, K. (2011). *Self-compassion: The proven power of being kind to yourself.* HarperCollins.

Norcross, J. C., & Alexander, E. F. (2019). A primer on psychotherapy integration. In J. C. Norcross & M. R. Goldfried (Eds.), *Handbook of psychotherapy integration* (3rd ed., pp. 3–27). Oxford University Press. https://doi.org/10.1093/med-psych/9780190690465.003.0001

Norcross, J. C., & Goldfried, M. R. (Eds.). (2019). ***Handbook of psychotherapy integration*** (3rd ed.). Oxford University Press.

Norcross, J. C., Krebs, P. M., & Prochaska, J. O. (2011). Stages of change. *Journal of Clinical Psychology, 67*(2), 143–154.

Norcross, J. C., & Lambert, M. J. (2019a). Evidence-based psychotherapy relationships: The third task force. In J. C. Norcross & M. J. Lambert

(Eds.), *Psychotherapy relationships that work: Volume 1: Evidence-based therapist contributions* (3rd ed.). Oxford University Press. https://doi.org/10.1093/med-psych/9780190843953.003.0001

Norcross, J. C., & Lambert, M. J. (2019b). *Psychotherapy relationships that work: Evidence-based therapist contributions* (3rd ed.). Oxford University Press. https://doi.org/10.1093/med-psych/9780190843953.001.0001

Norcross, J. C., & Lambert, M. J. (2019c). Psychotherapy relationships that work III. *Psychotherapy, 55*(4), 303–315. https://doi.org/10.1037/pst0000193

Norcross, J. C., & VandenBos, G. R. (2018). *Leaving it at the office: A guide to psychotherapist self-care* (2nd ed.). Guilford Press.

Norcross, J. C., & Wampold, B. E. (2011a). Evidence-based therapy relationships: Research conclusions and clinical practices. *Psychotherapy, 48*(1), 98–102. https://doi.org/10.1037/a0022161

Norcross, J. C., & Wampold, B. E. (2011b). What works for whom: Tailoring psychotherapy to the person. *Journal of Clinical Psychology, 67*(2), 127–132. https://doi.org/10.1002/jclp.20764

Norcross, J. C., & Wampold, B. E. (2018). A new therapy for each patient: Evidence-based relationships and responsiveness. *Journal of Clinical Psychology, 74*(11), 1889–1906. https://doi.org/10.1002/jclp.22678

Norcross, J. C., Zimmerman, B. E., Greenberg, R. P., & Swift, J. K. (2011). Do all therapists do that when saying goodbye? A study of commonalities in therapy termination. *Psychotherapy, 48*(1), 22–27. https://doi.org/10.1002/jclp.20758

Oyserman, D. (2009). Identity-based motivation: Implications for action-readiness, procedural-readiness, and consumer behavior. *Journal of Consumer Psychology, 19*(3), 250–260. https://doi.org/10.1016/j.jcps.2009.05.008

Pennebaker, J. W. (1997a). *Opening up: The healing power of expressing emotions* (Rev. ed.). Guilford Press.

Pennebaker, J. W. (1997b). Writing about emotional experiences as a therapeutic process. *Psychological Science, 8*(3), 162–166. https://doi.org/10.1111/j.1467-9280.1997.tb00403.x

Ponterotto, J. G., Casas, J. M., Suzuki, L. A., & Alexander, C. M. (Eds.). (1995). *Handbook of multicultural counseling.* Sage Publications.

Pope, K. S., Vasquez, M. J. T., Chavez-Dueñas, N. Y., & Adames, H. Y. (2021). *Ethics in psychotherapy and counseling: A practical guide* (6th ed.). Wiley. https://doi.org/10.1002/9781394259038

Porges, S. W. (2011). *The polyvagal theory: Neurophysiological foundations of emotions, attachment, communication, and self-regulation.* W. W. Norton.

Prochaska, J. O., & DiClemente, C. C. (1983). Stages and processes of self-change of smoking: Toward an integrative model of change. *Journal of Consulting and Clinical Psychology, 51*(3), 390–395. https://doi.org/10.1037/0022-006X.51.3.390

Ratey, J. J. (2008). Spark: The revolutionary new science of exercise and the brain. Little, Brown.

Rebar, A. L., Stanton, R., Geard, D., Short, C., Duncan, M. J., & Vandelanotte, C. (2015). A meta-meta-analysis of the effect of physical activity on depression and anxiety. *Health Psychology Review, 9*(3), 366–378. https://doi.org/10.1080/17437199.2015.1022901

Rogers, C. R. (1951). *Client-centered therapy: Its current practice, implications, and theory*. Houghton Mifflin.

Rogers, C. R. (1957). The necessary and sufficient conditions of therapeutic personality change. *Journal of Consulting Psychology, 21*(2), 95–103. https://doi.org/10.1037/h0045357

Rogers, C. R. (1961). *On becoming a person: A therapist's view of psychotherapy*. Houghton Mifflin.

Rogers-Sirin, L., Melendez, F., Refano, C., & Zegarra, Y. (2015). Immigrant perceptions of therapists' cultural competence: A qualitative investigation. *Professional Psychology: Research and Practice, 46*(4), 258–269. https://doi.org/10.1037/pro0000033

Rousmaniere, T. (2016). *Deliberate practice for psychotherapists: A guide to improving clinical effectiveness*. Routledge.

Rupert, P. A., & Dorociak, K. E. (2019). Self-care, stress, and well-being among practicing psychologists. *Professional Psychology: Research and Practice, 50*(5), 343–350. https://doi.org/10.1037/pro0000251

Rupert, P. A., & Kent, J. S. (2007). Gender and work setting differences in career-sustaining behaviors and burnout among professional psychologists. *Professional Psychology: Research and Practice, 38*(1), 88–96. https://doi.org/10.1037/0735-7028.38.1.88

Rupert, P. A., & Morgan, D. J. (2005). Work setting and burnout among professional psychologists. *Professional Psychology: Research and Practice, 36*(5), 544–550. https://doi.org/10.1037/0735-7028.36.5.544

Safran, J. D., Muran, J. C., & Eubanks-Carter, C. (2011). Repairing alliance ruptures. *Psychotherapy, 48(1)*, 80–87. https://doi.org/10.1037/a0022140

Saleebey, D. (2012). *The strengths perspective in social work practice* (6th ed.). Pearson.

Schneider, K. J., & Krug, O. T. (2017). *Existential–humanistic therapy* (2nd ed.). American Psychological Association. https://doi.org/10.1037/0000042-000

Schön, D. A. (1983). *The reflective practitioner: How professionals think in action.* Basic Books.

Schottenbauer, M. A., Glass, C. R., Arnkoff, D. B., & Gray, S. H. (2008). Contributions of psychodynamic approaches to treatment of PTSD and trauma: A review of the empirical treatment and psychopathology literature. *Psychiatry: Interpersonal and Biological Processes, 71*(1), 13–34.https://doi.org/10.1521/psyc.2008.71.1.13

Seligman, M. E. P. (2011). *Flourish: A visionary new understanding of happiness and well-being.* Free Press.

Shapiro, S. L., Brown, K. W., & Biegel, G. M. (2007). Teaching self-care to caregivers: Effects of mindfulness-based stress reduction on mental health of therapists in training. *Training and Education in Professional Psychology, 1*(2), 105–115. https://doi.org/10.1037/1931-3918.1.2.105

Shedler, J. (2010). The efficacy of psychodynamic psychotherapy. *American Psychologist, 65*(2), 98–109. https://doi.org/10.1037/a0018378

Siegel, D. J. (2010). *The mindful therapist: A clinician's guide to mindsight and neural integration*. W. W. Norton.

Siegel, D. J. (2020). *The developing mind: How relationships and the brain interact to shape who we are* (3rd ed.). Guilford Press.

Skovholt, T. M., & Trotter-Mathison, M. (2016). *The resilient practitioner: Burnout prevention and self-care strategies for counselors, therapists, teachers, and health professionals* (3rd ed.). Routledge. https://doi.org/10.4324/9781315737447

Stricker, G., & Gold, J. (2003). Integrative approaches to psychotherapy. In A. S. Gurman & S. B. Messer (Eds.), *Essential psychotherapies: Theory and practice* (2nd ed., pp. 317–349). Guilford Press.

Streltzer, J. (Ed.). (2016). ***Culture and psychopathology: A guide to clinical assessment*** (2nd ed.). Routledge.

Sue, D. W., Cheng, J. K. Y., Saad, C. S., & Chu, J. P. (2012). Asian American mental health: A call to action. ***American Psychologist, 67***(7), 532–544. https://doi.org/10.1037/a0028900

Sue, D. W., Rasheed, M. N., & Rasheed, J. M. (2016). *Multicultural social work practice: A competency-based approach to diversity and social justice* (2nd ed.). Wiley.

Sue, D. W., & Sue, D. (2016). *Counseling the culturally diverse: Theory and practice* (7th ed.). Wiley.

Swift, J. K., & Greenberg, R. P. (2012). Premature discontinuation in adult psychotherapy: A meta-analysis. *Journal of Consulting and Clinical Psychology, 80*(4), 547–559. https://doi.org/10.1037/a0028226

Swift, J. K., & Greenberg, R. P. (2015). Premature termination in psychotherapy: Strategies for engaging clients and improving outcomes. American Psychological Association. https://doi.org/10.1037/14469-000

Town, J. M., Abbass, A., & Hardy, G. (2011). Short-term psychodynamic psychotherapy for personality disorders: A critical review of randomized controlled trials. *Journal of Personality Disorders, 25*(6), 723–740. https://doi.org/10.1521/pedi.2011.25.6.723

Tummala-Narra, P. (2016). *Psychoanalytic theory and cultural competence in psychotherapy.* American Psychological Association. https://doi.org/10.1037/14800-000

Vaillant, G. E. (1992). *Ego mechanisms of defense: A guide for clinicians and researchers.* American Psychiatric Association.

van der Kolk, B. (2014). *The body keeps the score: Brain, mind, and body in the healing of trauma.* Viking.

Wachtel, P. L. (2011). *Therapeutic communication: Knowing what to say when.* Guilford Press.

Walker, M. P. (2017). *Why we sleep: Unlocking the power of sleep and dreams.* Scribner.

Walsh, R. (2011). Lifestyle and mental health. *American Psychologist, 66*(7), 579–592. https://doi.org/10.1037/a0021769

Wampold, B. E., & Imel, Z. E. (2015). *The great psychotherapy debate: The evidence for what makes psychotherapy work* (2nd ed.). Routledge. https://doi.org/10.4324/9780203582015

Weisz, J. R., & Kazdin, A. E. (Eds.). (2017). *Evidence-based psychotherapies for children and adolescents* (3rd ed.). Guilford Press.

Williams, M. T., Metzger, I. W., Leins, C., & DeLapp, C. (2018). Assessing racial trauma within a DSM–5 framework: The UConn Racial/Ethnic Stress & Trauma Survey. ***Practice Innovations, 3(4)***, 242–260. https://doi.org/10.1037/pri0000076

Witkiewitz, K., & Marlatt, G. A. (2004). Relapse Prevention for Alcohol and Drug Problems: That Was Zen, This Is Tao. *American Psychologist, 59*(4), 224–235. https://doi.org/10.1037/0003-066X.59.4.224

Yalom, I. D. (2002). *The gift of therapy: An open letter to a new generation of therapists and their patients*. HarperCollins.

Zur, O. (2007). *Boundaries in psychotherapy: Ethical and clinical explorations*. American Psychological Association.

APPENDIX A

Applied Tools for Integrative Clinical Practice (YIA)

The following tools are designed to support clinicians as they apply the Yanni Integration Approach in real time. Each resource emphasizes flexibility, clinical attunement, and the adaptive, moment-to-moment nature of an integrative model. These tools are not scripts. They are guiding structures that complement clinical intuition and help therapists stay grounded and organized while working with complex cases.

1. YIA Rapid Case Formulation Grid

A flexible, 5-minute way to synthesize information across domains and update your clinical understanding as sessions evolve.

Sections to Reflect On

Presenting Problems
Brief summary of concerns bringing the client to treatment.

Current Triggers or Stressors
Situational, relational, or internal factors activating symptoms.

Core Beliefs and Emotional Themes
Blend CBT and Psychodynamic thinking to identify:

- How the client perceives themselves and the world
- Emotional narratives or wounds influencing reactions

Relational Patterns
Attachment themes, defenses, reenactments, and how these appear interpersonally and in the therapeutic relationship.

Strengths and Protective Factors
Sources of resilience, internal resources, and external support.

Values and Motivators
Humanistic and Person-Centered anchors guiding meaning and direction.

Lifestyle Influences
Sleep, nourishment, movement, digital habits, structure, and rest.

Clinical Priorities

A flexible focus area for upcoming sessions, subject to change depending on what emerges in the room.

2. YIA Session Flow Map

A natural, adaptive rhythm for structuring sessions without imposing rigidity.

Session Flow

Opening Connection

Ground, attune, and slow the nervous system.

Anchored Purpose

Collaboratively identify what feels important today. This serves as a compass, not an agenda.

Model Focus for Session

Rather than choosing a modality in advance, observe where the session pulls you. This may include:

- Cognitive structuring (CBT)
- Emotional depth (Psychodynamic)
- Grounding presence (Humanistic)
- Empowered pacing (Person-Centered)
- Systemic stabilization (Lifestyle-based)

This focus can shift fluidly at any time.

Deepening or Redirecting
Follow emotional threads, clarify patterns, or adjust pace based on the client's readiness.

Integration or Action Step
Identify what the client wants to carry forward. Insight alone can be enough.

Closing Reflection
Name themes or emotions to create safety, containment, and closure.

3. Therapist Self-Check for Model Switching

A grounding tool to help therapists recognize when the session is naturally signaling a shift in therapeutic emphasis.

When to Lean Toward Psychodynamic Exploration

- Emotional activation without clear cause
- Old relational patterns surfacing
- Defenses or reenactments appearing in the room

When CBT Structure Is Supportive

- Cognitive spirals
- Heightened anxiety
- Need for clarity and containment

When Person-Centered Pacing Is Key

- Client overwhelmed
- Resistance or emotional hesitancy
- Alliance repair or strengthening

When Humanistic Presence Matters Most

- Shutdown or dysregulation
- Shame or self-criticism
- Acute emotional vulnerability

When Lifestyle Stabilization Supports the Work

- Sleep, nutrition, or digital habits impacting mood
- Physical depletion
- System destabilization that interferes with deeper work

4. YIA Lifestyle Assessment Conversation

A soft, non-judgmental set of prompts exploring how daily rhythms shape emotional health.

Guiding Questions

- How are you sleeping lately?
- What does your morning energy feel like?
- What are your eating patterns like during the day?
- What is your relationship with screens?
- What movement or physical activity is part of your week?
- What creates stress for you most often?
- Who supports you emotionally?
- What helps you restore yourself?
- What does a typical weekday feel like?
- How do you intentionally rest?

This framework allows lifestyle factors to emerge organically.

5. YIA Values and Direction Finder

A reflective guide for clarifying meaning, direction, and emotional alignment.

Explore Through Conversation

- What qualities in yourself do you value most?
- What do you value in relationships?
- What type of daily life feels meaningful to you?
- Where do you feel disconnected from your values?

- What small shift would move you closer to the life you want?

This supports deeper identity work without forcing behavioral homework.

6. YIA Intervention Selector

A flexible guide pairing client presentations with blended therapeutic responses.

If Rumination Is Present

- CBT reframing + Psychodynamic exploration of underlying fear

If Emotional Numbness Appears

- Humanistic presence + gentle lifestyle activation

If the Client Is Overwhelmed

- Person-Centered pacing + grounding + stabilizing routines

If Relational Patterns Repeat

- Psychodynamic mapping + CBT behavioral planning + empathy-building

If Anxiety Spikes

- Somatic grounding + thought organization + lifestyle stabilization

This selector reflects the fluid, responsive nature of integrative work.

7. YIA Termination Readiness Check

A compassionate, practical way to identify when treatment is naturally approaching closure.

Internal Indicators

- Emotional awareness improves
- Distress regulation increases
- Independent problem-solving strengthens

External Indicators

- Consistent skill use between sessions
- Greater lifestyle stability

Relational Indicators

- Ability to tolerate conflict or discomfort
- Less dependence on therapy for immediate emotional relief

Termination becomes a transition into self-trust, not an endpoint.

8. YIA Therapist Burnout Screening and Reset Guide

A grounding practice to help therapists maintain emotional balance, clarity, and well-being.

Burnout Signals to Notice

- Emotional exhaustion

- Compassion fatigue
- Cognitive fog
- Irritability
- Dread before sessions
- Emotional detachment

1–3 Minute Reset Ritual

- Ground feet
- Release tension in jaw and shoulders
- Lengthen exhale
- Name one emotion
- Name one intention

Weekly Prevention Prompts

- What boundary needs reinforcing?
- What restores me physically or emotionally?
- What connection am I craving?
- What workflow adjustment would reduce strain?

This supports long-term therapist sustainability and presence.

APPENDIX B: Printable YIA Tools

Printable Clinical Tools for Therapists Using the YIA

The following tools are designed as clean, ready to print clinical resources for therapists applying the Yanni Integration Approach in real world settings. Each tool reflects the practical, flexible, integrative structure presented throughout this book. Therapists are encouraged to use these forms during sessions, between sessions, in supervision, or as part of their own reflective practice.

These worksheets are clinician-facing. They are intended to support clinical decision-making, case formulation, treatment planning, real time intervention choices, and therapist wellbeing.

Each page may be photocopied or reprinted for personal clinical use.

Tool 1: YIA Rapid Case Formulation Grid

A one-page, quick reference form for synthesizing clinical information.

Client Name: ____________________

Date: ____________________

Presenting Problems

____

____

____

Current Triggers / Maintaining Stressors

____

____

Core Beliefs and Emotional Themes
(CBT + Psychodynamic)

____

____

Relational Patterns / Reenactments

____

____

Client Strengths and Protective Factors

Values, Priorities, and Motivators

Lifestyle Influences (Sleep, movement, routines)

Focus for the Next Session

Tool 2: YIA Session Flow Map

A simple guide to structure a flexible, grounded therapy session.

Client Name: ______________________________

Date: ______________________________

1. Opening Connection
(1–3 sentences)

____

____

____

2. Anchored Purpose / What Feels Most Important Today

____

____

3. Model Focused on for This Session

- ☐ CBT
- ☐ Psychodynamic
- ☐ Humanistic
- ☐ Person Centered
- ☐ Lifestyle-based
- ☐ Mixed / Adaptive

Reason for the focus:

____

____

4. Deepening / Redirection Notes

____

____

5. Action Step or Integration for the Week

____

____

6. Closing Reflection

One insight, one feeling, or one theme that stood out:

____

____

Tool 3: Therapist Self-Check for Model Switching

A rapid guide for real-time therapeutic decision making.

Client Name: ______________________________

Date: ______________________________

Is it time to switch models?

Psychodynamic

Client is emotionally activated but unclear why

☐ Yes ☐ No

Repeating patterns or themes

☐ Yes ☐ No

CBT

Client is looping in thoughts

☐ Yes ☐ No

Client needs structure or clarity

☐ Yes ☐ No

Person Centered

Client overwhelmed by pace

☐ Yes ☐ No

Client appears guarded or unsure

☐ Yes ☐ No

Humanistic

Client is dysregulated or collapsing

☐ Yes ☐ No

Shame or rupture is present

☐ Yes ☐ No

Lifestyle

Sleep issues, poor routines, depleted energy

☐ Yes ☐ No

Next Step / Pivot I Will Make

____

____

____

Tool 4: YIA Ten Question Lifestyle Assessment

A conversational screening tool for lifestyle-based interventions.

Client Name: ____

Date: ____

Rate or describe each area:

1. Sleep consistency: ____________________________________

2. Morning energy level: _________________________________

3. Daily nutrition pattern: ________________________________

4. Movement / physical activity: ____________________________

5. Screen habits: _______________________________________

6. Weekly stress level: __________________________________

7. Supports / connection: ________________________________

8. Hobbies or restorative outlets: ___________________________

9. Daily structure / routines: ____________________

10. Intentional rest practices: ____________________

Lifestyle Targets Identified:

____

____

Plan for Integration in Therapy:

____

____

Tool 5: YIA Values & Direction Finder

A guided reflection to help clarify values and align treatment.

Client Name: ____________________

Date: ____________________

What do I value most about who I am?

____

What do I value most in my relationships?

____

What do I value most in my daily life?

____

Where do I feel misaligned right now?

____

One small weekly action that moves me toward the life I want:

____

____

Tool 6: YIA Intervention Selector Form

A practical crosswalk between symptoms and integrative interventions.

Client Name: ______________________________

Date: ______________________________

Primary Issue Today (Check all that apply):

- ☐ Rumination
- ☐ Emotional Numbness
- ☐ Overwhelm
- ☐ Intrusive Thoughts
- ☐ Avoidance
- ☐ Relational Conflict
- ☐ Anxiety Spike
- ☐ Low Motivation
- ☐ Other: ________________

Recommended YIA Interventions (Check all that apply):

CBT Interventions

- ☐ Reframing
- ☐ Thought tracking

- ☐ Decatastrophizing
- ☐ Behavioral activation

Psychodynamic Interventions

- ☐ Exploratory questions
- ☐ Pattern mapping
- ☐ Defense identification

Humanistic Interventions

- ☐ Grounding presence
- ☐ Reflection of emotion
- ☐ Embodied awareness

Person Centered Interventions

- ☐ Pacing
- ☐ Validation
- ☐ Autonomy strengthening

Lifestyle Supports

- ☐ Sleep routine
- ☐ Movement plan
- ☐ Digital hygiene
- ☐ Nutrition / hydration
- ☐ Stress-management activity

Why these interventions were focused on today:

Tool 7: Termination Readiness Checklist

A quick assessment to determine if treatment is nearing completion.

Client Name: ______________________________

Date: ______________________________

Internal Readiness

Identify/communicate emotions independently

☐ Yes ☐ No

Regulate distress with learned strategies

☐ Yes ☐ No

External Readiness

Using skills consistently outside sessions

☐ Yes ☐ No

Lifestyle stabilized

☐ Yes ☐ No

Relational Readiness

Tolerates discomfort without withdrawing

☐ Yes ☐ No

Handles conflict without collapse
☐ Yes ☐ No

Termination Plan / Notes:

____

____

Tool 8: YIA Therapist Burnout Screening & Reset Tool

A protective guide to help clinicians remain grounded and effective.

Therapist Name: ______________________________

Week of: ______________________________

Burnout Screening (Rate 1–5)

Emotional exhaustion: ☐
Compassion fatigue: ☐
Cognitive fog: ☐
Irritability or frustration: ☐
Dread before sessions: ☐
Disconnection from clients: ☐

If the total score is 20 or higher, engage the Reset Plan below.

Grounding Reset (1–3 minutes)

- Feet on the floor
- Unclench jaw and shoulders
- Inhale for 4, hold for 2, exhale for 6
- Name one emotion you feel
- Name one intention for your next session

Burnout Prevention Plan

One Boundary to Strengthen:

____

One Recovery Activity This Week:

____

One Connection to Prioritize:

____

One Workflow Adjustment:

____

APPENDIX C

YIA Supervision Guide & Tools for Supervisors

This appendix provides structured tools and frameworks to support supervision using the Yanni Integration Approach. It is designed for supervisors working with interns, early career clinicians, and trainees. These tools support clinical integrity, flexible integrative thinking, ethical decision-making, cultural sensitivity, therapist wellbeing, and supervisee development.

---

1. Supervision Session Template

A flexible guide to structure supervision sessions while allowing for emergent clinical issues, ethical questions, and cultural considerations.

Supervisee Name: ____________________

Client/Case ID: ____________________

Date: ____________________

a. Case Overview / Current Status

Client presenting issues / symptoms:

____

Progress since last session / key shifts:

____

Contextual or cultural factors impacting treatment:

____

Any ethical considerations or boundary concerns:

____

b. Formulation Update (Using YIA Rapid Case Formulation Grid)

What is the presenting problem now?

____

Maintaining factors (stressors, identity dynamics, patterns):

____

Any shifts in beliefs, emotions, relational themes, lifestyle stability, or safety concerns?

____

Therapist observations or countertransference notes:

____

c. Intervention Strategy Discussion

Which modality or combination naturally emerged this week?

☐ CBT ☐ Psychodynamic ☐ Humanistic ☐ Person-Centered ☐ Lifestyle ☐ Mixed / Adaptive

Rationale for this focus (clinical, ethical, cultural, relational):

____

Interventions used:

____

Recommended next steps:

____

Between-session tasks (if any):

---

d. Supervisee Self-Reflection & Therapist Self-Check

What went well in the last session?

What was confusing or challenging?

Any emotional or identity-based reactions?

Ethical or boundary concerns that came up?

Signs of burnout or compassion fatigue?

Which grounding or self-regulation strategies were used?

---

e. Professional Development & Learning Goals

Which clinical skills need strengthening?

Which cultural or identity-awareness skills need strengthening?

____

What ethical decision-making areas need attention?

____

Resources or consultation suggested:

____

f. Next Steps Plan

Clinical goals for client:

____

Learning/skill goals for supervisee:

____

Next supervision date & focus:

____

____

2. Supervisee Progress Tracker

A long-term tool to track supervisee development across clinical, ethical, cultural, and self-awareness domains.

Supervisee Name: ____

Date Started Supervision: ______________________________________

Session #	Client/ Case ID	Primary Focus	Progress / Key Changes	Ethical / Cultural Notes	Next Session Focus

3. Supervision Discussion Map

A structured flow for supervision sessions that blends clinical work with ethics, culture, and professional sustainability.

Opening Check-In

- Therapist emotional and physical state
- Any stress, burnout, or boundary concerns
- Any cultural or identity-related moments from the week
- Any ethical questions

Case Presentations
Each supervisee presents:

- Brief case summary
- What worked / didn't work
- Where cultural dynamics showed up
- Any ethical dilemmas
- Which YIA modalities emerged and why

Group Reflection & Feedback

- Case conceptualization
- Identity awareness
- Ethical reasoning

- Therapist internal reactions
- Alternative integrative pathways

Skill Building & Didactic Learning

- Short teaching moment (integration topic, ethics, culture, trauma, lifestyle)
- Optional role-play or modeling

Self-Care & Professional Sustainability

- Burnout indicators
- Grounding strategies
- Boundary reinforcement

Future Planning

- Clinical goals
- Skill-building goals
- Recommended resources
- Next session date

4. YIA Supervision Competency Grid

Includes clinical, ethical, cultural, and self-regulation competencies.

Competency Area	Emerging	Developing	Proficient	Comments
Case Formulation (multi-domain)	☐	☐	☐	
Model Flexibility & Integration	☐	☐	☐	
Intervention Selection & Adaptivity	☐	☐	☐	
Therapeutic Alliance & Presence	☐	☐	☐	
Self-Regulation & Therapist Awareness	☐	☐	☐	
Ethical & Boundary Management	☐	☐	☐	
Cultural Humility & Identity Awareness	☐	☐	☐	
Lifestyle & Context Planning	☐	☐	☐	
Reflective Practice / Self-Evaluation	☐	☐	☐	

Use this grid quarterly or during formal evaluations.

5. Countertransference & Therapist Reflection Sheet

A guided tool for recognizing emotional, ethical, identity, or cultural reactions.

Therapist: ______________________________

Date: ______________________________

What emotions arose during the session?

____

Did I observe or react?

____

Did cultural or identity dynamics influence my response?

____

Did anything conflict with my boundaries or ethical responsibilities?

____

What grounding strategies did I use?

____

What support or clarification do I need in supervision?

____

6. "Stuck Point" Problem-Solver Worksheet

A decision-making tool incorporating clinical, ethical, cultural, and therapist factors.

Client/Case ID: ______________________________

Date: ______________________________

What is "stuck"?

____

Symptoms, resistance, relational tension, environmental barriers:

____

Possible Contributing Factors (YIA Domains)

- Cognitive patterns
- Emotional/trauma blocks
- Relational dynamics
- Cultural / identity dynamics
- Lifestyle stressors
- Ethical concerns
- Therapist burnout or countertransference

Possible Intervention Pathways

List 2–3 possible paths:

____

____

____

Plan

Intervention to try first (and why):

____

What to monitor and when to revisit:

____

____

7. Supervision Burnout & Well-Being Log

A weekly check-in tool for therapist sustainability.

Therapist Name: ______________________________

Week of: ______________________________

Self-Assessment (Rate 1–5)

- ☐ Emotional exhaustion:
- ☐ Compassion fatigue:
- ☐ Cognitive fog:
- ☐ Irritability or emotional reactivity:
- ☐ Motivation / engagement:
- ☐ Work-life boundary satisfaction:

If total score ≥ 20, implement a reset plan.

Reset Options

- Adjust boundaries
- Increase grounding/self-regulation
- Peer supervision
- Restorative time
- Consult with supervisor regarding workload

About the Author

Joseph R. Yanni, Psy.D., is a licensed psychologist, school psychologist, private practice owner, clinical supervisor, and author. He is the founder of Psychological Services of New York, P.C., a practice based in Westchester County that provides therapy for children, adolescents, adults, and families.

Dr. Yanni's clinical work integrates cognitive behavioral, psychodynamic, humanistic, person-centered, and lifestyle-based approaches to help clients better understand themselves, manage emotional challenges, and develop healthier patterns in daily life. His work is grounded in the belief that effective therapy requires more than knowledge of individual models. It requires clinical judgment, flexibility, emotional attunement, and the ability to meet each client as a whole person.

In addition to his private practice, Dr. Yanni has extensive experience as a school psychologist, giving him a broad perspective on child development, family systems, school-based concerns, emotional regulation, anxiety, and the real-world challenges children and families face. He also supervises developing clinicians and emphasizes practical, thoughtful, relationship-centered clinical work.

His writing focuses on helping therapists bridge theory and practice in a way that feels grounded, human, and clinically useful. Through his work, he aims to support clinicians in developing a more flexible, thoughtful, and integrated approach to therapy.

Learn more at: www.psychologicalservicesofnewyork.com

www.ingramcontent.com/pod-product-compliance
Lightning Source LLC
LaVergne TN
LVHW080028210926
848481LV00011B/3123
* 9 7 9 8 9 9 6 0 9 5 4 0 7 *